C000182006

THE SPIRITS

RICHARD GODWIN

For Johanna

Contents

THE COCKTAILING DAY

To everything a time and a place. (Disclaimer: this is merely a guide to match appropriate drinks with appropriate hours; you will kill yourself if you attempt them all.)

7am	Corpse Reviver #2 (page 156)
8am	English Breakfast Martini (page 94)
9am	Bloody Mary (page 193)
10am	Sherry Cobbler (page 210)
11am	Gin Fizz (page 74)
Noon	Spritz (page 75)
1pm	• LUNCH •
2pm	Mexican Jumping Bean (page 172)
3pm	Aviation (page 146)
4pm	Pousse-Café (page 235)
5pm	Martini (page 57)
6pm	Gin & Tonic (page 90)
7pm	Negroni (page 62)
8pm	• DINNER •
9pm	Stinger (page 136)
10pm	Vieux-Carré (page 139)
11pm	Sazerac (page 134)
Midnight	Champagne Cocktail (page 222)
1am	Mai Tai (page 202)
2am	Nuclear Daiquiri (page 174)
3am	Absinthe Suissesse (page 145)
4am	Espresso Martini (page 163)
5am	Eye-Opener (page 116)
6am	Last Word (page 170)

INTRODUCTION

'Most any afternoon at five
We'll be so glad we're both alive
Then maybe fortune will complete her plan
That all began
With cocktails for two

Spike Jones, 'Cocktails for Two' (1934)

OF ALL THE SKILLS you might acquire in life, learning how to make strong, effective cocktails is the least likely to be a waste of your time. No one will complain if, at 2.43am, when all the mainstream stimulants have been exhausted, you announce to the dying house party that you are going to make Gin Sours. No lover will think any less of you should you present them with a well-iced El Presidente when they walk through the door. No guest will be offended if you offer them a glass of whatever drab wine happens to be around and then add, with a glint in your eye: 'Or I could fix us all a round of Charlie Chaplins?' They will want to come to your house again. (Assuming these people are not devout or teetotal, in which case, what were you thinking?)

What I mean to say is that compared to improving your score on World of Warcraft, or perfecting your fish-gutting technique, or working up to bench-pressing 60 kilograms, upping your cocktail-production is a surer way to increase the sum of human happiness. It's almost selfless. It takes far less time to master than, say, learning to play the guitar, and when you announce to a room that you are going to play a suite of Leonard Cohen songs, people make their excuses. When you say: 'I'm going to make Rum Punch now', they are pleased. Trust me, I have tried both.

My intention with this book is to demystify cocktail-making for the interested amateur – to give you the simple means to be the one to spread that happiness. I have tried to translate the mixological bibles into plain English and put the wisdom of the prophets into the hands of you, the people. Because it's not as hard as you might think. You will need liquor, though not much to begin with – I reckon six bottles, at a combined cost of about £80, is enough to see you through the first term's syllabus (if you're not already peeping ahead to part two). You'll need equipment, though I bet you've the ready tools in your kitchen right now. You'll need a little technique, but nothing that you can't learn in an afternoon and certainly not so much as any Thrice-Blessed Order of the Mixologists would have you believe. Remember, you're an amateur – you're not charging your loved one £8.50 for their Pisco Sour, so he or she won't complain to your manager if it's a touch tart. And if they do, dump them.

I first began to take cocktails seriously – no, 'seriously' isn't the right word. Cocktails should never be taken *too* seriously, unless you're intending to open a bar (and even then…). I mean, I first vowed to get *good* at cocktails a few years ago now. I had tried a proper Manhattan for the first time in my late twenties and thought 'I could drink more of these!' and 'Why wasn't I drinking these before?'

I suppose I had always been fascinated by those antique and out-of-reach bottles on the bar (Roald Dahl's *George's Marvellous Medicine* leaves a strong impression on every inner child) but there was something about this whole business of spirits that seemed forbidding. Higher cost, higher proof, higher risk, perhaps? Still, all it really takes is an entry point – a sundown Negroni in Florence; a White Lady at London's Savoy – and the world opens up. At the same time, I was getting a little tired of post-beer hangovers (the *worst*) and felt that drinking less but drinking better was a more grown-up way of drinking. And the austere and uncertain climate of the early 21st century seemed to call for something with a bit more kick – hard liquor and hard times have a definite affinity. As I googled the recipe for my first 'Martini' one night and sipped the results with my wife in front of *Mad Men* (I'd used the wrong sort of vermouth, but still, not bad), I'd guess a lot of people were going through a similar process of discovery.

At the time of writing, cocktailing is in vogue in a way it hasn't been since F. Scott Fitzgerald coined 'to cocktail' as a verb in 1928 (I have cocktailed; we were cocktailing; I would have had to have cocktailed; etc). Some say we are in the Silver Age of the cocktail – if you count the era around American Prohibition as the Golden Age. In the major international cities, new bars seem to open each week, ranging from faux-speakeasies (which try to recapture something of the illicit dash of Fitzgeraldian drinking) to hyper-modern molecular establishments with Rotavapors and sous-vide machines. There are bars devoted to gin, rum, tequila – even to spirits that were all but unheard of a decade ago, such as pisco and mezcal. There is a cheering resurgence in independent producers, such as London gin distillers Sipsmith and Sacred, a development that has challenged the dominance of the corporate behemoths that for many years concentrated more on marketing than distilling. But all over the alcohol 'industry', you will now find people who care deeply about their craft. Such is the demand that bartending is one of the very few honest trades in which Britain faces a genuine skills shortage.

Still, considering how many customers seem happy to spend £8.50 (and often twice that) on cocktails when they're out, I still find it surprising that so few acquire the simple means to do so for themselves at home – which is always where the lasting revolutions happen. As I finally got round to discovering cocktails myself – documenting my first attempts on my blog, The Spirits, and later in my column in the *London Evening Standard* – I made two discoveries. One, it's not that hard. Seriously. Serving 500 perfect drinks to exacting patrons in a bar with very low profit margins: that's hard. Serving four Negronis to guests before dinner: that's easier than making toast. Two, there's a lot of unnecessary, intimidating and confusing information out there, enough to make you think: 'You know what? I always did like wine…'

For I swiftly found that there are plenty of people who take this stuff very seriously: a whole webosphere of bloggers and geeks, who do not drink drinks but *imbibe libations*, document their journeys through vintage recipe lists, and cultivate strong opinions on Batavia arrack. There are books written by bartenders… sorry, *mixologists*… who seem to assume you too have a ready supply of acid phosphate and mallow root and place 'craft cocktails' on a par with creating a collateralised debt obligation. They're often in the pay of major alcohol brands too, which means you're never sure you can trust them when they say that such-and-such a rum is the only rum you can possibly use. Then there are books from the 1920s that are charming, but which could be subtitled '500 ways of mixing gin and vermouth'. And there are some really horrible books with neon fonts and blue monstrosities that will make you think cocktails are really naff.

All of this makes me fear that cocktailing has suffered a similar fate to cookery in general. A relatively small number of people have become proficient, even obsessive cooks – often with the questionable aim of creating 'restaurant quality cooking at home' (one would far sooner encounter home-quality cooking in restaurants, but that's another story). However, these obsessive 'foodies' are the exceptions to the general rule, as all the surveys show that most people cook less than they used to. For all the cookery shows on TV, for all our familiarity with exotic cuisines and poncy techniques, the ready-meals section of the supermarket is still expanding.

My suspicion is that the 'drinkies' (the foodies' alcoholic counterparts) are outliers too; I'll bet the average person makes fewer cocktails than they used to. It's a shame, because I get the impression that in the not-too-distant past, people not only kept reasonable selections of spirits – they knew what to do with them, too. But how often have you visited someone's home and seen the same bottle gathering dust in the corner (often quite a nice one, often one that YOU BOUGHT THEM). Perhaps it will end up getting slathered in Coca-Cola at a party; perhaps it will be consumed as a dare. It would be such a simple thing to turn it into some punch.

Mixing drinks is not really an art, let alone a fine one. It is a craft. With a little application, a child could learn it. Your child! Or, at least, your inner child. And while learning the chords for Leonard Cohen's 'Famous Blue Raincoat' might have a more nourishing effect on the soul, you should not discount the spiritual refreshment of cocktails, which are not unlike songs, if you think about it. They pass in about the same amount of time. They transport you to somewhere else. They are rich in variety: there are ancient folk songs that are open to everyone, jazz-age standards that you can use for improvisation, kitsch songs and exotic songs, quaint songs and silly songs, communal songs and disco songs, and modern masterpieces that rely on complicated production techniques. Like songs, cocktails combine the wild and the cultivated, the spiritual and the profane... in short, they distil the human experience. They provide the feeling that this moment is special and that 'feelings' and 'moments' are important.

But really, the only thing you need to know is that cocktails make people happy. Honestly, people really light up when you offer to make them a cocktail. If there's one thing that you need to know to make good cocktails, it's that. Why would you not want that happiness for as many people as possible?

A BRIEF HISTORY OF COCKTAILING

'Civilisation begins with distillation'
William Faulkner (1897–1962), attributed.

The development of alcohol

You do not need to know who invented the Zombie (see page 214) or the Corpse Reviver #2 (see page 156) to appreciate their effects, but knowing a little history will lend them a dimension beyond mere taste and effect. The history of alcohol is ultimately the history of sociability. If you want to understand why we drink the way we do now, you need to peer back long ago.

Before there were cocktails, there were spirits; before there were spirits, there was wine, beer and mead; before there was any of that, there were piles of fruit turning funky in the sun. Monkeys couldn't get enough of that fruit. Elephants too. In fact, most living creatures seem to like getting pissed. When laboratory rats in cages are offered an unlimited supply of booze, apparently they incline to the same rituals that we do, including aperitifs, nightcaps and twice-weekly binges.

What is happening in that funkifying fruit is fermentation, a form of natural alchemy. In crude terms, a special strain of yeast consumes the fruit's natural sugars and farts out ethanol as a by-product. Ethanol has many remarkable properties: it works as a solvent and so it can preserve things; it is flammable so it may be used as fuel; it kills bacteria so it can disinfect (all of these properties have their uses in cocktails by the way). However, most magically, the alchemy that produces ethanol in the first place is mirrored in the psychoactive effects that ethanol has on the creatures who consume it. Alcohol is not only (mostly) beneficial to health. It also transforms us from earthbound creatures into seers, magi and visionaries. It has long been man's favourite mind-altering substance and his most holy too, the flame of Dionysus, the blood of Christ, the muse of poets.

We can assume that Homo sapiens first encountered alcohol by accident – but we soon learned how to create a more reliable supply. As alcohol production developed, so society itself changed. The invention of brewing seems to have coincided with the invention of agriculture, and with it, the invention of the city – for fermenting grains into beer not only helped to make water safer to drink, but also drew people together for rituals and storytelling. The rise of wine production (which requires two stages of fermentation) coincided with rise of the great empires of antiquity, as well as the spread of organised religion. What was the first thing Noah did when he got off the ark? He planted a vineyard, of course.

It took the genius of Arabian science to produce the more concentrated forms of alcohol required for spirits. The discovery of distillation (the separation of alcohol from water) is generally credited to the 9th-century Persian physician, Muhammad ibn Zakariya Razi, who was the first to isolate ethanol in its pure form. The science seems to have crept into Europe in the Middle Ages via eastern perfumers and medicine men, who used the new, stronger forms of alcohol to capture and preserve the 'spirits' of beneficial herbs and plants.

It was only really in the 15th century that distilling techniques became widespread, allowing ordinary farmers to turn grain and fruits into high-proof alcohol. This is when the early versions of the 'national' spirits that endure to this day were first developed. Dutch genever was grain spirit macerated with juniper. Irish *'uisge-beatha'* (whiskey) was malt barley spirit distilled from beer (Scotch whisky came later). Northern European schnapps and aquavit were produced from fruit and often flavoured with caraway; German and French brandy was distilled from grape wine; Italian grappa from grape pips; Russian and Polish 'bread wine' (the precursors of vodka) from rye, barley and wheat; East European slivovitz from plums; etc.

Many of the early spirits and liqueurs were first used as medicine, and some recipes from this period are still in existence today. Bénédictine, a herbal liqueur sweetened with honey and numerous other good things, is still made to a 1605 recipe. Chartreuse, a proprietary liqueur from the French Alps containing 131 herbal extracts, dates back to the 16th century, when it was made by Carthusian monks as an 'Elixir for Long Life'. Bols Genever has been in production since 1575, when they thought that the juniper that is the principal flavour was good for kidneys. In these cases, it's as if the alcohol has acted as a sort of meta-preservative, safeguarding the techniques as much as the aromas for posterity – how many products could you try today that are the same as they were more than 400 years ago?

Still, the bottles in the contemporary bar owe as much to politics as they do to anything so trivial as taste. William of Orange made genever fashionable among the English aristocracy to cement Anglo-Dutch relations (in English hands, it would become gin, the most important cocktail ingredient of all). Scotch whisky distilleries only really came to life during the Napoleonic wars, when a new home-grown alternative was needed to French cognac. Rum was a by-product of the sugar – and slave – trade, and thus stands as one of the earliest products of globalisation. In recent years, as international trade routes have become ever more interwoven, we have seen the gradual assimilation of still more exotic products, such as Mexican tequila and mescal, Peruvian and Chilean pisco, Brazilian cachaça, Chinese baijiu, Japanese shochu and Korean soju.

So if brewing helped to create human society, and winemaking wet the head of civilisation, distilling ushered in what we might see as modernity – and all the anxieties that go with it. The first great moral panic surrounding alcohol came with the Gin Craze of the 18th century, when backstreet distillers began to imitate genever and sell it dirt cheap to the urban poor, including, shockingly, children, and even more shockingly, women. The corrupting effects of 'Madame Geneva' were usually held in unfavourable contrast with the wholesome, rural qualities of beer. Even when the epidemic was brought under control, the gin palaces of 19th-century London were reviled for their gaudy gaslight and seductive architecture – as if the spirits served within set off temptations that could never quite be brought under control.

Early mixed drinks
Long before anyone shook up a cocktail, our ancestors were raiding their medicine chests to give a bit of kick to their cups. During the gin craze, the 'blue ruin' was more often than not drunk neat ('a flash of lightening'; 'a kick in the guts') or else mixed with water ('crank').

However, more wholesome treats endured in the Purl (stout, gin and spices, heated with a poker from the fire; see page 228), the Flip (warm ale with egg, spice and often gin; see page 164) or the Rumfustian (hot gin with sherry, ales and spices). Later, the proprietors of the gin palaces discovered that the new Old Tom and London Dry styles went with pretty much anything. The prostitutes who frequented them seem to have drunk gin with cream and sugar.

The classy way of consuming spirits, however, was Punch (ten recipes are given in these pages). The society ritual of gathering around the 'flowing bowl' dates back at least to 16th-century India and returned to Britain (along with its secret ingredients, nutmeg and tea) with the East India Company writers. The word 'punch' comes from the Hindi word *panch* which means 'five', referring to the five elements: alcohol, sweetness, sourness, dilution and spice. The drink attained peak popularity in the late 18th century, when every good household would have had its own recipe. According to the Victorian uber-housekeeper, Mrs Beeton, Punch fell out of favour only when wine became more widely available. By 1847, Charles Dickens (a great punchmaker) was trying to arrest the decline by using his novels to promote his own cherished recipes.

This didn't mean that mixed drinks weren't widely enjoyed – or given names that sound suspiciously like today's cocktails. Mrs Beeton provided recipes for Mint Juleps, Gin Slings and Sherry Cobblers, as well as Ching-Chings, Flosters and Locomotives. At the time, however, many modern ingredients would have been either impossible to obtain or prohibitively expensive. Citrus fruit was an exoticism: the old punch recipes make a lot of play of obtaining every last drop from every lemon, and suggest citric acid or 'oil of lemon' if the real thing wasn't available. Ice would have had to be cut from stagnant pools, so it would have been unthinkable to place it in your drink; most drinks were therefore served hot or at room temperature. Gin and rum were the most economical spirits to buy, cognac and whisky a luxury – which more or less holds true to this day.

Other mixed drinks were made out of expedience. From 1740, the sailors of the British Navy were given a daily tot (half a pint!) of rum, which they took to mixing with their lime rations, giving rise to sailor's Grog (see Navy Grog, page 204) and an early version of the Gimlet (page 84). In the sugar plantations of the Caribbean, wealthy colonials would teach their houseboys the proportions for what became known as Planter's Punch, made with lime, sugar, rum and tea: 'one of sour, two of sweet, three of strong, four of weak' (see pages 227 and 208). Rum was also the preferred drink of the early colonists in America – at least until the British dramatically raised duties to protect their own market share. This led not only to the development of American whiskey, but also indirectly to the foundation of the American state itself, as 'no taxation without representation' became a rallying cry for the Founding Fathers. And it was in the melting pot of the new nation that strong liquor was to find its spiritual home, mixed with greater enthusiasm and showmanship than anywhere else in the world.

The first cocktails

No one has ever come up with a definitive theory of where the word 'cocktail' comes from and how it relates to the rear-end of a male hen. Still, while we use it today as a general term for what our ancestors would have called 'fancy drinks', it originally denoted something much more specific. The first recorded use was in London in 1798, but it was in America that the cocktail first became associated with an agreed recipe. A cocktail was defined in 1806 as a 'bittered sling'. A sling was spirit sweetened with sugar and diluted with a little water; it was the addition of aromatic bitters, flavoured with root, bark and spice, that made it a cocktail. Since bitters up to that point had been used exclusively as medicine (or snake-oil, more properly), the first cocktails were generally seen as health drinks, a bit like kale juice or coconut water are today. Classically, the spirit used would have been Dutch genever. Over time, however, American rye whiskey became the standard base and, once refrigeration machines were introduced in the mid-19th century, ice was preferred to water. This is why today's Old Fashioned (see page 63) is called the Old Fashioned. Only it wasn't old-fashioned then. It was spankingly new.

The earliest cocktails evolved from this basic genome. Gin, whisky (or whiskey) and brandy were the most common spirits used. The sweetness, when it didn't come from raw sugar, often arrived in the form of curaçao (an orange liqueur from the Dutch Caribbean) and/or maraschino (a sweet liqueur made from marasca cherries and pits, from the Dalmatian coast of Croatia). Bartenders made additional use of fruit syrups (otherwise used for sodas), shrubs (fruits preserved in vinegar) and tiny doses of such exoticisms as absinthe to impart additional flavour.

By the time Jerry Thomas came to write his *Bartender's Guide* in 1862 – the first true cocktail book – there was clearly enough variety and demand to make it all worth noting down. Thomas opened his first saloon in New York in 1851 and soon earned fame as a travelling showman. In 1859, he toured Britain with a set of silver utensils, the publicity promising: 'The real genuine iced American beverages, prepared by genuine Yankee professor'. One of his signature 'sensation drinks' was known as the Blue Blazer and involved him 'throwing' ignited brandy from one mug into another in an arc of blue flame. If you think the wallies lobbing peach schnapps around in B@1 in Milton Keynes are all trying to be Tom Cruise in *Cocktail*, you are wrong. They can claim a far nobler heritage.

The Golden Age of cocktailing began in the late 19th century – and it required a little old-world sophistication to usher it along. Vermouth is a form of fortified wine, infused with spices and herbs, and traditionally made in south-east France and northern Italy. When used in cocktails as a sweetener in place of the curaçao or maraschino, it brought far subtler interplays of flavour. The first drink in this new style is generally deemed to be the Manhattan (c1870s; see page 59). In its wake came the Martinez ('Same as Manhattan, only you substitute gin for whiskey' – O.H. Byron's *Modern Bartender's Guide*, 1884; see page 125) and eventually the Martini (see page 57), which was first listed in the second edition of Harry Johnson's delightful *Bartenders' Manual* (1888).

Part of the charm of these early books lies in the glimpse they give into the cosmopolitan barrooms of America at the time – as the

American Dream had it, it was only in the promised land that an ambitious young gin from London could marry a nice young vermouth from France and hope to make an honest living. It seems the bartender's job was as much to interpret his patrons' orders as to prescribe what they should be drinking. The 19th century, after all, was the high period of taxonomy. Naturalists such as Charles Darwin set about classifying the natural world into species; novelists such as Charles Dickens and Honoré de Balzac attempted to do the same for human society. It fell to Thomas, Johnson and their contemporaries to organise the world's drinking. How else would we know that Burnt Brandy and Peach was used in the Southern States as a cure for diarrhoea, or that Swiss people would be annoyed if you served them absinthe the French way?

Johnson went a little further, including in his *Bartenders' Manual* meticulous detail on how to run a bar. His readership clearly had problems keeping ants out of their mixing bottles (he recommends you stand them in a bowl of water), as well as training 'boys', keeping books and handling deliveries of ice. For all that has changed, it's interesting to see what has not. Johnson's publishers clearly realised that money can be made from product placement ('In all First-Class Bar Rooms Boker's Genuine Bitters is still in demand as much as ever'). Johnson also seems to have had a portal into early 21st-century east London hipsterdom. 'The swaggering air some bartenders have, and by which they think they impress the customers with their importance, should be studiously avoided.'

The Jazz Age and Prohibition
Cocktail culture was at its zenith in the great American cities in 1919 when the Volstead Act came into force, prohibiting the sale of all alcohol. Europe had had its own moral panics over the abuse of alcohol, from the gin pandemic of 18th-century London to the absinthe scandals of early 20th-century France. Hard liquor had been forbidden in the new Soviet Union, but generally, the Temperance movements lost out to the Moderators. Only America went so far as an outright ban, thanks in no small part to the determined efforts of the Anti-Saloon League and the Women's Christian Temperance Union.

The 18th Amendment to the US Constitution was unpopular from the start, particularly in the cities, where people saw it as a few rural puritans imposing their will on the metropolitan classes just as they had cracked the proportions for a really decent Martini. Not that Prohibition stopped America drinking. It simply created a billion-dollar criminal industry overnight. 'I violate the Prohibition law, sure... Who doesn't?' the moonshine magnate Al Capone would reason with the Chicago press. 'The only difference is I take more chances than the man who drinks a cocktail before dinner and a flock of highballs after it.' Capone's gang, by the way, drank Southsides – a surprisingly unmacho combo of gin, lemon, sugar and mint (see page 212).

If Prohibition made drinking more hassle – and eye-wateringly expensive, too – it also made it more fun. Once you'd schlepped through Fat Sam's Grand Slam for a nightcap, you may as well make it seven after all. The speakeasies also helped to broaden the range of people drinking cocktails. Prohibition coincided with the era of the flapper – a new kind of liberated woman who discovered a taste for smokes, bobbed haircuts, casual sex and Pink Ladies (see page 178) that would soon spread to the masses of American females. The era also saw a tearing down of traditional boundaries, as jazz resounded through the dancehalls, and brought the debutantes and slickers into contact with Harlem players and Brooklyn mobsters, all with authority as their common enemy. 'Prohibition has set a great many dull feet dancing', observed the English journalist and prolific author Beverley Nichols. 'Who would prefer, to these excitements, a sedate and legal dinner, even if all the wines of the world were at his disposition?'

Meanwhile, the loss of America's overground drinking culture was the rest of the world's gain. As great New York bars such as the Algonquin and the Waldorf-Astoria switched to serving lemonade, their bartenders crossed the Atlantic to seek employment elsewhere. Harry MacElhone, a Scot who learned his trade in New York, moved back to Europe after the First World War and set up Harry's Bar at 5 Rue Daunou in Paris. Here, he claimed to invent the Sidecar, the Bloody Mary and the French 75 (see pages 181, 193 and 72). Harry Craddock (also British born, but an American citizen), came to England with his young family to take a position at the new-fangled American Bar at London's Savoy Hotel.

In Britain, cocktails were initially viewed with suspicion as 'sensation drinks' or, at best, with mild curiosity. 'Cocktails are compounds very much used by "early birds" to fortify the inner man, and by those who like their consolations hot and strong', wrote William Terrington in *Cooling Cups and Dainty Drinks* (1869). '"Cocktail" is not so ancient an institution as Juleps &c, but, with its next of kin, "Crusta", it promises to maintain its ground.' Even if the more hidebound Englishman mourned the decline of the pub and the good sing-song rituals that went with it, the opulence of venues such as the Savoy (which opened in 1889) lent enough glamour and respectability to drinking that women were finally trusted with a modicum of gin. Indeed, the first head bartenders at the American Bar were women – Ruth Burgess and Ada Coleman. Craddock succeeded them in 1925 and the *Savoy Cocktail Book* to which he lent his name remains the quintessential document of the era. It's also, presumably, where a good Jeeves would have turned when his Wooster requested a Between the Sheets (page 149). 'The cocktail is best drunk cold while it is still laughing at you', was Craddock's immortal advice.

As American bartenders fled their country for booze, many of their most loyal patrons did the same. For many years, Ernest Hemingway propped up the bar at La Florida in Havana (now El Floridita), the home of the Daiquiri (see page 158). The writer and adventurer Charles H. Baker made a fortune before the Wall Street Crash and duly spent Prohibition travelling around the world on steamships, compiling the recipes for what would become his *Gentleman's Companion* – not least the famous Singapore Sling and the Mojito (see pages 211 and 203). Still, by the time Prohibition was repealed at the height of the Great Depression in 1933, the damage had been done. Hundreds of distilleries had gone bust. Ireland's whiskey industry was almost dead. A culture had been destroyed. The few companies that remained standing were in a position to manipulate the changing market – and not always for the better.

The post-war decline

The prevailing mood immediately post-Prohibition in American might be best summarised as: 'Well that was a lot of silly nonsense: let's get drunk!' It's part of what makes the movies of the period so appealing – a determination to show that consuming six Martinis with your spouse (as in *The Thin Man*, 1934) was not only harmless but also wholesome. What were those puritans thinking?

However, as the Second World War came and went, the high spirits began to feel a little misplaced. In Britain, war led to austerity, rationing and a desire for a quieter life. In America, the economy boomed, but the focus of consumer culture had shifted from the city to the suburbs, from youth to the family, from the bar to the home. This was arguably the high point of the amateur. The best cocktail writing of the period is addressed to the home drinker, notably David Embury's *The Fine Art of Mixing Drinks* (1948) and Bernard DeVoto's *The Hour* (1948).

Cocktails were made with less finesse than before but perhaps more regularity. Consider little Sally Draper in *Mad Men*, expressing her daughterly affection for Don by mixing him his Old Fashioneds. Or, indeed, the prodigious number of spirits drunk by Frank and April Wheeler in Richard Yates's novel *Revolutionary Road* (1961). Frank is always thinking about the 'three fingers of bourbon' he will be drinking when they get home, to a living room adorned with a 'white wrought-iron table set with ice and cocktail mixings'. Not that the Wheelers' marriage is anything to aspire to, exactly. Or the Drapers', for that matter. But still.

It was also a time of family nights out. In Hollywood, a former bootlegger named Ernest Gantt changed his name to Don the Beachcomber and opened the first of his Polynesian theme restaurants in 1934. He and his rival, Trader Vic Bergstrom, would set a trend for kitsch escapism that would endure for decades. The appeal lay in the lavish sets (fibreglass waterfalls; fake tropical storms; girls in hula skirts) as much as the rum-laced 'exotics' that they served, such as Mai Tais (see page 202) and Zombies (see page 214). Caribbean drinks, Cantonese food, Polynesian décor – who cares about authenticity as long as it makes you smile?

It was in the 1960s that all of this began to decline. Blame sex, vodka and rock'n'roll. For the babyboomers, the cocktail was a throwback to their parents' generation, the quietly shellshocked souls who had emerged from the Second World War with modest dreams and military habits. It was speed that kept the rock clubs going, beer that the confident new working-class youth drank on nights out, and marijuana and LSD that opened their minds. Rum and Coke, gin and orange, neat Jack Daniel's were fine. The fiddly business of icing a Sidecar (see page 181) did not tally with the spirit of the age.

At roughly the same time, a new product gained ascendancy. Vodka is not really like other spirits, at least in its modern form (which was only actually introduced to Russia in 1895... see the Kangaroo, page 121). It owes its existence to the development of the rectification column by the chemicals industry, a piece of engineering that allows you to distil alcohol from pretty much anything organic. It creates a spirit that is colourless, nuanceless and more of an intoxication delivery system than a drink. As such, vodka proved wildly popular with people who wanted to get wasted without it actually tasting like they were getting wasted. The Moscow Mule (see table, page 190) was invented Los Angeles in 1941 as way of marketing Smirnoff and proved madly popular. Soon, vodka was being mixed with Coca-Cola, tonic (ahead of gin) and whatever else was to hand. It remains by far the world's best-selling spirit to this day.

There were spasms of life in the 1970s, which saw a rise of the package holiday in Europe; sophisticated ladies now liked to be seen drinking Cinzano or Campari. For the most part, these were glum years of Tequila Sunrises (see page 240) and Harvey Wallbangers. The Roaring 80s also saw a partial revival, as the emerging financial elite spent their evenings in glass-walled bars talking into enormous mobile phones. However, vodka had wiped the floor with gin in the Martini wars – and the vermouth that is so essential to the drink's subtlety was reduced in quantity until it disappeared altogether. Hence the Martini became a glass of iced vodka, the alcoholic equivalent of cocaine, more of a macho prop than the subtle and poetic drink it once was (see page 57).

This was nothing compared with the rise of flavoured 'Martinis'. Someone worked out that if you serve a yuppy vodka in a triangular glass, lace it with sugar and fruit and pretend it's frightfully sophisticated, you can charge them handsomely. The French Martini – a fruit-laced concoction that is neither French nor a Martini – is typical of the period. By the 1990s, industrial pre-mixed cocktails, such as Smirnoff Ice or WKD, were vying with stimulants such as vodka Red Bull to keep people dancing all night. In Britain at least, people were consuming alcohol to mimic the effects of ecstasy. Bars in general became noisier and stickier. The sensible option was to stick to beer.

Revival

It was only really in the 21st century, that cocktails began to reacquire their former glory. We should credit two drinks, not much admired now, as important staging posts. In New York, the Cosmopolitan (see page 157), as toted by *Sex and the City*'s Carrie Bradshaw, began to connote sass – and marked the cocktail's transition to 'luxury' product, a bit like a designer handbag. (It is no coincidence that the world's leading luxury brand, LVMH, makes handbags *and* spirits.) The rise of the Mojito (see page 203), which relies on fresh mint and lime for its flavour, obliged bar owners to start using organic plant matter in their drinks as opposed to processed commercial mixtures. At this point it was standard practice to squirt something called 'sour mix' from the 'gun' as opposed to actually squeezing lemons or limes.

The revival rode a number of parallel trends. A few venues, such as Dick Bradsell's Atlantic Bar in London and Dale DeGroff's Rainbow Room in New York, reminded everyone how it should be done. Middle-class people became a lot fussier about what they shoved down their gullets in general. A new globetrotting generation thirsted for Caipirinhas from Brazil (see page 153) and Pisco Sours from Peru and Chile (see page 179), as well as continental crazes such as Spritzes from Venice (see page 75) – now only a £24.99 EasyJet flight away.

Meanwhile, the more ambitious bartenders, such as Audrey Saunders of Pegu Club in New York, took to their kitchens. A top chef would never rely on pre-made Bisto; she would use her own stock to make her own gravy. Why should a bartender, therefore, use grenadine that's laced with corn-syrup and E-numbers? Wouldn't Jerry Thomas have made his own? Other bartenders, such as Tony Conigliaro of London's 69 Colebrooke Row, looked to molecular gastronomy for inspiration. If the fanciest chefs were using sci-fi equipment to make food, why shouldn't he use it to make drinks?

The web opened a new form of cosmopolitanism. We now have a huge database of information and imagery from bygone ages at our fingertips – and take comfort in the idea of fleeing into a simpler age. Social media now allows us to compete, often unwittingly, about whose experience is the most authentic, the most exclusive, the most glamorous. Always photo-ready and up-for-it, the cocktail has become established as the lifestyle accessory of the age.

The cocktail today

Seen against the broader currents of history, certain patterns begin to emerge in cocktail trends. For one, there is a notable correlation between the popularity of cocktails and economic inequality. The high point of cocktails in the 1920s coincided with some of the most outrageous financial philandering the world has ever seen. The low point for cocktails coincided with the 'post-war settlement' from 1945 to 1979 or so, when the western democracies sought to create a more egalitarian society. The cocktail revival began with the deregulation of the financial markets in the 1980s, reaching ordinary suburban centres in the 1990s (in slightly dodgy form), and truly got going in the boom years of the 2000s.

Following the great global crash of 2008, as lucky westerners drink cocktails with ever-greater abandon, where does this leave us now? Well, here are some items I've sampled in London bars recently. Pickled onion Monster Munch-infused vermouth. A chocolate digestive and stilton-flavoured Martini (really). A Mustard Martini. Salt Beef Beigel-infused Sazerac, complete with gherkin. A 'Bone' Martini where a distillate made from pulverised chicken bones provides the element of dryness. A cocktail that is supposed to taste like putting your tongue on a 9V battery.

I suppose you could see these baroque and Instagrammable creations as evidence of the boundless creativity of the modern bar scene. To me, they suggest that somewhere along the line, we've lost our way. We've allowed novelty to eclipse all other virtues (and having tasted all of the above, I wouldn't order any of them again... but why would anyone?). We're also using drinks to show off, to make distinctions between ourselves and others, rather than to commune around booze as people once did. We're abusing our hard-won rights to get merry in public, men and women, by behaving like children. Or worse: cutesters.

So as I see it, the challenge of 21st-century drinking is not to see who can create a Spherical Negroni or a Coco Pops Sazerac, but to ensure that the funky fruits of civilisation are open to all. We should see the sum of cocktail craft less as a way of boosting our own Twitter status, and more as a potable Wikipedia, allowing us a multisensory appreciation of who we are and how we got here. For there is no more instant way to conjure the gaudy thrill of a 19th-century gin palace than a tot of Old Tom gin and water. The jitterbugging dash of Prohibition is right there in the Scofflaw (see page 180). Even something as brazenly inauthentic as Don the Beachcomber's Zombie captures the reinvention available in midcentury California. It's all there in the spirits, if you only know how to set them free.

What we need is a liquid equivalent of the Arts and Crafts movement, led by some bibulous William Morris, to make good-quality, unwanky drinking available to all. Morris wanted everybody's homes to be touched by the beauty of good artistry and craftsmanship. 'Beauty, which is what is meant by art, using the word in its widest sense, is, I contend, no mere accident to human life, which people can take or leave as they choose, but a positive necessity of life.' I like to think of cocktails in the same way. They are the distillation of human ingenuity, not so much luxuries as essential pleasures. So next time I come round your house, I want you to make me a really goddam excellent cocktail.

PRELIMINARIES

'Try never to get drunk outside your own house'

Jack Kerouac, who never took that advice

10 THINGS YOU SHOULD KNOW ABOUT MAKING COCKTAILS

1. Start with the classics.

In Haruki Murakami's novel *Norwegian Wood* (1987), the character of Nagasawa only reads books that are more than 40 years old; if it's still in print after all that time, it's probably worth reading. (Follow the policy rigidly and you will not be able to read *Norwegian Wood* until 2027, but you get the idea.) A similar principle applies to cocktails. There are modern classics, true, but they're mostly indebted to the classic classics, which are classics for good reason. They're great! What's more, the classics are built on simple principles that, once learned, will lend structure to your own experiments.

2. Alcohol is the most important ingredient.

It should go without saying, but so many people persist in the belief that a cocktail should be a liquid pudding or a naughty milkshake, it is worth repeating. A proper cocktail should not disguise its booziness; it should celebrate it. As a rule of thumb, a cocktail is 50ml of the 'base' spirit (that's a double shot), plus a couple of other bits and bobs. Use a generous hand with spirits and a stingy hand with bits and bobs. It's easy to make a cocktail more sweet or sour or dilute; it's harder to make it unsweet or unsour and undilute. A lot of bartenders pour the alcohol into the shaker last for this reason – if you mess up with the cheaper ingredients, you haven't wasted the good stuff.

3. Ice is the second most important ingredient.

Do not even think about throwing a cocktail party unless the contents of your freezer could sink the Titanic. Do not ever ask as English publicans often do: 'Ice with your G&T?' There is a certain kind of Englishman who still sees ice either as overly fussy (upper-class) or a way of cheating him out of drink (lower and middle class). But when ice is freely available in your own home and you have already purchased the liquor, there is no excuse. Ice serves a dual purpose in cocktails, chilling the drink as well as providing a little (but not too much) dilution. If you use insufficient ice, it will melt much more quickly, resulting in insufficient chilling and too much dilution. The ice should always poke above the alcohol line both in the shaker and in the glass. How much ice do I need? More.

4. Mixers? Where we're going we won't need mixers.
How many times have you heard someone say: 'Ngah, we've got a bottle of rum, but we haven't got any mixers...' Oh yeah? What about that *massive bowl of limes over there*? (Assuming there's a massive bowl of limes over there.) What I mean is, cocktails should be comprised of ordinary fresh ingredients. Alcohol, other kinds of alcohol, ice, lemons, limes, sugar... maybe some eggs or berries or mint... and preferably not Diet Coke or concentrated orange juice. Study the labels of pre-made sodas and syrups carefully before you introduce them to your best bourbon. Do you really want saccharine, xanthan gum and E-numbers in there?

5. Keep it simple.
You do not need a whole tray of liqueurs, you do not need an orchard of fruits, you do not need some obscure variety of pisco, you certainly do not need all of these things at the same time. 'Many a cocktail has been hoist on the petard of its own casual plurality', as Charles H. Baker once wrote. Use ingredients that you understand, generally no more than two or three per drink. Think of your core cocktails like scrambled eggs or spaghetti sauce (*i.e.* something you might make each week and perfect over many years) rather than lobster thermidor or game pie (*i.e.* something you might make once and never know if you got quite right).

6. A cocktail should be balanced.
Aim for a harmonious blend of flavours, so neither sweetness nor sourness nor bitterness dominates the whole. The question is less whether it tastes good on first sip – it's easy to make something that makes you go 'Hot *damn*!' The question is more whether it still tastes good on the last sip: it's harder to make something that makes you go

'Hot *damn*! Same again!' Your taste buds are your guide here; keep tasting at all stages of preparation.

7. A cocktail is supposed to look nice.
You don't have to be a perfume ponce about it, but you should take time and care over presentation. It's part of the ritual. A little lemon-zest twist here, a frosted glass there – it makes whoever you're making the cocktail for feel special. Even if it's yourself, it's 1am, and no one came to your birthday.

8. Only shake cocktails with fruit juice in them.
It's a simple but more or less binding rule. Certain international super spies occasionally break it *cough James Bond with his 'special Martini' cough tosser*. However, it will serve the rest of us well. When you break it down, there are essentially two kinds of cocktail: aromatic cocktails, which contain only alcoholic ingredients; and sour cocktails, which contain citrus fruit (or occasionally other fruits, cream, egg, coffee, etc). The former kind (which are often dry, boozy and occasionally bitter) should be stirred with ice, which results in even dilution and a smoother texture. The latter kind (which are often tangy, fruity and occasionally creamy) require shaking, which results in more amalgamation, more dilution and a slightly altered texture. Both kinds can be diluted with water, soda, tea, champagne and so on, to form a third category: long drinks. Pretty much all else is variation.

9. All the pieces matter.
Every single component you add to the cocktail makes a difference. David Embury, the great amateur cocktail maker, insisted that no drink was better than the worst ingredient therein. That, to me, is a denial of the basic point of making a cocktail – your labour and ingenuity adds value – but you see the principle. The brand of rum you buy makes a difference; the particular limes you pick out in the supermarket make a difference; the time of year you buy your limes makes a difference. There are fewer variables in making a Daiquiri (see page 158) than in, say, cooking meatballs, so what you put into the glass matters (and how

much, and what kind of glass, and what side you part your hair, etc). On the other hand, see rule 10.

10. But they also don't matter.

By which, I mean, you are making cocktails, not safety speccing an Airbus, so who really gives a damn? The main task in hand when drinking cocktails is to have a fun time. If you're out of bourbon and use Scotch, no one will die. If you get the proportions slightly wrong, use more orange next time – you don't learn unless you make mistakes. If you can only afford supermarket gin, who cares? It's still gin. There is nothing more boring than someone who is boring about things that aren't boring. On the other hand, see rule 9. Etc.

THE BASIC CABINET

The cocktail menus in posh bars may leave you feeling a little deficient, booze-wise: lavender-infused this, barrel-aged that, triple-filtered-through-Kate-Middleton's-gymslip whatnot. As you wait to be served and eye the bottles of Suze and Chartreuse VEP and Umeshu and what-even-is-that, you may think, 'Oh God I'll have to spend at least a million pounds if I'm to make this stuff at home!'

You don't. You are not in competition with these guys. What you need to get started yourself is actually very simple. A bottle of gin will do, frankly. However, the best strategy is to pick one cocktail you really like, and then a second one you also like, buy the ingredients for those and see what you can make with the overlap. If the cocktails you like are fairly classic (see rule 1, page 30), there will be a lot you can do with the overlap. In the period when most of the classic cocktails were invented, there weren't all that many bottles to choose from anyway. To make the cocktails listed in Jerry Thomas's *Bartender's Guide*, for example, you only actually need eight alcoholic ingredients – brandy, whiskey, gin, curaçao, maraschino, vermouth, bitters and absinthe – plus a few syrups.

The cabinet I began with was based around what I considered to be my three favourite cocktails and which still are, pretty much: the Martini, the Manhattan and the Negroni. Whatever else comes and goes, and whatever little twists I might apply to them, I would like to be able to make them at all times, in the same way that, as a cook, I always want there to be onions and eggs and lemons in the kitchen. All this requires is six bottles – gin, bourbon, Italian vermouth, French vermouth, Campari and Angostura bitters – available in reputable emporia for about £80 combined.

The overlap of Martinis, Manhattans and Negronis is large. With a few kitchen ingredients and the odd passing bottle of wine, the six core bottles open up Whiskey Sours and Gin Fizzes, Spritzes and Smashes, plus Old Fashioneds, Juleps, Bronxes, Bees Kneeses, Americanos, French 75s, Southsides and many more things that look weird when you pluralise them. If you take the minimal effort to make your own syrups, you can add Gimlets, Ward Eights, Clover Clubs and Army & Navys to the list. With a bit more effort, we're into Bacon Old Fashioneds and Ramos Gin Fizzes. The 25 classic cocktails listed from page 56 represent the range of possibilities – but since these are the bottles we'll be drawing on time and again, it's worth looking at each of them in a little more detail.

Gin

London's great contribution to regret, gin is simply the most useful cocktail ingredient there is. Like your BFF on your birthday, it gets along with everyone and always brings something along to the party in its own right. Gin is the English corruption of a spirit named genever from Holland, the original Dutch courage, named after the Dutch word for juniper. Once William of Orange had fiddled with a few laws to allow landowners to profit from selling excess grain for distillation, England went mental for the stuff. A whole bunch of 18th-century Walter Whites began to synthesise it in the backstreets of Georgian London and soon, women were selling their children's clothes to buy more gin, 11-year-olds were knifing strangers for a 'kick in the guts' and gin was blamed for all manner of social ills for which it was perhaps merely the symptom.

To my mind, the charm of gin lies in its interplay of mayhem and melancholy, as dictated by the particular ingredients used in each example. The modern stuff is made from grain spirit in a manner not dissimilar to vodka, and then redistilled with a variety of herbs, fruits, spices and flowers (known as 'botanicals') for flavour. The only real rule is that juniper must dominate, but the supporting cast may involve coriander, lemon, cassia, cardamon, cinnamon, angelica, orris, licorice, almond and the odd curveball like cucumber or rose or London rainwater. This spectrum of flavours is part of the reason gin is so good for mixing. You might think of each gin as a little music box, where the various botanicals form notes and chords that various different mixers will use to harmonise; lemon will bring out its citrusy notes, lime will draw out the tropical flavours, vermouth will pick out floral notes, etc.

Gin fell out of fashion from the 1960s, and little was made in London until very recently. When the distiller Sam Galsworthy applied for a licence to make his Sipsmith in 2009, he had to wait for two years, with the eventual excuse that no one had asked since 1823. This state of affairs is now happily remedied with a cacophony of small producers all vying to prove that their particular combination of botanicals is the *sine qua non*. I like more gins than is seemly, but I would give honourable mention to Hayman's, Martin Miller, Sipsmith, Sacred and Half Hitch, which all come in at £20–£25. Still, you can get decent enough gin for less than that. Of the big brands, I'd always choose Tanqueray over Bombay Sapphire and at the cheapest end, Beefeater over Gordon's – though if you do go for Gordon's try to make it the yellow-label stuff they sell abroad, which comes in at a slightly higher proof (as a general rule, the higher alcohol, the more flavourful the gin).

These are all examples of the London Dry style, which came into fashion in the late 19th century. The sweeter Old Tom dominated in Victorian times and would have been used in many older cocktails, notably the Tom Collins (Hayman's makes a wonderful Old Tom). Plymouth Gin is in a category all of its own and has a special citrusy charm that's great in Martinis.

Bourbon

If gin is the English mother of the cocktail, bourbon is the all-American dad. Actually, that honour would probably go to rye whiskey, but since it is annoyingly hard to find in Britain, rye's slightly more approachable younger brother is your go-to guy. Does that make bourbon the uncle of the cocktail? Who cares, I'm getting bored of this metaphor. Like rye, bourbon has a moody glare and a five o'clock shadow, but it also has a malty lick of sweetness that makes it combine well with sugar, spice, nuts, chocolate, honey and, you know, nice things. Certainly, the American whiskeys are far more companionable than Scotch, which tends to stand aloof in cocktails.

It was Scottish, Irish and Welsh settlers who first brought whiskey distilling and barrel-ageing over the Atlantic. While Scotch is made from malted barley (and often smoked with peat), American distillers threw in other grains too, notably corn (perky, sweet), rye (hefty, peppery) and occasionally wheat (creamy, bright). However, it was the barrel that lent the really distinct flavour to American whiskeys. When charred on the inside, they impart a delicious woody roundness to spirits aged inside them, as well as a darker hue. The discovery of this happy quality was most likely an accident. Now it is law: all bourbon must be made in brand-new charred barrels. The bourbon distilleries often end up selling them to the Scots when they're done with them.

The word 'bourbon' comes from Bourbon County in Kentucky, named in honour of the French who fought alongside the Yankees in the War of Independence. And once the pesky English had all but killed the nascent American rum industry with their taxes, American whiskey became the national spirit, sipped by cowboys, farmers, pioneers, good-time girls, tycoons and working men alike. It's rough stuff that comes over all sweet. It's also the cornerstone of two of the most important cocktails ever created, the Old Fashioned and the Manhattan.

Brandwise? Don't make the common mistake of thinking that Jack Daniel's is bourbon (it's not, it's Kentucky Straight Whiskey... though to be fair, you can still use it in a Manhattan and no one will get hurt). Jim Beam is the entry-level bourbon and Maker's Mark is a good step up. Personally, however, I like the ones that have a good strong rye backbone and offer a bit more proof, such as Wild Turkey 101, Buffalo Trace and (if you can afford it) George T. Stagg. If you opt for a pure rye, the peppery Rittenhouse 100 is beloved of American bartenders and cheap in the States ($20) but not here (£35). So book a holiday.

Italian vermouth (aka sweet vermouth)
French vermouth (aka dry vermouth)

These are heady times in the world of vermouth. Not since the 1880s have drinkers gone so mad for the stuff. London's fashionable Chiltern Firehouse literally has a vermouth menu. In Barcelona, vermouth bars are very much where it's at. New vermouth brands are popping up all over the shop. Put it this way: if Kim and Kanye launched their own vermouth, I would not be surprised.

It's a cheering reversal of fortunes, since not so long ago, vermouth had a huge image problem. It was partly, I suspect, due to the word 'vermouth' itself – it sounds like a condition you might get from tonguing rats. Wine-people got far more excited about sherry. Spirit drinkers preferred something with higher ABV than vermouth. But the cocktail would be in the ditch without it. Vermouth is a much subtler way of adding sweetness and aroma to spirits than the sugar or liqueurs used in the first cocktails. It was vermouth creations that provided the gateway to the cocktail's golden era. What's the difference between a glass of gin and a Martini? Vermouth.

So WTF is it? Essentially, vermouth is wine that is first flavoured with aromatic plants such as gentian and wormwood (the German name for which, *Wermut*, gives the drink its name) and then fortified with small quantities of brandy or grappa. There are many different styles, but for our purposes we'll need two, Italian and French.

'Italian' vermouth (traditionally made near Turin) is the red stuff and is otherwise known as rosso or rouge. It is sweet, heady with aroma and takes its colour from caramel since it's actually made with white grapes. It's the first stuff that would have made it to American bars. 'French' (traditionally made in Chambery and Marseille) is light-coloured, much steelier and lemony and less sweet – hence, it is sometimes known as dry or extra dry. It lends an extra layer of intrigue to cocktails and often serves as an intermediary between spirits and fruitier flavours.

To confuse matters, there is also a sweeter style of light vermouth known as 'white' (aka bianco/blanc), which is used in cocktails less often; rosé and amber styles are becoming more common too. To make matters even more confusing, most producers turn their hands to all styles – so French producers make Italian vermouths and Italian make French vermouths. My advice for the ver-gin is to begin with Italian Italian and French French. Martini Rosso is the most common Italian (about £10 a bottle) and it is rosy and boisterous and friendly and versatile. More luxurious is Carpano's Antica Formula (about £15 for a half bottle), which is rich and syrupy and dark and moody and marries with higher-proof spirits in just the most heavenly way. Punt e Mes, also made by Carpano, brings its own bitter rasp and is worth seeking out (about £8 a bottle).

As regards French, Noilly Prat (c£10) is my go-to dry vermouth, the lasting representative of the aromatic Marseille style. Dolin Dry is a fine example of the bone-dry Chambery style and now more widely available (also c£10). Martini Extra Dry (c£10) is OK, but less interesting.

Remember that vermouth is wine and while the fortification will extend its natural life, it will not keep all the flavours fresh forever. I suspect that vermouth's low reputation had a lot to do with the fact that people used only a tiny amount at a time and then it went stale at the back their cupboards and then they were like: 'Why would I put *this* in my Martini?' Buy it in half-bottles if you can, vacuumise it with one of those wine stopper things and keep it in the fridge.

Campari

OK, I admit, Campari is a personal indulgence, not a 'classic' ingredient and still not applicable to more than a handful of cocktails. But what cocktails! The Negroni, the Spritz, the Sbagliato, the Americano, the Rosita, the Boulevardier… these are some of the finest drinks known to man. Like Coca-Cola and Heinz Ketchup, Campari is one of the great proprietary recipes and it will lend Continental sophistication to all these uncouth American drinks.

Campari is an Italian liqueur made near Milan in a style known as 'amaro' (which is Italian for 'bitter'). It is made to a secret formula that was originally said to contain

60 ingredients, including quinine, rhubarb, ginseng and bitter orange peel. Its most distinctive feature, apart from its refreshing bitterness and sophisticated *je ne sais quoi* (or whatever that is in Italian), is its plasma-red colour, which means that almost everything you make with it will look fetching. Since the Campari family aren't telling, we don't really know what makes it red. Heaven forbid that it be food colouring.

Classically, it's mixed with gin and vermouth, but actually, it will go with a whole variety of other flavours, from tequila to chocolate and strawberries. Aside from its cocktail uses, it's a handy bottle to have around. It is so good with fizzy water as Campari and Soda, you needn't even bother with cocktails. It is also very fine with (*fresh*) orange juice and even better with grapefruit juice. Moreover, it goes incredibly well with all manner of white wines, sparkling or otherwise, so if any guest ever brings a substandard bottle around, you can say: 'Great, I'll make Spritzes!' and not worry about offending them.

While Campari is Campari is Campari (around £15 a bottle), you can at a push use the similar Aperol (£15) in its place – it's sweeter and lighter and more of a crowd-pleaser, but lacks the astringent intensity of the original. Other amari tend to be darker and more syrupy, more suited to after-dinner drinking, but if you get the chance, seek out the divine Cynar (which includes artichoke in its list of ingredients; £15) and the tar like Averna (£15-£20).

Aromatic bitters

Once upon a time, bitters were thought of as a miracle cure. They are the most enduring legacy of alcohol's medicinal past, compounded by macerating beneficial herbs, spices and roots in high-proof alcohol, and touted as a tonic for everything from liver complaints to dyspepsia, rheum to stomach cramps. Look in any 19th-century newspaper and you'll find an advert for some brand or other, each making promises that would make the Advertising Standards Authority displeased today.

To the best of my knowledge they do naff all to cure scrofula, but when it comes to cocktails, aromatic bitters have a magic way of making everything better. In fact, it was a few drops of bitters that transformed the mere 'sling' into the first true Cocktail – and when I say a few drops, you really only need two or three shakes of the bottle. People often compare the role of bitters in cocktails to that of salt and pepper in cooking, less of a flavour, more of a way of amplifying other flavours and binding them together. That's a bit of a simplification, since different sorts of bitters have different effects – making them more like a spice rack – but certainly, with the aromatic style of bitters that is most commonly used, the general effect is to deepen the flavour, lending a fourth dimension. With any cocktail made with bitters, it's worth tasting the mixture before and after adding them to appreciate their effect; a Manhattan without bitters, for example, feels a little two-dimensional.

There are many kinds of bitters (orange, anis, peppermint, chocolate, lavender, peach, cardamom... many). However, to all intents and purposes, there is just one brand of aromatic bitters and it is Angostura, which was invented by a German apothecary in Venezuela in 1824. It is readily available and only about £8–£10 for a small bottle that will take you a long time to get through. If you're a little more adventurous, I can recommend the Bitter Truth's Traveler's Set: it offers the beginner five miniature bottles to get to know, including the aromatic-style Jerry Thomas's Own Decanter Bitters, which is made to the master's 1862 recipe, plus a useful orange bitters, Creole bitters (which are a bit like the more famous Peychaud's bitters) and an interesting celery number to provide a little uplift.

THE BASIC STORE CUPBOARD

Since we're starting with a fairly limited range of bottles, I'm going to take more or less the same approach with the non-alcoholic ingredients too. There is no reason to go hunting around for sumac or persimmon or liver sausage to embellish your creations when lemons will do. Just to warn you: the most hard-to-source ingredients among the 25 classic cocktails listed from page 56 are citric acid and orange blossom water, both of which I have found in numerous local grocers as well as all the normcore supermarkets. Although familiar, these basic provisions have specific cocktail uses, so need a little elaboration.

Citrus

Citrus fruits, especially lemons and limes, are the most common 'other' ingredients in cocktails. They are used not only for their sour juice but also for their skins, which are used both as garnish and to extract the fine spray of bitter oils contained in the bubblewrap of their pores. **Lemons** vary one to the other and they also vary from month to month, since vendors change suppliers according to where in the world is having a harvest at that particular moment. It's worth tasting the cocktail to ensure you haven't chanced upon a notably sour lemon. If you are using lemons for their skins, try to buy unwaxed lemons.

   Limes are still harder to get right than lemons. Some of them are barren and mean and yield nary a drop of juice. Some positively explode when you stick a knife in. Since lime is mainly used for juice, not zest, buy thin-skinned ones that feel plump and ready to burst. Before you slice down the middle to juice, roll around under your palm on the worktop to break down the cavities between the segments.

   Oranges appear in a few cocktails for their juice (orange-juice cocktails tend to disappoint, I find) but more often for their skins, which impart a Christmassy warmth. Blood orange, which is a little more tart, generally tastes better and looks prettier too. Do not countenance using carton orange juice unless it's of the finest quality. **Grapefruits** are more useful to have around, both for their bitter juice (which finds its way into numerous cocktails) and for their skin, which makes a superior twist. Bear in mind that pink grapefruits are sweeter than yellow ones.

Do experiment with other citrus too. Clementines and especially mandarins are good in place of orange juice. The huge pomelo provides a bland juice, but makes up for it with a bumper amount of twists.

Sugar

There is a bit of a witch-hunt aimed at sugar at present. This is understandable in one sense (too much sugar makes you fat and irritable) but silly in another. Sweet is one of the four components of taste, along with sour, bitter and salt; to try and go through life without sugar is a bit like choosing a three-legged horse when healthy quadropeds are at your disposal. For sugar does not provide merely sweetness; it provides balance too. Try making a Sour without sugar – it's unpleasant. Try making alcohol without sugar for that matter. No! Sugar is essential. Just don't add too much.

Still, it's worth bearing in mind too that all refined white sugar is ever going to add to your cocktail is sweetness. For this reason, I prefer to use unrefined sugars, which retain some of the richness of the tropical sun and thus improve the flavour of the cocktail. As a general rule, darker sugars pair better with darker spirits – but golden caster sugar will cover most of the bases.

Whichever sugar you use, you must first dissolve it into a syrup to mix it, otherwise you will end up with nasty little granules at the bottom of your cocktail glass. Recipes tend to call for one of two kinds of syrup. **Simple syrup** is one part sugar to one part water (1:1). **Rich simple syrup** is two parts sugar to one part water (2:1), therefore sweeter (though actually only 16.67 per cent sweeter). Personally, I like to use 2:1 syrup, partly because it keeps for longer, partly because you need less of it, and partly because that's just what I'm used to using. Just use a stingy hand when pouring as there's nothing worse than an over-sugary cocktail. Here's my go-to syrup recipe that will work throughout this book.

Golden sugar syrup (2:1)
Place a saucepan on a low heat. Pour in 2 cupfuls of golden caster
sugar, then 1 cupful of fresh water. Stir until the sugar is completely
dissolved. As soon as it is dissolved, remove the syrup from the heat and
allow it to cool – on no account allow it to boil. Once cooled, decant
into a jar or bottle and it should keep for six weeks or so – do give it a
little taste before you add it to you spirits if you're in doubt.

Fizzy water

Many cocktail recipes call for something called soda water. Most
people do not have a soda syphon in their homes and there is no
meaningful difference between bought 'soda' water and your average
sparkling water. So I just call it fizzy water. There's no real need for an
expensive brand, though if you go for smaller bottles, then the water's
more likely to be fizzy when you come to use it. Honourable mention to
Perrier, which is super-bubbly, thus provides respectable effervescence
when only a small amount of fizzy water is required.

Eggs

For cocktail purposes, use only eggs fresh from a hen's bum. You can tell
a tired egg from how watery the white is when you crack it. If it's very
watery, make a different cocktail or simply do without. Unless you have
the tastes of a 19th-century coachman, you will probably be drinking
only the whites so retain the yolks for spaghetti carbonara (Nigella
Lawson's recipe is the best and involves Noilly Prat dry vermouth).

Others

I like to think of other ingredients as passing through – so when I
happen to have **mint** in the kitchen, I might go: 'Ooh, I could make
Mint Juleps', while fresh **cream** means Ramos Gin Fizzes all round
(see pages 71 and 87). **Pineapple** juice is a useful ingredient (buy
good-quality pressed juice) and the fruit itself makes a fetching garnish.
Other ingredients called for in this preliminary section are **basil, passion
fruit, tonic water, marmalade, maple syrup** and, erm, **bacon**. There are
also syrups made from **almonds** (orgeat; see Army & Navy, page 86, to

make your own), **pomegranates** (grenadine; page 83) and **raspberries**, while the lime cordial recipe (see Gimlet, page 84) calls for citric acid, coriander seeds and green cardamom.

Garnishes

The garnish is a crucial part of what makes a cocktail a cocktail: a drink over which some special effort has been made. You may use anything that looks pleasing, from nasturtium flowers to basil leaves, pineapple and papayas and mangoes and kiwis, even plastic toys – but do bear in mind that simplicity is often best. With frothy cocktails, a few drops of bitters look good drizzled on top. Sometimes, no garnish at all is what's best. However, these are the most common.

Twists: If in doubt, garnish with a lemon-zest twist… or maybe an orange- or a grapefruit-zest twist, but probably a lemon-zest twist. A twist is a paper-thin length of peel, at least 1.5cm wide and 2.5–5cm long. To make one, you should place a serrated knife flush against the skin of an unwaxed fruit and saw away from your face, taking care to get as little of the white pith as possible. You can also use a vegetable peeler to do this, though in both cases exercise caution. It seems like an innocuous task, but it is easy to slip and create a twist from the skin on your thumb instead. The little round cavities on the peel contain bitter oils that provide uplift to a drink; to enhance the effect, rub the twist around the inside of the glass first or else twist it over the finished drink before dropping it in. Aesthetes will cut twists into rectangles or parallelograms for effect.

Wedges, wheels and slices: Lime garnishes usually take wedge form, and occasionally lemon garnishes do too. Slice the fruit in half lengthways and again into thirds or quarters. Make a further incision at 45 degrees into the flesh and slide on to the glass. Often, I've noticed, people assume they should remove this and squeeze it into the drink. Tell them not to, unless they really want their drink to be tart. Oranges are sometimes cut cross section to form a full-circle 'wheel' garnish; a lemon slice is typically a semicircle.

Cherries: Do not buy the lurid red 'cocktail cherries' you often find in supermarkets. It's better to have no cherry than a disgusting cherry.

At Christmas, you'll occasionally find jars of cherries in kirsch quite cheaply – these are preferable. Even better are the proper maraschino cherries made by Luxardo. If it's cherry season, it's easy enough to make your own: carefully pit 20 or so cherries, trying to keep them as intact as possible, place in a jar with a splash of sugar syrup and cover with vodka. Be warned though: hardly anyone ever eats the cherry so your effort may be in vain.

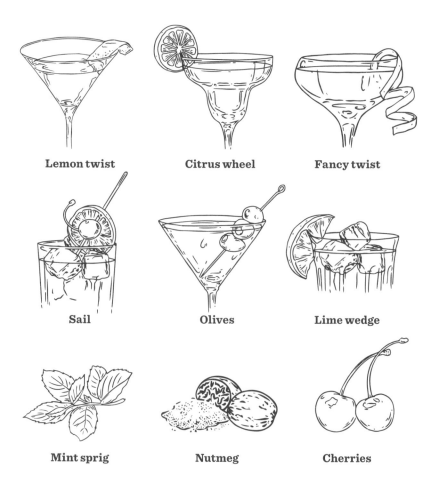

Lemon twist   **Citrus wheel**   **Fancy twist**

Sail   **Olives**   **Lime wedge**

Mint sprig   **Nutmeg**   **Cherries**

THE BASIC EQUIPMENT

A similar principle applies to equipment as applies to alcohol – you don't need as much as you think you do. Many people have cocktail shakers already that they never use (a bachelor friend tells me that he unfailingly receives three every birthday). However, you don't even need a cocktail shaker for most cocktails. The main thing you need, and sorry to bang on about this, is ICE.

Ice production

I mentioned in rule 3 (see page 30) about ice. I wasn't joking. You're going to need more of it. At least a tray *per person* per evening, since each tray is really only good for two cocktails. The easiest way to ruin a party is to have insufficient ice.

So you have three options. The first is to buy one of those huge American fridges with a built-in ice-maker… though don't assume that throwing money at the issue is the best remedy. While these machines produce copious ice, they have a tendency to issue stale and unsavoury ice that you really wouldn't want influencing your gin.

The second option is to buy fresh bags of ice from the shops… which is not a terrible idea if you're entertaining at short notice, though the ice that come in those bags often comes in very small pellets – which isn't ideal. In most cases, you want as large lumps as possible. Science: ten 10g ice cubes will melt more quickly than will one 100g ice cube because they have a larger surface area. This makes a huge difference to the dilution of the drink. Here, you can learn a lot from the experts. Careful study of the bartenders at the Savoy's American Bar in London reveals that they keep a huge lump of ice on the bar and hack off a single large lump with an ice-pick for shaking purposes. This makes for more cooling and less dilution.

The third and best option is to re-examine the relationship you have with your freezer. Devote a whole shelf solely to ice. Use only large ice trays, not little piddly ones. And think of ice trays less as storage vessels for ice and more as machines for making more ice. Once a tray has frozen, empty its contents into some freezer-based plastic container, and

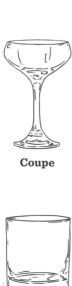

Coupe

Martini glass

Margarita glass

Old fashioned glass

Collins glass

Julep tin

Wine glass

Fancy glass

Champagne flute

Tiki Mug

Hurricane glass

Sherry glass

fill the tray up again. Do this each and every time you pass the freezer. Do it now, in fact.

Even better, make large Savoy-style ice of your own. Treat yourself to an enormous takeaway and hope that it comes in those plastic containers with lids. (If it doesn't, maybe just buy some plastic containers with lids.) Wash out these containers well, fill them with fresh water, replace the lids and put them in the freezer. After a few hours, you will have great blocks of ice. To cut a slab down into manageable pieces, remove it from the container and run it very quickly under a tap. Great fissures should creak into being. Place the block on a clean chopping board. It should now be easy to hack apart with a short sturdy knife or a fork. Use whichever lumps you need and return the rest to the freezer.

Not only does large ice make for more efficient shaking, it also looks excellent when you serve someone a drink with a rugged lump of Arctic in it as opposed to a few stingy cubes. Though for God's sake be careful. Careful study of the Savoy bartenders makes me worry that someday, someone will hurt themselves with that ice-pick.

Glassware

It is not essential to serve your cocktails in the correct glassware, but it is preferable (see rule 9, page 32). Here, the home bartender has a clear advantage over the pro. You don't have to ensure your glasses match, so you can pick up odd glasses in charity shops and at antiques markets. My only real advice is don't be tempted by coloured glasses, since they will upstage the colour of your cocktail, and don't spend too much on them as one day, someone will drop/sit on your beautiful glass and it will smash into tiny pieces. Also, smaller is better: it's better to leave people wanting more.

Posh bars keep numerous kinds of glasses, using different vessels for sours and flips and Margaritas and so on. The more styles you have, the better your Instagram feed is going to look, obviously, but this book only really calls for four.

A **cocktail** glass is the classic fancy long-stem glass and the first item on your shopping list. The most common style is the V-shaped Martini glass but to my mind the rounded coupe is more elegant. The idea is that you hold it by the stem so your hand doesn't warm the drink while the wide opening allows you to appreciate the aroma. Drinks served in these glasses are served 'up', with no ice, since they have already been chilled in the shaker.

An **old fashioned** glass is a short fat tumbler, sometimes called a rocks glass, ideally fairly sturdy. They are generally used for drinks that you mix in the glass itself, but occasionally shaken drinks are poured over extra cubes in the glass. Drinks served in this way are 'down' or 'on the rocks'.

A **tall** glass is a long thin glass, sometimes called a Collins glass or a Highball glass. These are used mainly for fizzes, since the length of the glass allows the bubbles further to travel.

A **flute** is a long-stemmed Champagne glass and is used for champagne cocktails.

Other vessels you might need are regular **wine** glasses (quite good for G&Ts), a copper **julep** tin, a **mug** for hot drinks and a novelty **tiki** cup in the shape of a carved tribal figurine, the dafter the better. And remember: only morons serve cocktails in **jam jars**.

Measuring devices

If you buy one special piece of equipment, make it a very small 60ml measuring jug with measurements that go all the way down to 5ml. Oxo make a useful one that you can read from above and from the side. Baby bottles are a good substitute, as they come printed with small measurements down the side.

Most bartenders will use a jigger: a little thimble that measures single shots (25ml) and/or double shots (50ml). Using a jigger has the advantage of being fast and much more debonair than squinting at a little jug. However, jiggers are problematic for the novice – not least because most taper inwards towards the bottom, which makes it far harder to gauge where the halfway mark is (let alone the 10ml or the 35ml mark). For this reason, I prefer a straight-sided jigger. For smaller measurements, use spoons. Generally, a teaspoon holds 2.5ml, a dessertspoon 5ml, a tablespoon 7.5ml, no matter what you read in other, less scrupulous recipe books.

Incidentally, as a proud European I have opted for millilitres for the purposes of this book, with 25ml as a basic 'shot'. American bartenders tend to express measurements in ounces, half ounces and so on – one ounce is about 30ml. Most of the cocktails in this book are built from a base of a 50ml double shot, but occasionally, I've rounded up or down to express the proportions without having to use fiddly decimal points.

Jigger

Measuring jug

Shakers

You can busk cocktails with no shaker. For cocktails that you stir, use a jug or a large glass to make the cocktail instead, then carefully strain out. For cocktails that you shake, you may use a large, well-cleaned jar and strain with a sieve.

But it's much easier with a shaker. The standard **three-part shaker** consists of a flask, a strainer and a cap. You assemble the cocktail in the flask, lob in the ice, ram on the strainer plus cap, shake it up and then remove the cap to strain into a glass. The built-in strainer isn't particularly discerning, so expect to use an additional strainer – a tea-strainer works well – to sift out those fine shards of ice. It should all fit together snugly so that it doesn't leak when you shake it but not so snugly that it becomes stuck when you try to prise it apart. Alas, both of these are common problems.

Pro bartenders often favour a **Boston shaker**, for speed and utility. It consists of a metal flask, a pint glass and a separate handheld

Hawthorne strainer, which is like a small metal ping-pong bat with holes in it and a spring round the edge. Here, the basic technique is to measure the liquids into the metal flask, wedge the ice-filled glass in it, give it a shake, and then bang them apart. The cocktail is then strained from the glass through the Hawthorne strainer.

Personally, I find the regular strainer less hassle. In all cases, remember that the longer you shake, the more cold but also the more dilute your drink will be. Five seconds is generally enough.

Boston shaker

Three-part shaker

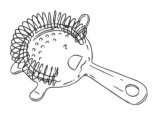

Hawthorne strainer

Tea strainer

Other equipment

...is mainly decorative. **Swizzlers** and **absinthe spoons** and **stirrers** and all that. **Barspoons** are long and come with swirly handles that makes them pleasing to stir with – but you can do pretty much the same thing with any other spoon. More useful is a hand-held **citrus squeezer**, sometimes known as a **Mexican elbow**. It saves a lot of time when you're making large quantities of punch or a platoon of sours. **Muddlers** are useful for bashing ginger, berries, herbs and so on, while a **blender** is called for in certain tropical drinks – the on-trend Nutri-bullet serves cocktailing purposes well.

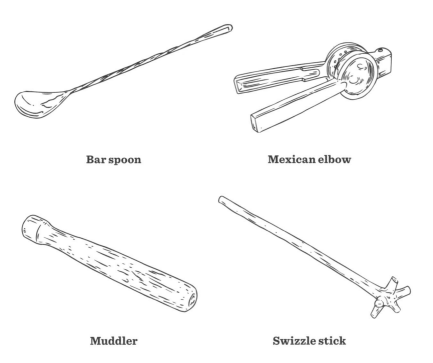

Bar spoon   Mexican elbow

Muddler   Swizzle stick

THE 25 CLASSICS

'For God's sake develop a little skill
and then do the job unostentatiously.'

Bernard DeVoto, *The Hour* (1948).

THE 25 COCKTAILS listed here between them show the breadth and depth of what you can do with your spirits. Each recipe is designed to illustrate some basic principle of stirring or shaking or egging or grenadining. Think of them as modules in your first year at cocktail university. Once you attain some basic proficiency, you can then go on and pluck all the fruits of the cocktailing orchard at your leisure – they are listed in the second half of this book (from page 100).

1. MARTINI

The Martini was not the first cocktail. It was not even the first Martini (that honour goes to the Martinez, see page 125). And yet there is something pre-eminent about it all the same. Perhaps it's best to think of it as the *quintessential* cocktail. At any rate, it's a fine place to start.

You could do worse than adopt the approach of Nick and Nora Charles in *The Thin Man*, the classic 1934 screwball comedy starring William Powell and Myrna Loy as a husband-and-wife detective duo. Released soon after the repeal of Prohibition, it is a celebration of both drinking and matrimony. Nick, a warm-hearted sophisticate, and Nora, the model 'modern' woman, both consume a ridiculous amount of alcohol, but it only ever makes them more sparkling, more fond of each other. In fact, the whole film could be an advertisement for Martinis, as if to say, 'how on earth did we ever do without them?'

> *Nora:* [settling down opposite her husband with a Martini]
> How many drinks have you had?
> *Nick:* [who has been drinking all afternoon]
> This will make six Martinis.
> *Nora:* [to the waiter] All right. Will you bring me five more
> Martinis, Leo? Line them right up here.

Though its ingredients are mostly English (gin) and a little French (vermouth), the Martini is an all-American invention – and its mixture of strength and sophistication, directness and delicacy captures the contradictions of its homeland. It looks sort of poncy; it makes you feel all fancy; and yet you are millilitres away from drinking a glass of neat spirit. You need to be a pioneer, a cowboy, a tycoon to make it through a half-dozen. But then again, I wonder if the key to its mysteries lies in its European ingredients? A background of Thomas Paine with just a dash of Alexander de Tocqueville? It is possible to over-think these things after a few.

There is a certain amount of mystique attached to Martini construction. Perfection, as ever, is less a matter of technique than of timing. By which I mean, the efficacy of any given Martini is far more to do with who you're drinking it with than whether your stirring method is quite up to scratch. Still, with such a simple drink, the little things matter.

The first thing to get right is the proportions. The earliest Martinis tended to be very 'wet', *i.e.*, long on the vermouth (a ratio of 1:1 in some of the old books). Over the century, the vermouth part came to be seen as an inconvenience. Noël Coward used to quip that you only need to wave the vermouth in the general direction of the cocktail; Winston Churchill liked to shine a light through the bottle; the Queen Mother, God rest her pickled soul, favoured an 11:1 ratio of gin to vermouth. Once the vermouth is discarded, you may as well lose the aromatics in the gin, too, and replace it with vodka. No! While I am in favour of a strong Martini, the vermouth should not hide. I find 5:1 to have the most compelling combination of aroma and heft but in certain moods, I will go all the way to 3:1. If I'm in the mood for neat spirit, I'll simply pour myself a glass of gin. (Try it sometime!)

The second point is that the cocktail must be ice, ice cold, a process which will ideally involve freezing your glass – but preferably not your gin, because that kills all the subtlety. The third point is that you shouldn't shake it, whatever James Bond or Nick in *The Thin Man* says. You should stir it very patiently. If there is any secret to Martinis, it lies in the methodical business of stirring for at least half minute, which binds it, chills it and dilutes it just a touch. In fact, water is the silent partner in a Martini. It should be present enough to take the alcoholic burn from the gin and help it to slip by almost unnoticed. If you are ever served a Martini with a little too much rasp, it's usually the result of a time-pressed bartender not having the patience to stir properly; try dropping a little water in it and sipping again.

You may garnish a Martini with a lemon-zest twist or green olive depending on your mood, and if you drop in some olive brine, it becomes a Dirty Martini. I have no real preference, it just depends on how I'm feeling. A few further Martini mysteries. The second is always better than the first. Two is never enough, three is always too many ('after three I'm under the table, after four I'm under the host', as

Dorothy Parker once said). Two olives on a cocktail stick are considered bad luck but three are fine. And another: I know hardened boozers who find Martinis way too strong, and yet my wife, who gets all la-la after a soupçon of wine, has a formidable capacity for them – a fact that makes me strangely proud. Perhaps, nodding to *The Thin Man* again, this explains why I always think of the Martini as a rather romantic drink.

50ml gin
10ml French vermouth
Dash orange bitters (optional)

First of all clear a little space in your freezer for a cocktail glass (if there's no room, throw out some ready-meals – they're always disappointing anyway). Leave it there, just chilling, while you make your lemon-zest twist or alternatively, thread an olive or three onto a cocktail stick.

Now carefully measure your ingredients into a shaker or jug, then add tons of ice cubes, as big as possible, well above the gin line. Stir the cocktail well for at least 30 seconds, running the bowl of the spoon around the edge of the mixing vessel. Remove the glass from the freezer and strain the alcohol into it. Twist the lemon zest to release a light spray of bitter liquid over the glass, then drop it in. Or drop in the olive(s), forgetting about the lemon stuff I just mentioned. Drink swiftly, in good company.

2. MANHATTAN

'Bartender, I'd like a Manhattan, please', coos Bette Midler at the beginning of the old Tom Waits song 'I Never Talk to Strangers'. Once the piano has bluesed up the scene, a sax squawks and Waits announces his presence, making it clear that this is a duet. 'Aaaargghghghghmmmm', he says. Or perhaps it's more of a 'Hi... rgghrgh...umm'. At any rate, you get the picture: downtown bar, grizzled barfly spots classy lady at ten o'clock, sidles up to her, clears his not inconsiderable throat and tries his luck: 'Stop me if you've heard this one…'

I'm not sure what Waits is drinking, probably Scotch and razorblades. ('I'd rather have a bottle in front of me than a frontal lobotomy', he once explained to a chat-show host). But we can be fairly certain that it is a Manhattan that fuels Bette Midler's worldly put-downs. 'Now tell me do you really think I'd fall for that old lie?' she teases. 'I was not born just yesterday.'

And yet her choice of drink gives her away. Wow, a Manhattan. That's a serious drink. Waits clearly detects that she's seeking a shade of oblivion with which he is familiar. 'You're bitter 'cos he left you, that's why you're drinking in this bar', he surmises. It turns out they know each other all too well. And so they fall in love, with the romance foreshadowed by the cocktail order – hard, sweet, bitter.

The Manhattan is generally agreed to be the very first cocktail made with vermouth, which was a novel ingredient in American bars in the late 19th century – a bit like liquid nitrogen is today, perhaps. It has spawned numerous variations (not least the Martini, see no.1) and it has barely slipped off cocktail menus since, which is hardly surprising because it is delicious. While it is the vermouth and whiskey that form the drama of the drink, it is the bitters that sew it all together – it's worth tasting without to see what a difference a little dash makes.

I wonder, in a contemporary version of 'I Never Talk to Strangers', what would the Bette Midler character have ordered? Perhaps a glass of Pinot Grigio? And if she had, would she have ended up wandering into the night with Tom Waits? Then again, while people often think of the Manhattan as a masculine, after-dark, aftershave-y sort of drink, one that goes well with smoke, steak and Miles Davis, you could make a good claim for it as the original 'girly drink'. There is a persistent rumour that it was actually invented by Winston Churchill's mother in the 1870s. Then there's that wonderful scene in *Some Like It Hot*, where Marilyn Monroe fixes a round of Manhattans for an entire female orchestra on a train after lights out. Her resourcefulness when faced with a bottle of bourbon is impressive: 'Who's got some vermouth?'; 'Run down to the pantry car and get some ice would ya?'

I suppose that's why everyone fell in love with her.

50ml bourbon (or rye)
20ml Italian vermouth
Dash Angostura bitters

The method is more of less the same as for the Martini (see page 57), right down to freezing the glass. Stir with plenty of ice and strain into a cold cocktail glass. Garnish with a cherry or an orange-zest twist (lemon will do at a push).

For a Perfect Manhattan, use a mixture of French vermouth and Italian vermouth. For a Dry Manhattan, use all French vermouth. Embellish and vary to your bitter heart's content.

3. AMERICANO

The Americano is what James Bond liked to order when he visited 'a mere café'. His reasoning? 'In cafés you have to drink the least offensive of the musical comedy drinks that go with them.' I've tried to order an Americano in cafés and they always assume I want a watery coffee. They're a little more civilised on the continent, where ordering *un caffè* or *un café* will get you a decent cup of java, and asking for *un Americano* will result in a simple, crisp, refreshing aperitif.

The Americano is not American, but Italian (which is why they spelled it with an 'o'). It used to be known as the Milano-Torino on account of the origins of its two main ingredients: Campari from Milan and Martini Rosso Vermouth from Turin. American soldiers stationed in Florence after the First World War were fond of it, and so the name stuck.

For many, the Americano is merely a stepping stone to the much more grown-up Negroni (which follows). However, provided you don't add too much fizzy water, it has a sprightly charm all of its own and the low alcohol content makes it a pleasant option for moments when you need to keep your wits about you. It's also so simple – not really a cocktail at all – that you can usually instruct even the most haphazard teenage temp to make one for you in an English pub, provided they have the ingredients. One shot of this, one shot of that, splash of water. Not so hard!

> *25ml Campari*
> *25ml Italian vermouth*
> *50ml fizzy water*

Simply pour each of the ingredients into a tall glass filled with ice and stir. Alcohol has a tendency to sit at the bottom of the glass (a common problem in long drinks), so be sure to stir 'up and down' as well as round and round. Garnish with a lemon slice.

4. NEGRONI

You can tell a lot about a decade by what people order in cocktail bars. Currently, one drink rolls off the tongue like no other. What the Cosmopolitan (see page 157) was to the sugary Nineties and the Mojito (see page 203) was to the minty-fresh Noughties, the Negroni has become to the bittersweet 2010s. It is the order of the epoch, the drink that seems to capture, in its aromatic majesty, something of the spirit of the age. These days, you're almost as likely to be served one at a vicarage BBQ as you are at an East London speakeasy.

Its appeal can be explained on multiple levels. Foremost, the Negroni is delicious – complex, not-too-sweet, strong and refreshing, the perfect portal between work and play. The classic *aperitivo*, it whets the appetite like nothing else. Its bitterness (thanks to the Campari) and its retro hue (also thanks to the Campari) feel all Continental – just the thing to give your gathering a certain *sprezzatura*.

Like so many modern crazes, it is vintage, too. Its origins lie in the Americano (see previous recipe), which was a well-established drink when the redoubtable Count Negroni walked into a Naples bar and announced that he wanted something a mite stronger. The barman added gin instead of soda, which is never a bad idea, and in this case, was a wholly inspired one. 'Let-a me show you how an Italian drinks!', I can imagine the Count exclaiming to the assembled servicemen.

As Orson Welles discovered when he was filming in Italy, the Negroni acheives a rare equilibrium. 'The bitters are excellent for your liver; the gin is bad for you; they balance each other', he remarked. Still, while Italophiles have been sipping Negronis for years, it has never enjoyed anything like its current vogue – which gives it the appeal of a lost classic, a bit like that moment when 'Pink Moon' by Nick Drake was played on a Volkswagen advert.

Even more importantly for bar managers, it is cheap and easy to make – much less time-consuming than a Mojito, for example. Many London establishments now offer Negroni on tap, but before you call your plumber, do bear in mind that the Negroni is pretty easy to make from scratch. As long as you keep to the formula of one part strong, one part aromatic wine, one part bitter, it is adaptable too.

25ml gin
25ml Italian vermouth
25ml Campari

Pour all of the ingredients into an old fashioned glass filled with large cubes of ice. Stir. Garnish with a lemon- or orange-zest twist and consume with something salty just before dinner. It's also surprisingly good in an airport lounge at 7am.

5. OLD FASHIONED

The Old Fashioned is so called as it descended from the very first cocktail known to man, which consisted of liquor, sugar, bitters and water. They used to call it the 'Cocktail', since there wasn't anything to be Old Fashioned about at that stage. As we all know, the Old Fashioned is what Don Draper drinks. We even get to see his own personal recipe, as he makes one in season three of *Mad Men*, in the episode where Roger Sterling has his party.

Shortly after his boss has serenaded his guests and shortly before Peter Campbell dances in such a charming fashion that you begin to wonder whether he isn't the debonair, Gatsby-esque hero of the whole series, Don escorts his heavy soul away from the main action and finds himself at Roger's own personal bar. Since there is no barman around (only the millionaire hotelier, Conrad Hilton, also looking for a drink), Don is forced to take matters into his own hands. 'Is rye OK with you?' he asks Hilton. Rye *is* OK (in fact, it is much more authentic than bourbon). He then proceeds to make two Old Fashioneds.

This is Don's method. He drops a pair of brown sugar cubes into a pair of glasses and douses them in bitters. He fills a separate glass with ice and pours in the rye, topping up with soda water. He lets this chill while he crushes the sugar cubes with a muddler. After creating a quick rumpus in the rye and soda with a bar spoon, he distributes the liquid among the two glasses, ice cubes and all, before dropping in a lemon wedge. Then, he drinks it.

You should know that this is a really bad way to make an Old Fashioned. Despite its simplicity, its rusticity, its versatility, the original Cocktail is a difficult drink to get right. (The Manhattan, no.2, *looks* more sophisticated but it leaves a lot more margin for error.) The idea of an Old Fashioned is to draw out the qualities of base spirit you use (it doesn't necessarily have to be bourbon either). You want the sweet notes to be that bit sweeter; you want the dark notes to be that bit darker; you want the smooth notes to be that bit smoother. In short, you are looking for balance. Master an Old Fashioned and you are well on the way to mastering cocktails.

Why do I say Don Draper is all wrong? He is impatient. Watch him muddle that sugar cube. Do you think it is really crushed? Don't you think the drink needs a bit more stirring, Don? Don't you think your wife needs a little more loving? What will Hilton say when he gets to the bottom of the glass and encounters all that undissolved sugar? But Don gets away with it. That's charm for you. As all this is going on, Pete is dancing a blinder in the other room, and everyone still thinks he's a tit. Here is how I make an Old Fashioned.

> *50ml bourbon (or rye)*
> *5ml golden sugar syrup (2:1, see page 44)* *
> *Dash Angostura bitters*

Pour half the bourbon in the glass and add the sugar syrup* and bitters. Add two ice cubes and stir, allowing the cubes to melt a little. Pour in the second shot of bourbon and two more ice cubes and continue to stir. Then finally add two more ice cubes, stirring some more. It is the ice that provides the necessary dilution – but by introducing the bourbon in stages you are ensuring that it is never too dilute.

Now twist a length of orange (or lemon) peel over the drink to release a fine spray of oil and drop it in, along with a cherry, if you fancy. Drink; have sex with your secretary; have a cigarette; shout at Pete; shout at Peggy; etc.

* You can use a teaspoon of brown sugar in preference to the sugar syrup if you like; just be sure to dissolve it properly in half the bourbon before you add any ice.

6. SOUR

The Sour is one of the most useful cocktail recipes you can know, for it contains within it a formula that applies to a high proportion of all the cocktail recipes in existence. While the Whiskey Sour has a special New York-y sort of romance all of its own, you can make a Gin Sour too or a sour with any spirit you could care to name. In fact, I bet you can make a Sour *right now* with stuff you already have in your kitchen. In *The Seven Year Itch*, Tom Ewell's character Richard Sherman draws on this expedience to make Whiskey Sours for breakfast when he's left home alone for the summer. He chases his down with a peanut-butter sandwich. However, you can also have Sours for lunch or dinner, or at three in the morning at a party, to the unfailing appreciation of your fellow revellers.

Contemporary sours evolved from a 19th-century preparation called a Crusta, which requires you to peel an entire lemon and cement it to the glass with sugar. To me, that sounds like an awful hassle, but the drink they served within their special lemon cup was a simple enough combination of spirit, lemon, sugar and ice. Bear in mind that to our ancestors, the merest taste of fresh lemon would have been startling; a sour is not supposed to be sour so much as tangy, with the tartness of the citrus tempered by the sugar syrup. Once you master this delicate business, you will be on your way to making Daiquiris, Margaritas, Sidecars, and indeed, about half of the drinks in the canon, since they all work on a similar principle.

Every good bartender has his or her own preferred ratio for sours. David Embury, in his *Fine Art of Mixing Drinks*, insisted on a booze-heavy 8:2:1 ratio (two shots of spirit, half-shot of lemon, quarter-shot of rich sugar syrup). However, many bartenders prefer higher proportions of lemon and sugar. Another common ratio is 8:3:4, which translates as two shots of spirit, three-quarter-shot of lemon and a whole shot of *simple* syrup (ie 1:1 syrup, see page 43). After much experimentation, I've settled on 10 parts spirit, three parts lemon and two parts rich simple syrup, or 10:3:2. You can also express that as 50ml/15ml/10ml, or two shots of spirit, a generous half-shot of lemon and a stingy half-shot of sugar syrup. I like this ratio as it allows the flavour of the spirit to dominate and finds a nice poise between sugar and citrus.

The Sour is the first cocktail we will shake. Shaking not only cools the drink, it also adds texture (in the form of tiny air bubbles) and dilution (in the form of the melting ice). Technique is a matter of personal preference – you will find your rhythm, just be sure to hold tight – but do bear in mind that the longer you shake, the more slushy the ice will become and therefore the more diluted the drink will be. If you have opted for higher amounts of lemon and sugar, you will probably want to shake for a little longer. Likewise, if you use a bourbon that is 50 per cent ABV, the drink will benefit from more dilution than a bourbon that is 40 per cent ABV. If you want a good strong drink that is still cold, you should use larger lumps of ice (which will melt less) and shake for a briefer period.

Whatever kind of ice you use, the shaking will tease off little shards of it, which you do not want to end up in your drink. Therefore shaken cocktails should be double-strained by holding a tea-strainer or a sieve above your glass while pouring. As for glassware, you can serve a sour up or down (see page 50), but the fact that you have shaken it with ice does not negate the need for ice when you serve it down. With all that in mind, here is a simple Whiskey Sour... which suddenly doesn't seem so simple any more.

> *50ml bourbon (or gin, or whatever)*
> *15ml lemon juice*
> *10ml golden sugar syrup (2:1, see page 44)*

Measure your ingredients carefully and pour them into the shaker. Add plenty of ice (enough to come above the alcohol line) and then shake hard for five seconds. Double-strain into either a cold cocktail glass or an old fashioned glass filled with ice. The traditional garnish is a cherry and a lemon slice on a cocktail stick, which is known as a 'sail'. It may be easier to go for a cherry in the bottom of the glass or a lemon wedge.

You can leave the sour at that. Or you can get a little fancier. A little egg white shaken up with the drink makes it taste like lemon meringue pie, and imparts the silken texture of Marilyn Monroe's negligée. When made with whiskey, this is known as a Boston Sour. However, my preference with Whiskey Sours is to add a 'claret snap', which turns it into a New York Sour: once you have poured your cocktail, take a dessertspoon of red wine (classically, a Bordeaux) and carefully touch the edge of the spoon to the inner rim of the glass just above the cocktail line. The red wine will trickle down the side, and should 'float' on top of the cocktail. It makes the drink look *right gorgeous*, as they say in New York. As you sip the cold Sour through the rich wine, you get a beautiful contrast of flavours and temperatures. Do not neglect the Gin Sour either. Here, a dash of Angostura bitters will provide you with a Fitzgerald. Or turn to the next pair of recipes.

7. GREEN PARK

Erik Lorincz, the head bartender of the American Bar at London's Savoy Hotel, created this summery pleasure, foremost among contemporary classics to my mind. (I have never known it to disappoint anyone.) The secret ingredient is fresh basil, which any cook will tell you has a wonderful summery affinity with lemon. Here, it brings a herbaceous, liquorice scent to an ordinary Gin Sour (see previous recipe) and shows how a minor tweak can transform a basic template into something memorable. Erik's original recipe called for Hayman's Old Tom gin (which is slightly sweeter and more aromatic than an ordinary London Dry) and a dash of Bitter Truth's Celery Bitters (which lends a savoury vegetal uplift), but it is still worth constructing with our regular ingredients. Just don't omit the egg white.

'It is hard to think of anything more original than the egg', wrote Seb Emina in *The Breakfast Bible* and it's true. Eggs are miraculous things, capable of all sorts of culinary feats, from raising cakes to glazing pastry to binding forcemeat. In a cocktail context, eggs are used not for taste, but for texture – and as such should be thought of as a modifier rather than an ingredient. When you beat air into egg white, it creates tiny little bubbles. When you create enough bubbles – by shaking *really hard* – you transform it from a gloopy mess into a froth. This froth will float to the top of a drink and make it look attractive and feel all velvety and smooth.

The first thing to do with your egg is to ensure that it is fresh. Crack it carefully over a bowl, retaining the yolk in one half of the shell, but letting a little white slither out. If the white is watery, then it lacks the precise quality you want; make the cocktail without it. If it is good and stiff, separate white from yolk by pouring the yolk from one half of the shell to the other, letting the white slither into the bowl. Retain the yolk for some other purpose.

When shaking an egg cocktail, you need to create as many micro-bubbles as possible, so you need to agitate extra hard. You do not want extra dilution so most of your agitation should be done without ice. This is known as 'dry-shaking'. There are two approaches to dry shaking. Either you shake up everything without ice first and introduce the ice only after the egg has frothed (this is known as a 'double-shake'); or, shake everything *with* ice, double-strain, quickly rinse the shards of ice from the shaker, and then shake again without the ice. This is known as a 'reverse double-shake'.

Both methods have their pros and cons. With double-shaking, you create more froth in the first place, since room-temperature ingredients are more amenable to bubbling than very cold ones... but then you pop them by banging them around with the ice. With reverse double-shaking, you get more froth... but you have the hassle of doing washing up in the middle of preparation. All the same, the fact that you get a clean pour at the end (since you've already done your double-straining) makes me favour the reverse double-shake method.

Be careful with that egg white! Egg has a slightly 'wa-hey!' character when you try to measure it and if you include too much, you will be literally over-egging it. And relax. The chances of catching anything like salmonella from a cocktail are negligible.

50ml gin
15ml lemon
10ml golden sugar syrup (2:1, see page 44)
Dash celery bitters (optional)
6 fresh basil leaves
15ml egg white

Pour everything into the shaker except the egg white and taste... if you need to adjust the balance do so now. Now add the egg white and shake hard with large ice until your fingers are slightly numb. Double-strain out the cocktail into a spare vessel, empty the shaker and return the cocktail to the shaker without the ice, and shake like a demon to froth up the egg. Pour into a cold cocktail glass. Launch a basil leaf on top by way of garnish.

8. CLOVER CLUB

A bartender once told me that a Clover Club is what he offers to any woman who orders a Cosmopolitan (see page 157). It's not hard to see why. Both cocktails are, to use a retrograde term, 'girly drinks'. They are both fruity, are both sweet and both have a similar pinkish hue, though the Clover Club is more of an opaque pink, with a lacy frill.

The main difference is provenance. The Clover Club dates back to before Prohibition, when it was the house drink of a Philadelphia gentleman's club frequented by captains of industry. It is therefore a voguish and subversive reference point. The Cosmopolitan was sipped in pre-crash noughties when vodka was on the ascendancy and cranberry juice was a bit of a novelty – and there is nothing so unhip as the recent past. The Cosmopolitan is a blingy Louis Vuitton handbag. The Clover Club is a demure Mulberry satchel. They are both expensive – but one is a little more in tune with the age.

More importantly, the Clover Club tastes better, if you can get it right. This is not easy to do, since the precise proportions are a matter of some dispute. In fact, I'm not sure that I've read two Clover Club recipes that are the same. Some specify lime juice as opposed to lemon juice; some call for grenadine, some call for raspberry syrup; some call for vermouth, some don't; some involve egg white and some don't. My own recipe is the product of hours of arduous experimentation: a Gin Sour lengthened with a little vermouth and perfumed with raspberry. Ideally, the veil of egg-white foam will bind the garden notes of vermouth and raspberry into a liquid marshmallow, and then part, like the tendrils of a weeping willow, to reveal some good strong gin beneath, soured with just enough lemon to wake you up.

As for what my bartender offers any man who walks into his bar and orders a Cosmopolitan, I'm not sure... respect?

> *50ml gin*
> *15ml lemon juice*
> *10ml golden sugar syrup (2:1, see page 44)*
> *15ml French vermouth*
> *Three fresh raspberries*
> *15ml egg white*

The ingredient that usually presents difficulty with the Clover Club is raspberry syrup – but it shouldn't. All you really need is 10ml golden sugar syrup (2:1, see page 44) and three raspberries instead. Pour everything except the egg white into your shaker, swirl them around and taste. If it's not quite right, this is the best point to adjust the sweetness/tartness/strength. Now add the egg white and plenty of ice and shake hard for at least 10 seconds. Double-strain this into a spare vessel, give the shaker a quick rinse and then pour the cocktail back into the shaker without any ice. Shake it again for around 10 seconds to froth up the egg, and strain into a cold cocktail glass. Garnish with a lemon-zest twist or a fresh raspberry. A mint leaf on top turns it into a Clover Leaf.

9. MINT JULEP

The Mint Julep is one of the few American recipes that Charles H. Baker saw fit to include in his *Gentleman's Companion* of 1939, declaring it was 'a masterpiece in its own right, a true exotic of the Deep South'. When the thermometers are high and the motivation is low, the combination of hard liquor and fresh mint works like nothing else.

The classic recipe was recorded in the diary of the British naval officer Captain Frederick Marryat, a friend of Charles Dickens and author of many seafaring adventures. Even Mrs Beeton copied it. Marryat spent much of the 1830s travelling around the American South, during which time he became very fond of the local customs. The Mint Julep, he wrote, is 'one of the most delightful and insinuating potations that ever was invented, and may be drunk with equal satisfaction when the thermometer is as low as 70 degrees.'

The Captain's recipe called for a dozen tender shoots of mint, a spoon of sugar and equal parts peach brandy and ordinary brandy. You are to place the crushed ice on top of this and drink as the ice melts. Then, 'like the American ladies', the drink becomes irresistible, wrote Marryat.

The Julep has evolved and mutated since then. At some point, the peach brandy was discarded. At a later point, Kentucky bourbon replaced the brandy as a more patriotic choice. At various points, rum, lemon, berries, you name it has been thrown in.

While a Southerner might get particular about things, I see the Julep as one of those standards that each player may use to launch their own improvisation. The main thing to watch out for is the mint. It is a delicate herb but it is also prone to strops. You only need to tap it to release those ethereally fresh oils. If you pound it you will crush the loveliness away and be left with bitter leaf juices that aren't much good to anyone.

You also need to make crushed ice. Either buy ready-crushed from the frozen section, chip it away from a large block of ice, or fill up a couple of sturdy plastic bags with regular cubes and cudgel on your kitchen floor or appropriate surface until it is all broken up. The more high-tech method involves a blender, but I've broken blenders like this before so advise caution. If you can lay your hands on proper metal julep cups, these should be used, as the condensation does look mighty fine as it drips down the side. Maybe use a clean tin can with the label scrubbed away as a white trash alternative? You should also sip a Julep through a straw and garnish it with a mint sprig that tickles your nose as you drink.

> *10 or so fresh mint leaves*
> *50ml bourbon*
> *5ml golden sugar syrup (2:1, see page 44)*
> *20ml peach liqueur (optional)*

Gently bruise the mint in the bottom of your julep vessel, before adding the bourbon and sugar syrup. Add the peach liqueur, if required. Now add the crushed ice to just below the brim and churn the drink so that the ice and spirit are well combined. Heap more ice over the top, stick in a straw, garnish with more mint and sip.

10. FRENCH 75

Recently, my little sister texted me from a champagne bar to explain that she had found a new favourite drink. Champagne, she was already a fan of. Gin was held high in her estimation too. But it had never once occurred to her that they might actually go together, in the same actual glass.

Then again, the French 75 is decadence itself. It was named after the 75mm gun used by the French artillery in the First World War, and was supposedly invented by Harry MacElhone just after the First World War. Harry's Bar was among the most scintillating places in Paris, back when Paris was the most scintillating city in the world. I would like to imagine that on any given night, you'd have looked up from your French 75 to see Picasso and Cocteau and Chanel and Hemingway and the Fitzgeralds and Diaghilev and Stein and Stravinsky and Joyce and an inadvertently time-travelling Owen Wilson, all shimmering gently.

The French 75, which slides a spine of cold gin, lemon and sugar into a quivering body of champagne, is a simple and excellent way of improving bubbles. Admittedly you wouldn't want to use the best vintage Dom Perignon here but if you use half-decent bubbles, you should find the result sharp, steely and 'modern', in the way that Guillaume Apollinaire and Zelda Fitzgerald are modern. Certainly, with its sharp report, it is more satisfying than the more common methods of doctoring champagne – and I won't tell if you use prosecco.

30ml gin
10ml lemon juice
5ml golden sugar syrup (2:1, see page 44)
Champagne (or sparkling wine)

The most common fault with champagne cocktails is that they are too warm. Be sure to freeze your flutes first and shake the gin, lemon juice and sugar syrup over ice to combine (if you are opening a bottle of champagne, I'm assuming you're multiplying the quantities for guests, which may convince you it's worth the trouble). Double-strain a shot's worth of the mixture into each chilled glass and top up with champagne. Garnish with a lemon-zest twist – here, elegance is all, so I would use a knife to fashion each one into a neat little parallelogram.

11. TOM COLLINS & THE GIN FIZZ

A conundrum. If you look through old cocktail books you will learn that a Tom Collins is gin with lemon, sugar and fizzy water. A Gin Fizz is also gin with lemon, sugar and fizzy water. They're basically the same! The only significant difference, it emerges, is how you make them. The Tom Collins is less of a faff. You bung the lemon, sugar and gin in a glass and pour over fizzy water. With a Gin Fizz you make a Gin Sour in a shaker, then strain it into a glass and top it up with fizzy water.

Still, whichever way you prepare it, lemon, sugar and fizzy water is lemonade, so we're talking gin and lemonade. You can cut to the chase by throwing some gin in the bottom of a glass and topping it up with any decent brand of old-style lemonade. Job done! See you later.

If you're still reading, you probably want to do better than that. The good news is that you can. For a start you can make lemonade that is superior to any manufacturer's, since you have fresh lemons at your disposal and only you know how sweet you like it. (With any long-style sour, I'd advise using slightly more lemon and sugar than you would for a short-style sour, so that the lemon flavour withstands the extra dilution.) What's more, if you're going down the Gin Fizz route, with all the hassle of shaking, you can modify it any way you choose. Add some mint to the shaker and you have a Southside Fizz. Add some basil and you have a Green Park Fizz. You can add egg white (for a delicious Silver Fizz), egg yolk (for a not-sure-about-this Golden Fizz) or a whole egg (for a Royal Fizz… on second thoughts, no.) You can use cordial in place of the sugar syrup (for an Elderflower Fizz, say?). You can even throw in a scoop of lemon sorbet into the shaker (for a White Gin Fizz) or some vanilla ice cream (for a Silver Stallion).

As for the Tom Collins, well, it's hardly much hassle to squeeze a lemon into some gin, throw in some sugar syrup, is it? In fact, if you make it in a jug and multiply the proportions, it makes a swell cooler for a large tennis party or an awkward meeting with the in-laws. Why is it called a Tom Collins? Well, the drink is a variant on the John Collins which was originally made with Hollands Gin (which we now call genever) by a London bartender by the same name who served at

Limmer's Hotel in London in the mid-19th century. There's also a Jack Collins (made with applejack), a Juan Collins (with tequila), a Phil Collins (with pisco), etc. Who was Tom Collins? Well, I hear he's been badmouthing you in a bar down the road.

> Tom Collins
> *50ml gin*
> *25ml lemon juice*
> *15ml golden sugar syrup (2:1, see page 44)*
> *50ml fizzy water*

You can afford to be a bit sloppy with a Tom Collins. Take a tall glass. Pour in the gin, squirt in the lemon juice, lob in the sugar syrup and top with fizzy water. Stir. Garnish with a lemon slice.

This is a good drink to make in a jug if you're having visitors – simply multiply the quantities by the amount of visitors you have and then again by 1.5 so the greedy people can have seconds.

> Gin Fizz
> *50ml gin*
> *25ml lemon juice*
> *15ml golden sugar syrup (2:1, see page 44)*
> *50ml fizzy water*

Shake up the gin, lemon juice and sugar syrup over ice and double-strain into a tall glass filled with more ice. Top up with fizzy water and stir. Garnish with a lemon slice.

I'd recommend the Silver Fizz as a variation: add 15ml egg white to the mix and perform a reverse double shake (see page 68). Garnish this with a few drops of bitters.

12. SPRITZ

On a corner of Campo Santa Margherita in Venice is a small café containing the worst loos in town. It is frequented by local students, who call it Il Caffè Rosso on account of its colour (red) and its political leanings (also red) though its sign reads just Caffè. On most nights, it is so full of students with sockless loafers and thin cigarettes, that it is hard to make it to the bar – a plank supporting some sweaty-looking *cicchetti* and a brass espresso machine with an eagle embossed on it. It is tended by lightly perspiring bartenders. Most of their work consists of making the same cocktail, over and over. They place a tumbler on the bar top, and fill it with ice. From the bar tap comes a squirt of local dry white wine, straight from the barrel. Over this, they pour over a glug of Campari. Finally, they splash in the *seltz,* or soda. It is garnished with a lemon slice and a plump green olive on a stick, a 1960s innovation that many locals consider a voguish anomaly. It is called a Spritz. It is a local descendant of the classic Viennese way of watering down wine. Like the Caffè Rosso, the Spritz is red.

I happened upon this establishment a few years ago, when my wife and I spent a rainy few spring days and nights in Venice, sharing an umbrella in splashy little alleys, chasing down the rich honey-ish smell of a certain kind of dark green tree that we never did identify. On a serene evening, we ordered a pair of Spritzes and drank them outside, half-listening to the chatter of the students, wishing we spoke Italian bitter. I mean better. These students, I remember thinking, as our mouths puckered up to the sweet-bitter taste, are on to something.

A few years later, the Spritz had become London's summer drink of choice. Sadly, most places there serve it with Aperol (the tamer cousin of Campari) and prosecco (an easier substitute for dry white wine). If you want the pure item, the Caffè Rosso's recipe is transcendent. It is the sort of thing you could drink all evening and into the following morning too.

> *100ml dry white wine (Soave is appropriate)*
> *50ml Campari*
> *25ml fizzy water (Perrier is good, as it is super fizzy)*

You can make this in an old fashioned glass or a wine glass, as you wish. Either way, fill it with ice, pour in the wine, Campari and a splash of fizzy water and stir. Drop in a half lemon slice and a plump green olive on a long stick.

For a simpler version, pour a drop of Campari in the bottom of a bunch of flutes, drop in an ice cube and top up with prosecco.

13. BRONX

It's unlucky 13 for the Bronx, which is appropriate. Like ragtime and spats, the Bronx has fallen out of favour in recent decades. Back in the early 20th century, however, it was a serious rival to the Martini (see no.1) and the Manhattan (no.2), to be shaken to a two-step rhythm according to Nick in *The Thin Man*. 'The Bronx was fashionable', as Bernard deVoto wrote in *The Hour* (1948). 'The gay dogs of Murray Hill drank it, the boulevardiers who wore boaters with a string to the left lapel and winked at Gibson Girls as far up Fifth Avenue as 59th Street.'

DeVoto was, I must add, not a fan. In fact, he wasn't a fan of any cocktail other than the dry Martini (sans olive) and an Old Fashioned (no.5) at an absolute push, though he preferred straight Scotch. He described the Manhattan as 'an offence against piety' and the Bronx as the 'the most ominous' of a 'sore heritage of slops' that came to pass for American drinks at the time of writing, which was just after the Second World War. I may not be selling this drink to you, but bear with me.

The Bronx was invented in 1906 at the Old Waldorf Astoria hotel, a New York cocktailing institution which has since relocated uptown, where the present bartender Frank Caiafa makes a valiant attempt to uphold the old traditions in the face of a pianist playing Celine Dion covers. Back in the day, a barman named Johnny Solon is supposed to have added fresh orange juice and gin to the Duplex, a cocktail comprising both types of vermouth and orange bitters, thereby creating the first cocktail with fruit juice in it. It proved wildly popular – particularly during Prohibition when the poorer quality of gin needed to be masked and fruit juice did the job nicely. One assumes the parties in *The Great Gatsby* were kept afloat by trays of Bronxes, since we learn that Jay Gatsby has a machine in his kitchen, 'which could extract the juice of two hundred oranges in half an hour if a little button was pressed two hundred times by a butler's thumb'. I doubt they were drinking that OJ on its own.

As DeVoto sighs: 'Infection spread... And then swiftly, came the Plague and the rush of the barbarians in its wake and all the juices of the orchard went into cocktail.' DeVoto, in other words, saw the Bronx as the first step towards the fruity abominations that would so debase the name Martini in the 1980s. '[It] was not bathtub gin that came close to destroying the American stomach, nervous system, and aspiration toward a subtler life. Not the gin, but the fruit juices so basely mixed with it: all pestilential, all gangrenous, all vile. A cocktail does not contain fruit juice.'

Anyway, I don't mind a Bronx. The twin vermouths lend it a faraway note and the gin is still good and strong. It's not that sweet at all. Perhaps that's why the Bronx is not ordered too often these days. For after Prohibition, it never quite recovered its popularity. My suspicion is that too many barkeeps started making them with concentrated orange juice as opposed to the stuff that comes out of oranges. Those with sweet teeth found their thrills with Passion Fruit Woo Woos and Blue Hawaiians instead. Those who craved subtlety cleaved to their Martinis and Manhattans. In the context of the Bronx's general decline, it's quaint to read DeVoto railing against it. He's a little like the guy who shouted 'JUDAS!' when Bob Dylan went electric. You admire the force of his convictions but you would also like to place him in the midst of a dubstep rave. Or, indeed, see what he made of a Sex on the Beach.

40ml gin
20ml Italian vermouth
20ml French vermouth
10ml orange juice

Pour all the ingredients into a shaker, add plenty of ice and shake hard to a two-step rhythm, then double-strain into a cold cocktail glass. Garnish with an orange-zest twist, taking care to express the oils.

The addition of a few drops of Angostura Bitters turns this into an Income Tax cocktail.

14. JERRY THOMAS GIN PUNCH

Mankind has for centuries found punch to be an expedient way of lubricating a party. If you happen to find yourself entertaining a first XI or a corps de ballet, you too will find it far more convenient to place a flowing bowl in the middle of the room than to run back and forth preparing potations for all and sundry. The fact that punch is primarily a communal drink, and a very venerable idea at that, tells you that drinking was, and should still be, a sociable activity.

In Jerry Thomas's *Bartender's Guide* (1862), the punches come first. You sense that for his contemporaries, the punch is the important bit... there are also these new things called 'cocktails' but they can wait, we're dying to know how General Ford compounded his sherbert for his punch! There are warm punches and cool punches, punches on a grand plan and punches fashioned in the glass, punches of brandy and rum and whiskey and arrack, punches for sporting parties, Glasgow punches, punches by the celebrity chef Alexis Soyer, punches for champagne, sauternes, claret, port, hock, you name it. It seems our forebears used the word 'punch' a little like we use the word 'cocktail', to mean anything fruity with alcohol in it.

Nowadays, someone might announce that they are going to make punch, but it is as often as not, made in a 'so let's put some milk in it! And now fish sauce!' sort of way. It is nothing like the patient and proud business it was for the likes of General Ford (who was, incidentally, a commanding engineer who ran a by all accounts excellent inn at Dover).

Since we have gin at our disposal, the recipe here is for a cold gin punch, based on one in Thomas's book but enlivened with a couple of punch hacks purloined from other punches. To do it right, you should first heed Thomas's advice: 'To make punch of any sort of perfection, the ambrosial essence of the lemon must be extracted by rubbing lumps of sugar on the rind, which breaks the delicate little vessels that contain the essence, and at the same time abosorbs it. This, and making the mixture sweet and strong, using tea instead of water, and thoroughly amalgamating all the compounds, so that the taste of neither the bitter, the sweet, the spirit, nor the element, shall be perceptible one over the other, is the grand secret, only to be acquired by practice.'

Punch should be stirred, not shaken. With a hot punch, the spirits generally go in first; with a cold punch, last. It should look delightful. Be sure to account for a little melting ice in your dilution. As to the ice, it is an excellent idea to freeze it in large round bowls with berries encased in it. A large lump of ice will cool much more evenly than small cubes and the suspended fruits will look splendid.

> *For 10 people*
> *5 lemons*
> *150g raw cane sugar*
> *500ml cold black tea*
> *75ml raspberry syrup (or 50ml golden sugar syrup*
> *   (2:1, see page 44) muddled with 15 fresh raspberries*
> *   and strained; see also Clover Club, no.8)*
> *1 bottle gin (700–750ml)*
> *Oranges, pineapples, lemons, nutmeg, mint*
> *For the ice: a few raspberries*

Make a block of ice some hours before your party: place a few raspberries in a rounded bowl, fill it with water and place in the freezer.

Remove the skin from the lemons using a peeler, taking utmost care not to take the white pith with the zest (and also not to slice open your fingers). Place the skins in the bottom of your punch bowl with the sugar and pound them all together until you are sure all the sherberty goodness is extracted (the General Ford apparently did this for about half an hour). It's even better if you leave this to sit awhile in a tub. Remove the lemon peel.

Now prepare a pot of good black tea using boiling water, taking care to remove the teabags or leaves once it is brewed. Pour most of this over the lemon sugar and stir until it is dissolved. Add the juice of four of the lemons and the raspberry syrup. Finally pour in most of your gin but not all. Stir and taste. You should have a small amount of sugar, tea, lemon and gin left over. Use these to add more sweetness, dilution, acid or proof as required. Once the punch is balanced to your liking, introduce slices of orange, pineapple and lemon, grate over some nutmeg, cover and leave it to cool.

Just prior to serving, place the block of ice in the punch bowl. A few mint leaves will make it prettier still.

15. GINGER ROGERS PUNCH

The Ginger Rogers is a useful 'emergency' punch. It is the sort of thing you can prepare for a large party, safe in the knowledge that everyone will be a) grateful and b) impressed, and c) you won't have to spend hours messing around. It is a hybrid of two long drinks, namely a Gin Buck (which is gin, lime, ginger beer and bitters) and a Mojito (which is rum, lime, mint, sugar and soda). It is strong and spicy enough to appeal to all palates.

I made it up at a party once and was a teensy bit disappointed to find that someone else had already invented something very much like it. The name Ginger Rogers, I assume, is a play on the ginger beer rather than anything more specific, but it does dance nicely on the tongue. Proportions are here inexact – it should be mixed in a jug and as such, you should draw on your taste and intuition. As a rough guide, however, the following should fill a jug for six people.

For 6 people
6 sprigs of mint
3 limes
300ml gin
500ml ginger beer (the fiery Jamaican sort please!)
Angostura bitters

Gently bruise the mint in the bottom of the jug – no violence, please. Slice the limes into quarters, squeeze them in and throw in the spent shells too. Pour in the gin, add enough ice to comfortably rise above the gin line and churn. Top up with ginger beer and an indecent amount of Angostura, stirring carefully all the while.

You may leave people to serve themselves. If you want some ceremony, however, fill six glasses with additional ice and *strain* the mixture into each one. A lime wedge and/or a mint sprig is a logical garnish.

16. AVENUE B

The original Avenue cocktail is more of a curio than a classic – but its combination of bourbon, calvados, passion fruit, pomegranate and orange blossom was intriguing enough that I made a note when I discovered it in the *Café Royal Cocktail Book* of 1937. Here, I've replaced the calvados with more bourbon and played around with the proportions a little to create an Avenue B. (I suppose you could make it with just calvados and it would be an Avenue C.)

The Café Royal still exists, in suitably disappointing form on London's Regent Street, but it was once a glamorous place to be seen – good enough for Oscar Wilde, Virginia Woolf and Aleister Crowley at least. Certainly, the cocktails were wild, to judge from W.J. Tarling's book. Here, you will find not only blue curaçao but green curaçao and red curaçao, as well as weird and defunct liquids such as Forbidden Fruit pomelo liqueur and something called 'Pash', which seems to be some kind of passion fruit juice, evidently in vogue at the time and the sort of exoticism you might have expected at a chi-chi bar. People in the 1930s were just as mad for novelties as we are now.

These days the passion fruit has receded to baobab powder and goji berries but its gentle amber tartness makes it a useful ingredient in a whole range of cocktails, not just tropical ones. The advantage of the 2010s is that we don't need to buy cartons of adulterated passion fruit juice or bottles of E-number-rich passion fruit syrup, or even to unearth old bottles of 'Pash'. We can buy passion fruit fresh at the supermarket for little more than the cost of a lemon or lime. They may not be as luscious as the ones you find in the Caribbean, but they will do.

The intrigue of the Avenue doesn't end there, however. It also contains a few drops of orange flower water, which is a hydrosol made from orange blossom, used frequently in Middle Eastern cooking and French baking. You can pick this up in most supermarkets too (look in the baking section) or in Middle Eastern grocers.

The Avenue also requires grenadine, one of the great mysteries of the cocktailing world. Grenadine is pomegranate syrup. It is used not only to sweeten drinks (in the manner of sugar syrups) but also to lend a luscious berry roundness and a pinkish hue. There are literally hundreds of recipes that call for grenadine. It is one of the most in-demand ingredients there is. However, you cannot find good grenadine for love nor money. The leading brand retails at about £8 for a bottle and it is absolutely disgusting, the colour of a kill in Jaws 2. Respectable producers produce cordials in many flavours but never pomegranate, it seems. It's almost as if there is a conspiracy. The only choice, therefore, is to make your own.

Grenadine

Fortunately it's easy! All you need is pomegranate juice and sugar with optional flavourings. The easiest way to get the juice is to buy Pom 100% Pure Pomegranate Juice (don't be tempted by 'pomegranate juice drinks'). Or you could buy a large fresh pomegranate, cut it into eighths (on the x, y and z) and juice it as you would a lemon. Either way, collect the juice in a cup and pour it into a cold saucepan on a low heat. Take one-and-a-half times the volume of sugar and introduce it to the pan, stirring continually until the sugar dissolves – at which point remove from the heat. (Do not allow the mixture to boil.) For a richer flavour, you can dissolve a decent trickle of pomegranate molasses into it, which is also available from Middle Eastern shops. You can also add intrigue with the bitter juices from orange zest, scant amounts of orange flower water, rose water, and/or vanilla – but don't overdo it. Grenadine should look and taste red. It will be roughly the sweetness of our golden sugar syrup and can be used as a pink variant on all recipes made with it.

Now you are ready to make an Avenue B. It should come out like a lovely deep sunrise, luscious with the tropics, fragrant with blossom, rich with berry but with a good strong American kick.

50ml bourbon
20ml fresh passion fruit pulp (one fruit should suffice)
5ml grenadine (see above)
Dash orange blossom water

Put all the ingredients into a shaker, shake up with plenty of ice and double-strain into a cold cocktail glass. Garnish howsoever you choose.

17. GIMLET

A lot of people will swear there's only one way you make a Gimlet: with Rose's Lime Juice Cordial and gin. That is largely due to a story of its origins, which (as you might guess) is given particular credence by the people who make Rose's Lime Cordial – Coca-Cola Enterprises, these days. The cordial was originally invented by a Scottish man named Lauchlan Rose in 1867 as a way of preserving limes. It was a very useful patent for the British Navy, whose vitamin C deficiencies are well-documented, and often led to our scurvy-ridden sailors landing on the shores of the New World and snogging limes they were so desperate for the stuff. Hence: Limeys.

According to the corporate history, Rose's Lime Juice Cordial became part of the standard Navy ration, and, since gin was also part of that ration, the clever officers were soon mixing up Gimlets like billy-o. The Gimlet became a popular drink all over the British colonies – Charles H. Baker describes it as the 'Far Eastern Gimlet' and declared himself perplexed that it hadn't made it to America as yet. So Coca-Cola Entreprises says you should make your Gimlets with Rose's. So does Raymond Chandler: 'A real gimlet is half gin and half Rose's lime juice and nothing else', he counselled in *The Long Goodbye*, which is really one long ode to the Gimlet. I'm not so sure. I'm not sure that what those seadogs drank would have contained some of the E-numbers I saw listed on the Rose's label. I'm even less convinced that Chandler's proportions are ideal given the amount of sugar in the present-day cordial too. That would give you a Grimlet.

So how should you make a Gimlet? Well, you could go the fresh lime route and make a Gin Sour only with lime instead of lemon. I wouldn't advise against that course of action. A Fresh Lime Gimlet can be exquisite. However, I feel we would be getting away from the essence of the drink. It is supposed to have a certain cordial-like quality, surely... just maybe not one involving all those chemicals. No, the best course of action is to channel old father Rose and make your own. Actually, it really doesn't take that long. The only special thing you need to buy is citric acid, which you can find in most supermarkets and ethnic grocers (where it is often sold with the spices as 'lemon salt') and some coriander seeds, which lend a little warm spice to it.

Lime cordial

The tartness of limes makes the syrup-making process slightly different from that for grenadine (see previous recipe). You need a little extra water, which makes for a more dilute cordial. Place the zest of 4 limes (grated) into a saucepan with 1 teaspoon of coriander seeds and some green cardamom pods (optional). Add 100ml water. Heat slowly until it begins to boil. When it bubbles, remove from the heat and stir in about 200g golden caster sugar (twice the quantity of the water) until it is fully dissolved. Strain into a non-metallic bowl. Add a teaspoon of citric acid and stir until fully dissolved. Now add the juice from the four limes (i.e. about 100ml... you may need more limes if they're the unjuicy sort) and taste for balance. This will store in the fridge for a couple of weeks, possibly more if you add a splash of vodka, gin or rum.

Now, to the Gimlet:

> *50ml gin*
> *25ml lime cordial (above)*

Simply combine the gin and the cordial in your mixing vessel with plenty of ice, stir Martini-style until it is ice cold, then double-strain into an ice-cold glass and garnish with a fresh lime wedge.

Despite what Chandler says, it seems Gimlets were often diluted with a splash of cold water or soda, but sufficient stirring should lessen the need.

18. ARMY & NAVY

The Army & Navy was first featured in Harry MacElhone's *Harry's ABC of Mixing Drinks* (1919). It's one of those simple classics that's nigh on unimproveable, provided you make it with decent ingredients. The flavour rests on the pleasing combination of almond syrup – orgeat – and lemon, which is then lent a little complexity by the presence of the gin, making it a more grown-up version of the ever-popular Amaretto Sour (see page 145).

The tricky ingredient here is orgeat. It's a bit of effort to track down the commercial stuff and you'll likely be disappointed if you do, since most brands are kind of sickly and synthetic. However, if you like almond, it's well worth making your own. Aside from its abundant cocktail uses (it's used widely in Tiki-style drinks), it's great in cappuccinos and it makes a good summer refresher with a squirt of fresh lime, fizzy water and Angostura bitters.

Orgeat syrup

Take 100g raw almonds (skin on) and toast them in a dry pan for about 2–3 minutes, keeping a watchful eye over them to avoid them turning black. Allow them to cool. Now put half of the almonds into a blender and pulse them into powder. Transfer to a bowl. Pulse the other half for a shorter time so they're just a bit roughed up. Add these to the same bowl; the varying textures should make for different levels of almond flavour. (If you have no blender, use a combo of knife and rolling pin to bash them up.)

Now add about 150ml water to the bowl, cover and leave it to socialise for 3–6 hours, stirring occasionally. Then, strain the almonds from the water using a muslin cloth or a (clean!) tea towel, really wringing it out well to extract all the liquid. I'm sure you can use the almond mush for baking or something; look that up in some other book. What we're interested in is the almond water you have just created.

Use the almond water to make a rich sugar syrup: place 1 cup of almond water in a saucepan with 2 cups of golden caster sugar and heat slowly, stirring all the while, until the sugar is dissolved. It should have a rich, buttery almond taste and a lovely brown colour. You can pep up the flavour with a scant dash of orange blossom water if you like; I have been known to cheat mine to marzipan heights with a drop of almond essence so help me God. Remove from the heat, allow the mixture to cool and decant into a bottle. It should keep in the fridge for a month or so; a dash of vodka, rum or brandy will extend its life. It will tend to separate over time, so each time you use it you will need to shake it beforehand.

Incidentally, I've tried using commercial almond milk (increasingly in vogue) as a short cut to orgeat and it tends to curdle when mixed with citrus.

Now for the Army & Navy:

> 50ml gin
> 15ml lemon juice
> 10ml orgeat syrup (above)

Pour all the ingredients into a shaker, shake up with plenty of ice, then double-strain into a chilled cocktail glass. Garnish with a lemon-zest twist.

19. RAMOS GIN FIZZ

Ever since Henry C. Ramos created his eponymous cream fizz in New Orleans at the turn of the 20th century, it has had a reputation as a refined and exacting concoction. Simply to shake it up requires superhuman stamina – or, if eyewitness accounts of are to be believed, staff. 'The main secret of excellence was the platoon of eight or a dozen blackamoors who passed the shaker over shoulders to the next, after each had literally shaken his heart out chilling the drink', writes Charles H. Baker. 'Iced glass, and iced soda, also were vital factors of excellence.'

Even if you and eleven of your friends do *literally* shake your hearts out, it's still eminently fuckupable. (Ethnicity seems to make no difference here.) Common Ramos Gin Fizz-related mishaps include: smacking the shaker against your chin by mistake; loosening the grip and watching seven minutes' worth of effort go flying all over the kitchen; opening the shaker after the full 15 minutes to discover that it contains a revolting curdled mess as opposed to the silken whip of a drink that it is supposed to be. In New Orleans this is known as Ramos Gin Jizz.

It is only the legendary taste of the drink that inspires persistence. When you consider how many people must have expired in its production over the last 100 or so years, you have to conclude, it must be worth it. A correctly made Ramos Gin Fizz is indeed a thing of ethereal wonder, like a rich chord welcoming you into the pillowy yonder.

It took Ramos some persuasion before he gave up the secret. The fact that it contains lemon *and* lime hints that he spent much time perfecting the flavour (I can't think of many other drinks that call for both). Another secret note is the orange blossom water, which gives the drink a certain ethereal quality – something like a major seventh. Another is vanilla essence, which adds a richness that holds the whole thing together.

All the same, the mystique might have something to do with the fact that most published recipes are wrong. They generally ask you to put everything in a shaker and get busy. Chemistry dictates that if you put cream and citrus in the same shaker, the mixture will curdle no matter how long you shake it. The same thing happens if you 'cheat' and put it in a blender too. To stop this happening, the egg white needs to be aerated to the utmost before you add the lemon and cream. Shaking is a very laborious way of doing this. Whisking is far better. In fact, it leads me to suspect that Ramos was a sadistic marketing genius, putting his poor bartenders to a whole lot of unnecessary effort simply to impress people like Baker and increase the legend of his drink.

So here's an ethical and relatively pain-free Ramos Gin Fizz. Is it cheating? Probably! Is it delicious at any time of day? Definitely. I have given the proportions for two here as it really ought to be shared with lovers and if you're just making it for yourself, then you deserve twice the reward.

For 2 people
2 egg whites (approx. 80ml)
40ml golden sugar syrup (2:1, see page 44)
100ml gin
50ml single cream
Few drops orange blossom water
Few drops vanilla essence
25ml lemon juice
25ml lime juice

Place two tall glasses in the freezer, *pace* Ramos. Measure out your ingredients in advance for ease. Separate your eggs and place the whites in a mixing bowl with the sugar syrup. Whisk with an electric whisk until the batter becomes stiff (you should be able to turn the bowl upside down with nothing falling out). Continue to whisk as you slowly pour in the gin, the cream, the orange blossom water and the vanilla essence. (Pause to taste at this point. Yum, huh?) Only now introduce the citrus, whisking all the while. Transfer to a shaker filled with ice, shake very hard to cool and double-strain into your pre-chilled glass without ice. You may add a little fizzy water if you like (stir if you do), but it will taste fizzy without. Garnish with a lime wedge.

20. GIN & IT

OK, after the Ramos Gin Fizz you need something really simple, something your five-year-old can just throw together with a minimum of fuss. The Gin & It is probably the cocktail I make the most often, precisely for this reason. It is a cinch. It never fails. It's always time for a Gin & It. The world would be better if bartenders concentrated less on making Stilton Martinis and Lychee Woo-Woos and more on making Gin & Its.

The 'It', by the way, stands for 'Italian', *i.e.* Italian vermouth. According to the history books, the combination apparently dates back to pre-Prohibition America – which seems fair enough, since gin and

Italian vermouth feature in the Martinez (page 125) and the 'Sweet Martini'. However, to an Englishman, the Gin & It calls to mind Terence Rattigan plays and Agatha Christie novels and slim girls named Cecily in drawing rooms. The proportions are more or less the same as those of the Queen's favourite, Gin & Dubonnet, too. I wonder if it wasn't a combination that came about almost independently, or at least gained a different name over here. My mother-in-law remembers her own mother ordering Gin & Its in the pubs around the Portsmouth docks when she was small – suggesting it wasn't so much a cocktail as simply a pub drink, along the lines of Port & Lemon. All pubs have gin. The vast majority of them have Italian vermouth too. Why shouldn't they mix them together in a glass with a couple of ice cubes? And if they happen to add a dash of bitters, who's counting?

That's how I like my Gin & Its – as a sort of classic 'bunged-together' drink. You can take them to the peaks of deliciousness if you serve them 'up' (see page 50) and make them with a really decent vermouth. You can add a dash of pretty much any liqueur you could care to name and have yourself an interesting variation. However, sometimes simple and easy is best.

> *50ml gin*
> *25ml Italian vermouth*
> *Dash Angostura bitters*

Stir in an old fashioned glass with large ice and serve with a lemon-zest twist.

21. GIN & TONIC

My guess (my hope, at least) is that you already know how to make a gin and tonic, the spirit pairing that most readily rolls off the English tongue. So what's with the recipe you patronising arse? Well, I've been asked 'Ice and lemon?' at one too many bars, and feel a little refresher might not go amiss. Moreover, as I was reminded when I was served four or five of them outside the Foreign Correspondents' Club in New

Delhi a couple of springs ago, the G&T is one of the finest drinks known to man – and for all its fame, it deserves more appreciation.

The G&T rose to prominence not through the great cocktail bars of London and New York, but through the verandas and pavilions of British India in the 19th century, popular among sadistic colonels and East India Company bounders. It was necessary, under the circs. Tonic water was invented in 1858 as a way of making the anti-malarial drug quinine palatable, and gin too was supposed to have beneficial effects. It was a happy coincidence that together, they made medicine more tasty even than Calpol. Winston Churchill once credited the G&T with saving 'more Englishmen's lives, and minds, than all the doctors in the Empire'. Then again he was a drunkard. For most, it was a drink to accompany the lazy thwack of polo balls and corporal punishment, to be consumed around teatime, when the sun casts long shadows, the fever began to rise and the dream began to fade.

The basic G&T formula will serve for all such 'highballs' whether made with soda, ginger beer, Coca-Cola or what have you. You want to fill the glass with ice (a tall or old fashioned glass or even a wine glass if you're Spanish). You want the spirit to come up at least halfway. Then you want to top it up with tonic water.

The tonic water must be of excellent quality and freshly opened. I'd caution against Schweppes, which contains corn syrup in America and saccharine in Britain (but neither in France, which is why G&Ts taste much better there). Fever Tree or Fentimans are worth the little bit extra. The standard ratio of gin to tonic should be 1:2, but 1:3 is still acceptable. Remember, though, that when G&Ts were first mixed, the gin was used to make the tonic palatable, not the other way round. Was this the reason the Empire fell? Or the reason it endured for so long? Discuss. Over a G&T.

50ml gin
Squeeze of lime
100–150ml tonic

Fill a glass with plenty of ice and pour in the gin. Squeeze over the lime and drop the spent shell in too. Top up with tonic and give it a stir.

While the lime is the pre-eminent garnish, you might also use a length of cucumber, a basil leaf, a lavender sprig or a grapefruit wedge, so as to complement the particular botanicals in your gin.

22. 'PIN'

In Vladimir Nabokov's novel *Lolita*, the narrator Humbert Humbert proves himself to be very particular about his females (pre-pubescent, please!) and also his drink. We learn this in Chapter 17. 'The sun made its usual round of the house as the afternoon ripened into evening', he reminisces. 'I had a drink. And another. And yet another. Gin and pineapple juice, my favourite mixture, always doubled my energy.'

At this point, Humbert has been lodging with the widow Charlotte Haze for a few months. He moved in so as to be close to her 12-year-old daughter Dolores (alias Lolita); Charlotte, however, has fallen in love with him. When she takes Lo to summer camp, she leaves Humbert a letter, confessing her adoration and telling him to leave her home, never to return if he does not return her feelings. He does not return her feelings. And yet he stays. He resolves to marry the mother in order to be near her daughter, who will become his step daughter. So he buys 'good liquor' and awaits Charlotte's return. Before long, he is drunk and dreaming. 'A reek of sap mingled with the pineapple... the gin and Lolita were dancing in me.' Finally, Charlotte comes home, to find a new hubby. He stayed!

Humbert calls his gin and pineapple mixture 'Pin' and sometimes 'My Pin'. Since I cannot find any other reference to it, we must credit Nabokov with inventing the cocktail. I confess, the first couple of times I read Lolita this 'Pin' did not leave much impression, but that only goes to prove Nabokov's edict: 'There is no reading, only rereading.' Once you have detected it, the 'Pin' soon becomes as unmistakeable as the scent of pineapple mingling with sap. It is not much of a stretch to see its peculiar admixture of gin (stern, European, 'Mother's ruin') and pineapple (exotic, sweet, forbidden fruit) as one of the central motifs of Humbert's infatuation with Lolita.

The most significant 'Pin' appearance comes a little later, when Charlotte (by now Mrs Humbert) has just discovered Humbert's diary, and is horrified to discover that he refers to her as: 'The Haze woman, the big bitch, the old cat, the obnoxious mamma'. (She seems less concerned with his sexual obsession with her daughter). The game seems to be up for Humbert, and he tries to buy time by making her a Scotch ('She could never resist Scotch'). He goes to the kitchen, where the faucet whines and the ice box barks and bangs. 'I poured in the whiskey and a dram of soda. She had *tabooed my pin*.' Charlotte has clearly developed her own ideas about the appropriateness of Humbert's tastes.

What does 'Pin' taste like? Nabokov must have tried gin and pineapple in the course of his research. I certainly have and find it a surprisingly good combination, particularly in the slightly jazzed-up form below, I hope. Pineapple is an underrated juice, one that does not deserve to have fallen so far behind cranberry and pomegranate in the pantheon. They pick out unusual notes in each other, the gin ennobling the fruit, the fruit encouraging the gin to let its hair down.

Once Charlotte has died, and Humbert has eloped with Lolita as her sole legal guardian, he returns to his Pin only once. When he is summoned to Lolita's school by a concerned teacher, he assumes his nightly assaults on her have been discovered. 'I imagined all sorts of horrors, and had to fortify myself with a pint of my 'pin' before I could face the interview.' (A PINT!) Then as the affair reaches its melancholy, paranoid phase, he seems to drop the pineapple part. He shoots a squirrel for target practice, toasting it with 'a dram of gin'. When Lolita runs away, he lies in a lounge chair, 'swallowing pony upon pony of gin'. Finally, in that horrible fist fight with Clare Quilty – the other paedophile-wordsmith in Lolita's short life – Nabokov brings his gin/ pin/sin theme to its conclusion. 'It was a silent, soft, formless tussle on the part of two literati, one of whom was utterly disorganised by a drug while the other was handicapped by a heart condition and *too much gin*.'

I'd like to conclude, however, by revisiting that heartbreaking moment shortly before that clumsy showdown, when Humbert visits the semi-grown-up, pregnant Lolita. She is trying to begin a respectable life with a blue-collar husband named Dick Schiller. They serve him beer. ('The exquisite courtesy of simple folks.') Humbert begs Lolita to run away with him. She does not. He begins to cry. 'Stop crying, please', she tells him. 'You should understand. Let me get you some more beer. Oh, don't cry, I'm so sorry I cheated so much, but that's the way things are.' Beer, incidentally, was Nabokov's favourite drink.

> *50ml gin*
> *15ml lemon juice*
> *10ml golden sugar syrup (2:1, see page 44)*
> *50ml pineapple juice*
> *Fizzy water*
> *Angostura bitters*

Pour the gin, lemon juice, sugar syrup and pineapple into the shaker, add plenty of ice and shake until the mixture becomes nice and frothy. Double-strain into a tall glass filled with ice cubes, top with fizzy water (not too much) and stir. Pour a few dashes of Angostura onto the foamy head by way of garnish.

23. ENGLISH BREAKFAST MARTINI

I like this cocktail as it's the perfect example of how a spirit may be combined with workaday kitchen ingredients to create something unexpected. Its invention is often credited to the celebrated bartender Salvatore Calabrese. His version from the 1980s is essentially a White Lady (gin/Cointreau/lemon; see page 187) with a bit of marmalade in it. However, perhaps he failed to consult the *Savoy Cocktail Book*, otherwise he would have found the strikingly similar Marmalade Cocktail (gin/marmalade/lemon)?

A little experimentation tells me that marmalade is amply sweet and orangey in itself and, provided you are comfortable with its bitter notes, this renders the orange liqueur redundant. Who pours himself a Cointreau for breakfast anyway? Gin yes, but Cointreau? What are you, French?

No, simplicity is all. If you can reduce the number of expensive ingredients, why wouldn't you? While on the breakfast theme, however, you can make two small cocktail 'hacks'. The first is to introduce some egg white, which is appropriate only at breakfast time. The second is to infuse your gin with tea. Simply leave a teabag or even better, real tea leaves – Earl Grey works well – to steep in gin for around three minutes, prodding it now and then. In not much longer than it takes to make a decent cup of tea, you will have a richer, darker base spirit to play with. I would recommend 100ml of gin per teabag, enough for two cocktails, so hopefully you are having breakfast with a special friend.

> *50ml (tea-infused) gin*
> *15ml lemon juice*
> *15ml marmalade (approx 1 heaped dessertspoon*
> *   or a generous 5ml)*
> *15ml egg white (optional)*

If you are using egg white, shake all the ingredients hard without ice and then again with the ice before double-straining into a cocktail glass. Garnish with a copy of *The Times*.

24. BACON OLD FASHIONED

Among the most iconic contemporary cocktails is the Benton's Old Fashioned, created in 2008 by Don Lee at the famous New York bar, PDT. (PDT stands for 'Please don't tell', which must be the most abused instruction in history since anyone who's been there won't shut up about how they had to climb through a phone box to get there and it was really amazing...) The idea is simple but it goes to show how a little creativity and a soupçon of science can turn something very plain and old into something spankingly new.

Benton's is the name of a noted American bacon manufacturer and this concoction is essentially a bacon-infused Old Fashioned. You use the fat from a couple of rashers of streaky to 'fat-wash' your bourbon, infusing the spirit with those sweet bacon molecules. The principle will work for any number of animal fats, so theoretically you could try Goose Fat Gin, Chorizo Brandy, Haggis Scotch, etc... though remember kids: just because you *can* do something doesn't mean you *should*. Bacon and bourbon, however, is a droolsome combination. As for maple syrup? Yabba-dabba-do!

Bacon bourbon

To fat-wash 250ml bourbon you will need only two or three rashers of bacon. (Be sure to use fatty and smoky American-style bacon; English back bacon won't work as well.) To rend the maximum fat, start off with a cool pan. Warm the bacon slowly and then let it sizzle on both sides for a couple of minutes. The fat should slowly weep out. Drain the rendered fat into a jar and pour in the bourbon. (Consume the bacon.) Let the bourbon sit around for a while before transferring it to the freezer overnight. When you collect it in the morning, the fat will have congealed and it will look really gross. Pass this liquid through a coffee filter to remove all lumps (if you don't have a coffee filter, line a sieve with a couple of pieces of kitchen roll). The bacon bourbon will keep in the fridge for about a month.

Now make your cocktail.

> *50ml bacon-infused bourbon (above)*
> *10ml maple syrup*
> *Dash Angostura bitters*

Construct the drink Old Fashioned-style. Pour the bourbon into the glass, add the maple syrup and stir until dissolved. Add a large lump of ice or two and stir. Add some more ice and stir some more. Express the oils from an orange-zest twist and drop in the glass.

25. ANGOSTURA SOUR

You may have noticed a pattern emerging with your Angostura usage. In ordinary circumstances, all you really need is a dash. A shake. A few drops. All it takes is a flick of the wrist and the rusty elixir will work wonders. It's almost enough to make you believe that homeopathy is not utter horse manure. As such, I'm guessing there's a fair bit of Angostura left in the bottle?

Well not for much longer, pal. Today, we are going to jimmy off that little yellow dropper and go deep into the bitters. Today, we are going to make an Angostura Sour.

The Angostura Sour is a rare beast among cocktails in that it uses bitters as the base spirit. If you take a closer look at the paper wrapping, you will notice that Angostura bitters come in at 45% ABV, which is quite healthy. It's just going to need a little tempering.

Bitters cocktails have enjoyed a vogue recently, as everyone tries to reinvent the wheel and come up with the craziest thing. The game changer was a drink called the Trinidad Sour, which emerged from a cocktail competition in the mid-00s and tames the Angostura with a whopping amount of orgeat syrup, some lime and a little rye whisky (see page 184). I much prefer the Angostura Sour, which is simpler and better balanced, both of which are good qualities. The recipe here is adapted minimally from the one in *Beta Cocktails*, a piece of cocktail samizdat by a couple of radical American bartenders, Maksym Pazunia and Kirk Estopinal, who seem determined to make everyone drink tons of bitters. They call the drink 'a potable abstract of our entire philosophy'. However, the inspiration comes from way back. They credit Charles H. Baker, who noted down an Angostura Fizz recipe… but there's an even earlier one written down in a bar book called *Jack's Manual* from 1910. There is nothing new under the sun. But still, I doubt you've tasted anything like this before.

> *50ml Angostura bitters*
> *25ml lime juice*
> *25ml golden sugar syrup (2:1, see page 44)*
> *15ml egg white*

Shake hard with plenty of ice and double-strain into a cold cocktail glass. No garnish.

WHAT NEXT?

Congratulations. You have reached the end of the first world. 1-Up! If you have been working through the opening 25 cocktails methodically, taking careful notes as you go, you may suddenly feel at a loss. You may feel like going round getting your shirt signed, tearfully exchanging hugs with French vermouth like a kid on their last day of primary school. You may be slightly trepidatious about the mezcal and Fernet-Branca and crème de cacao that await in big school. You probably won't be, though.

However, if you are planning a shopping trip for a few strategic additions to the cabinet, I would make a few recommendations.

The best way to multiply your output is to increase your base material, *i.e.* spirits. The obvious next two spirits to go for would be rums – **light rum** *and* **dark rum**. You can make almost as many cocktails with rum as you can with gin and if you include the full canon of exotics, probably more. Light rum will open up the Daiquiri (see pages 158–161), which is commendation enough. (El Dorado 3-year, Flor de Caña Extra Dry and Havana Club 3-year are my favourites... don't settle for boring old Bacardi.) Dark rum will prise open Don the Beachcomber's Tiki treasure chest (see page 214) and provide the base for all sorts of warming punches and grogs.

If your tastes run more to classic, aromatic cocktails, you'll probably want **brandy** at some point. Cognac is the posh French stuff – and it is priced for posh people, alas. I'd recommend a good supermarket cognac if you want to economise; just don't go too cheap, otherwise it will lack the snobby refinement that is its *raison d'être*, and try to make it French.

The single most useful liqueur in cocktails is **orange liqueur**. There are two main styles, Dutch curaçao and French triple sec, as well as two leading producers (Cointreau and Grand Marnier) that are in classes of their own. There are differences, as there always are, but to all intents and purposes they're still orange liqueurs. I like Cointreau for its bright sharp rasp and its versatility. It's not cheap, but it's usually used sparingly, almost like sugar syrup, to impart a fruity sweetness to cocktails – so one bottle will see you through almost as many cocktails as would a bottle of bitters.

The other liqueur that you will reach for often is **maraschino** – not to be confused with the cherries. Well, it's made from cherries, sweet marascas from the Croatian coast, pits and all, and turned into a sweet and lively liqueur with a note of almond and a whole lot of funk going on. It was once a saloon staple (it's actually used more often than curaçao by Jerry Thomas) but fell way out of favour in the lean years. None of the major supermarkets seems to supply it, so you'll have to find a specialist or go online. Luxardo is the leading brand and it's great. Again, not cheap, but a bottle should last you a long time.

The other mainstay of the old books was **absinthe**. In cocktails, it is mainly used as an anise accent, like bitters, literally only a few drops. It's expensive, but if you can find a miniature bottle, that will suffice. Otherwise, surreptitiously decant a few shots into a hipflask next time you're at a party where there's a bottle. **Orange bitters** and **Peychaud's bitters** will provide you with the full bitters arsenal – neither should break a tenner.

That's about it for the basics. Ten big bottles, three bitters bottles and one purloined vial of absinthe. I would sooner buy different varieties of gin, bourbon, vermouth and amaro than add to the overheated property market that is currently my booze shelf. Still, if you want to go up to level three, **apricot brandy** is one of the few other fruit liqueurs you will use with any regularity (get good French stuff, never an American brand), and maybe also **crème de cassis** (which is quite cheap, about a tenner a bottle). Aside from certain fancies such as elderflower and pear liqueurs, I prefer to invest in alcohol that aims to taste of nothing but itself. Herbal liqueurs are more worthwhile. The holy duo of **Bénédictine** and **Chartreuse** are sacrosanct and versatile and worth saving up for.

As for base spirits, I'd go for **pisco** (unaged South American grape brandy) and **tequila** (I prefer the 'rested' reposado style). I've had more happy accidents with them than with any other spirits. Now we've reached an even 20 bottles and we risk breaking the bank... I'm thinking maybe **fino sherry** too... you see how this gets out of hand? See the index of ingredients (page 268) if you're in doubt as to whether a particular bottle is worth your while. Bear in mind that the most commonly used ingredient in cocktails is... lemon juice.

THE STIRRED

'Do a Stinger for the man.'
'Yaz-zuh.'

John Updike, *Rabbit Redux* (1971)

THE DRINKS in this section are aromatic in style. In many cases, that means seriously boozy after-dinner drinks but it can also mean light and fragrant aperitifs. They're all built on the principles of the Old Fashioned (page 63), the Manhattan (page 59) and the Martini (page 57) but make full use of the cocktail cabinet. See pages 268–315 for a full glossary of ingredients and page 246 for suggestions as to what to substitute if you're caught short.

ADONIS

The Adonis (named after the burlesque musical of 1884, in which a statue comes to life) is a lovely example of a 'shim' – a cocktail that is high in flavour but low in alcohol. So you can have two of them. Richer styles of vermouth, such as Antica Formula, will need to be balanced with a high proportion of sherry.

30ml Italian vermouth
30ml fino sherry
Dash orange bitters (optional)

Stir together with plenty of ice and strain into a cold cocktail glass. Express the oils from a lemon-zest twist and drop it in.

AFFINITY

A dry aperitif that leaves you plenty to ponder. Go for an approachable Scotch blend with a misting of something smokier.

25ml French vermouth
25ml Italian vermouth
25ml Scotch whisky
Dash Peychaud's bitters

Stir together with plenty of ice and strain into a cold cocktail glass. Express the oils from an orange-zest twist and drop it in.

ALASKA

The Alaska is a classic Martini variation with no relation whatsoever to the northernmost state of America ('it was probably first thought of in South Carolina', according to *The Savoy Cocktail Book*). Still, at the best parties it is served at the temperature of the Bering Strait in January and stirred with the tusk of a narwhal. For a drier variant known as a Nome, replace half of the quantity of the Yellow Chartreuse with fino sherry. For a Puritan, add 10ml of French vermouth.

50ml gin
15ml Yellow Chartreuse
Dash orange bitters

Stir slowly over large ice and strain into a cold cocktail glass. Garnish with a lemon-zest twist.

ALGONQUIN

The Algonquin Hotel is – or rather was – one of *the* places to drink in New York. Its oak dining room was the site of the Round Table, a group of humourists who had such fun together one lunchtime in 1919 they decided to exchange bons mots most weekdays for the next decade or so. (Can you imagine? *Out to lunch every day?*) The crowd variously included Dorothy Parker, Robert Brenchley, Edmund Wilson and Harpo Marx. The manager used to give them free celery. It was here that the *New Yorker* magazine was first conceived; here too that Edmund Wilson arranged a dinner so Parker could meet the honeymooning Scott and Zelda Fitzgerald, who duly turned up riding on the roof of a New York taxi...

Sadly, perishingly few writers can afford to dine at hotels anymore and when they do the management are less generous with celery. Then again, it's worth reflecting that the famous lunches would have been alcohol-free – unless the Algonquin contravened Prohibition? So there are some advantages to modernity.

50ml rye (or bourbon)
25ml sweet white vermouth
25ml pineapple juice
Dash Peychaud's bitters

Stir over plenty of ice (if you shake, the pineapple will become frothy) and serve in the same glass. Garnish with a cherry.

Most classical recipes call for regular French vermouth – to my mind, far too dry here.

AMPERSAND

A New York classic from *The Old Waldorf Astoria Bar Book* of 1935, the Ampersand is unusual in its combination of gin and brandy. I'd like to think the name comes from an indecisive patron ('Gin or brandy? Whaddya say to gin *and* brandy?') but no one really knows. Whatever, it has a lovely balance and a Fred Astaire sort of sweep. Try replacing the brandy with pisco too.

> *25ml gin (Old Tom if possible)*
> *25ml brandy (or pisco)*
> *25ml Italian vermouth*
> *10ml Grand Marnier*
> *Dash orange bitters*

Stir slowly over large ice and strain into a cold cocktail glass. Garnish with a lemon-zest twist.

ARSENIC AND OLD LACE

Arsenic and Old Lace is a classic black comedy of 1944 involving Cary Grant and some murderous aunts. The cocktail of the same name is a violet-hued Martini variation, better known as the Atty (*i.e.*, Attorney) or the Attention – but I find this name better suits its Sunday-afternoon melodrama, with absinthe playing the part of the poisoner and violette the shrieking victim. What chemistry!

> *50ml gin*
> *20ml French vermouth*
> *5ml crème de violette*
> *5ml absinthe*

Stir slowly over large ice and strain into a cold cocktail glass. Garnish with a lemon-zest twist.

ART OF CHOKE

A flash of genius from *Beta Cocktails* (2012) – one of the rare modern drinks that are not in debt to some old drink or other, and it is somehow more than the sum of its delectable parts.

> *Handful of fresh mint leaves*
> *25ml light rum*
> *25ml Cynar*
> *5ml Green Chartreuse*
> *2.5ml lime juice*
> *2.5ml golden sugar syrup (2:1, see page 44)*

Gently bruise the mint leaves in the bottom of an old fashioned glass. Add all the other ingredients and stir. Garnish with a mint sprig.

B&B

A simple equation: dark spirit + sweet liqueur = superior digestif. The B&B is one of those useful 'throw-together' drinks, perfectly OK to serve at room temperature too.

> *50ml brandy*
> *15ml Bénédictine*

Stir both ingredients in an old fashioned glass with large lumps of ice. Garnish with a lemon-zest twist, if you like.

BACON OLD FASHIONED

See The Classics, page 95.

BAMBOO

Like the Adonis (see page 103), but with French vermouth. Ago Perrone of London's Connaught Bar had the clever idea of infusing his with a few coffee beans, which works much better than you might expect.

5 coffee beans
30ml French vermouth
30ml fino sherry
5ml Grand Marnier

Leave the coffee beans to infuse in the vermouth for 15 minutes or so. Strain into a vessel with the other ingredients, stir over plenty of ice and strain into a cold cocktail glass.

BCC

BCC stands for Brandy-Cassis-Clove, which is a room-temperature cocktail, blind cc'd to me by Alex Kammerling (inventor of Kamm & Sons ginseng liqueur) as a good thing to put in a hip flask before a festival.

50ml brandy
10ml cassis
10 or so cloves

For the hip-flask version, simply combine and leave to infuse in your favourite container. For an instant version, muddle the cloves with the cassis and strain into a glass containing the brandy.

BIJOU

'Bijou' is French for jewel, innit. The Bijou cocktail is so named because all constituent parts apparently look like jewels (ruby-red vermouth, diamond gin and emerald Chartreuse). Once upon a time, they were layered carefully one on top of the other, Pousse-Café-style, to make a virtue of this fact. Then everyone discovered that life is short and decided to mix them together.

Unfortunately, when you combine the three ingredients in equal parts, you end up with a drink that looks and tastes nothing like a jewel. It's too rich and too sweet, and it comes out a weird brown colour. The Bijou is infinitely better if you up the gin and use the herbaceous Chartreuse as just a delicate grace note. This way, it comes out the colour of burnished copper.

50ml gin
20ml Italian vermouth
5ml Green Chartreuse

Stir slowly over large ice and strain into a cold cocktail glass. Garnish with an orange-zest twist and tell your guests once they have finished that you hope they appreciated the priceless jewel you placed in the bottom of the glass and what... you swallowed it?

BOBBY BURNS

A Scotch twist on the Manhattan (see page 59) – therefore, a Clanhattan? – from *The Old Waldorf Astoria Bar Book*. It's traditionally made with Bénédictine and Angostura bitters, while the current barman at the Waldorf Astoria, the redoubtable Frank Caiafa, insists on a dash of absinthe; here's the version I like best.

50ml Scotch (blended)
25ml Italian vermouth
5ml Drambuie
Dash Peychaud's bitters

Stir with large ice and strain into a cold cocktail glass. Garnish with a lemon-zest twist.

BOULEVARDIER

An classic variation on the Negroni (see page 62), with bourbon in place of the gin. It's obscene how good it tastes.

25ml bourbon
25ml Italian vermouth
25ml Campari

Stir all the ingredients over large ice in an old fashioned glass. Garnish with a slice of lemon or orange. By way of variation, try the Old Pal: the same but with French vermouth.

BROOKLYN

The Brooklyn is the third cocktail named after the five boroughs of New York City (Manhattan, page 59; Bronx, page 77... they didn't get round to Queens or Staten Island). Sadly, it is impossible to make a 'true' Brooklyn anymore since the crucial ingredient – Amer Picon – is no longer manufactured in the way it once was. You can still buy something called Amer Picon for about €10 in French supermarkets, however. It's a bitter orange liqueur, almost like a cross between an Italian amaro and Grand Marnier, and it's great when you mix it with beer (see the Biere Picon, page 192), but it's much lower-proof than the old stuff. Still, you can make an approximation as follows.

45ml rye (or bourbon)
15ml French vermouth
10ml Amer Picon (or a dark hued amaro)
5ml maraschino

Stir slowly over large ice and strain into a cold cocktail glass. Garnish with a cherry.

CELERY COCKTAIL

Pale and interesting, celery is surprisingly good as a cocktail ingredient. You can turn this liquid virtue into a sour by shaking it up with 15ml lemon juice and 10ml sugar syrup.

Ten or so thin slices of celery
50ml gin
10ml Lillet Blanc (or bianco vermouth)
Dash celery bitters

Muddle the celery in the bottom of your shaker with the gin and the Lillet. Stir over large ice, strain into a cold cocktail glass and garnish with a piece of celery.

CHARCO DI SANGRE

An idle afternoon's invention. The grapefruit-zest twists really lift it.

2–3 grapefruit-zest twists
40ml tequila reposado
20ml amontillado sherry
20ml crème de cassis

Bash the twists about in the bottom of your mixing vessel, before adding the alcohol. Stir with plenty of ice and strain into a cold cocktail glass. No garnish.

CHOCOLATE MARTINI

Not as sweet as you might think, the Chocolate Martini is a delightful way to appreciate the subtleties of Mozart Dry chocolate distillate. The intensity is softened by the vodka and sweetened just a touch by the vermouth (Cocchi Americano works well here). If you only have regular white crème de cacao but would like a similar effect, go up to 45ml vodka, take it down to 15ml cacao and use regular dry French vermouth instead of the sweet stuff.

30ml vodka
30ml Mozart Dry
20ml Cocchi Americano (or sweet white vermouth)

Stir slowly over large ice in the manner of a true Martini (see page 57) and strain into a cold cocktail glass. Garnish with an orange-zest twist.

CHOPIN

A happy Gin & It-inspired composition (see page 89) that has become one of my go-to aperitifs – I named it for its combination of Polish and French influences.

50ml Zubrowka
25ml quinquina (e.g. Byrrh or Dubonnet)
Dash orange bitters

Stir with plenty of ice in an old fashioned glass and serve just like that. Garnish with a lemon-zest twist.

CHRYSANTHEMUM

An elegant way of pimping up vermouth, originally listed in Hugo R. Ensslin's *Recipes for Mixed Drinks* (1917).

50ml French vermouth
10ml Bénédictine
Dash absinthe

Stir slowly over large ice and strain into a cold cocktail glass. Garnish with an orange-zest twist.

CONSOLATION

When you arrive home after an exceptionally shitty day what do you need? A Consolation, of course!

30ml amontillado sherry
10ml pisco
10ml crème de peche
10ml farigoule de thym (thyme liqueur)

Stir slowly over large ice and strain into a cold cocktail glass. Garnish with a lemon-zest twist or a sprig of thyme, if you happen to have one.

CORN N' OIL

A Caribbean drink of unknown origin, Corn n' Oil is almost like a summer Old Fashioned (see page 63). Traditionally, it is made with thick black molasses rum (which resembles engine oil) and falernum (which resembles corn oil). However, it works just as well with most good rich Jamaican rums. You can serve it without the squirt of lime, but I find that just a drop of the juice opens rum up nicely.

50ml dark rum
10ml falernum
Dash Angostura bitters
Lime wedge

Stir the rum, falernum and bitters together with a few large cubes of ice in an old fashioned glass. Squirt in a little lime juice and lob in the husk.

CORPSE REVIVER #1

It's hard to tell precisely what a Corpse Reviver is, exactly, as the various recipes that have come down have so little in common. However, like Bosom Carressers and Moustache Twisters, Corpse Revivers were foremost among the American 'sensation' drinks that bewildered English palates in the 19th century. As Henry Porter and George Edwin Roberts wrote in *Cups and Their Customs* (1863): '[The] source from which "eye-openers" and "smashers" come is one too notorious to be welcomed by any man who deserves well of his country: so we will pass the American bar, with its bad brandies and fiery wine, and express our gratification at the poor success which "Pick-me-ups", "Corpse-revivers", "Chain-lightning", and the like have had in this country.' Porter and Roberts will be gratified to note that the Corpse Reviver #1 was still going strong many decades thence, when Harry Craddock prescribed it 'to be taken before 11am' in *The Savoy Cocktail Book*.

40ml brandy
20ml apple brandy
20ml Italian vermouth

Stir over large ice and strain into a cold cocktail glass. Garnish with a paracetamol?

See also Corpse Reviver #2, page 156.

CUCUMBER COCKTAIL

A simple spring delight. The cucumberly affinities of Hendrick's gin make it the obvious choice here.

5cm cucumber
50ml gin or Zubrowka
10ml golden sugar syrup (2:1, see page 44)

Peel the cucumber and muddle it at the bottom of the shaker with the other ingredients. Add plenty of ice and stir carefully. Double-strain, express the oils from a twist of lemon zest and discard, garnishing instead with a mint leaf.

DUNAWAY

A warming and sophisticated sherry cocktail, invented by the celebrated Boston bartender Misty Kalkofen. Amontillado works just as well as fino.

50ml fino sherry
20ml Cynar
10ml maraschino
Dash Angostura bitters

Stir slowly over large ice and strain into a cold cocktail glass. Garnish with a lemon-zest twist, taking care to express the oils.

EARL GREY MARTINI

One for Mothering Sunday. You will not believe how easy this is to make or how delectable the results. A teabag will do at a push but I'd heartily commend Rare Tea Company's loose-leaf Earl Grey, which uses real bergamot oil.

> *Teaspoon Earl Grey tea leaves*
> *50ml gin*
> *10ml French vermouth*

Leave the tea leaves to infuse in the gin for no more than 1 minute. Strain into a mixing vessel and proceed as you would for a regular Martini (see page 57), stirring patiently over plenty of ice with the vermouth. Strain into a cold teacup and garnish with a lemon slice this time. For a party of four, serve from a teapot with cucumber sandwiches.

EAST INDIA

A beautiful creation when made accurately. Do be careful when measuring the homeopathic quantities of liqueurs required, since brandy is easily ruined by over-sweetening. A teaspoon contains about 2.5ml, a dessertspoon about 5ml, so I would recommend measuring that way.

> *50ml brandy*
> *2.5ml Grand Marnier*
> *2.5ml maraschino*
> *5ml grenadine (see page 83)*
> *Dash Angostura bitters*

Stir slowly over large ice and strain into a cold cocktail glass. Garnish with an orange-zest twist.

EDWARD I

I invented this on returning from the hospital, sleepless and drained, soon after my son Teddy was born. It is dry and bitter and sweet at the same time, the chocolate-orange connection very subtle.

> *40ml vodka*
> *20ml Cynar*
> *5ml Mozart Dry*
> *5ml orange liqueur*

Stir slowly over large ice and strain into a cold cocktail glass. Garnish with an orange-zest twist.

ELDERFLOWER MARTINI

Redolent of freshly mown grass and the first delicate flowers of the year, the Elderflower Martini is a fine cocktail for the arrival of spring. For an autumnal variation, use apple brandy in place of the Zubrowka – or try a mixture of both?

> *50ml Zubrowka*
> *25ml French vermouth*
> *10ml elderflower liqueur*

Stir slowly over large ice and strain into a cold cocktail glass. Garnish with a lemon-zest twist.

EL PRESIDENTE

A *muy elegante* way of serving rum – and a drink my wife commands me to make her almost hourly. It was named for the Cuban war hero-turned-not-that-nice-dictator, Gerardo Machado (1871–1939). There are as many variations as there are bartenders but I prefer the simpler, drier versions. You might add a touch of orange liqueur (Grand Marnier is good here) if you want a lick more sweetness.

50ml light rum
20ml French vermouth
5ml grenadine (page 83)

Stir slowly over large ice and strain into a cold cocktail glass. Garnish with a lemon- or orange-zest twist.

EYE-OPENER

The Eye-Opener, like the Corpse Reviver, is less a family of drinks than a band of orphans who decided it was them against the world. This is a particularly vicious example from Robert Vermeire's *Cocktails: How to Mix Them* (1922).

20ml brandy
20ml absinthe
20ml crème de menthe

I would personally stir this concoction but Vermeire's advice is: 'Shake… add plenty ice and shake some more; double-strain into a small wine glass and dust the top with a little chilli powder.' (Insanity.)

FERNANDO

A signature drink at the New York bar Employees Only, and a good example of the modern style of blending many complex ingredients.

25ml Fernet-Branca
35ml sweet white vermouth (Dolin Blanc recommended)
15ml Galliano L'Autentico

Stir awhile over plenty of ice and strain into a cold cocktail glass. Garnish with a mint leaf (gently bruise it to release the aromas).

GIMLET

See The Classics, page 84.

GIN COCKTAIL

The first known reference to a cocktail is not American but English. It dates back to a satirical snippet in the *Morning Post and Gazetteer* from 1798, speculating about William Pitt the Younger's tavern bills and imagining he might be fond of a 'cock-tail (vulgarly called ginger).' Hmm. This is a full eight years before the reference to the 'bittered sling' in America and suggests that 'cocktail' may once have had a different meaning. In his *Cooling Cups and Dainty Drinks* (1869), William Terrington refers to a Gin Cocktail as gin, water, ginger syrup and bitters. The missing link?

Ginger syrup
To make a first-rate ginger syrup you need fresh ginger juice. That's easy if you have a juicer. If not, simply peel a nice big root of ginger and grate it finely onto a clean tea towel or muslin cloth. Wring out the juice into a clean vessel and then use it to make a regular 2:1 sugar syrup (page 44), dissolving twice the volume of golden caster sugar into it on a low heat. Strain through a coffee filter, decant and store in the fridge. It's wonderful in many syrupy contexts, especially the Daiquiri (page 158). And the following:

> *50ml gin (Old Tom, properly)*
> *5ml ginger syrup*
> *Dash Angostura bitters*

A room-temperature cocktail. Simply combine in an old fashioned glass.

GIN & PINE

If you ever happen to be walking in a pine forest with a hand-axe and a bottle of gin in your knapsack, try this (and then come and find me): 'Split a piece of the heart of a green pine log into fine splints, about the size of a cedar lead-pencil, take two ounces of the same and put into a quart decanter, and fill the decanter with gin. Let the pine soak for two hours and the gin will be ready to serve.' (From Jerry Thomas's *Bartender's Guide*, 1862).

GROSVENOR

A serious after-dinner drink that's relatively light on alcohol.

> *50ml Kamm & Sons*
> *25ml Punt e Mes*
> *Dessertspoon (5ml) Islay whisky (eg Laphraoig)*

Stir over plenty of ice and strain into a cold cocktail glass. Garnish with a lemon twist.

HANKY PANKY

The Hanky Panky was invented by Ada Coleman, the celebrated female head bartender of the American Bar at London's Savoy, who got the job in 1898. The British patrons loved her and her (mostly female) bar team; it seems however, that American visitors found the presence of a woman in the saloon offensive. As she recounted, the actor Sir Charles Hawtrey came in one day and asked for something with a punch to it. When she presented him with this concoction, he cried, 'By Jove! That is the real hanky panky.' Sir Charles Hawtrey was not wrong. It *is* the real hanky panky. It is still very popular in Argentina, where Fernet-Branca is a naturalised citizen.

> *35ml gin*
> *35ml Italian vermouth*
> *5ml Fernet-Branca*

Stir all the ingredients with a large lump of ice and strain into a cold cocktail glass. Garnish with an orange-zest twist, taking care to express the bitter oils onto the drink.

HARRY'S COCKTAIL

One of Harry MacElhone's lesser-known gems – why it isn't offered at every Wetherspoon in the land is an enduring mystery.

50ml gin
25ml Italian vermouth
Sprig of fresh mint
Dash absinthe

Gently bruise the mint in the bottom of your mixing vessel. Add everything else, stir with plenty of ice and strain into a cold cocktail glass. Garnish with a stuffed olive.

HARVARD

See the Metropolitan, page 126.

IMPROVED BRANDY COCKTAIL

In Jerry Thomas's *Bartender's Guide*, the 'Cocktails' tend to appear in three iterations. There is the standard version: the Brandy Cocktail is made with brandy, sugar, curaçao and bitters and served over ice. There is the Fancy version, 'made in same way as the brandy cocktail, except that it is strained in a fancy wineglass, and a piece of lemon peel thrown on top, and the edge of the glass moistened with lemon.' And then there is the Improved Brandy Cocktail, which bears the closest resemblance to a modern cocktail and which Thomas asks you to shake. If you want to drink as people once drank:

50ml brandy
5ml golden sugar syrup (2:1, see page 44)
5ml maraschino
Dash absinthe
Dash bitters

Stir with plenty of ice (though Thomas would have shaken it) and double-strain into a 'fancy cocktail glass'. Moisten the edge of this glass with a little lemon and garnish with a lemon-zest twist, taking care to express the oils.

JAPANESE COCKTAIL

Dating back to the 1860s, the Japanese Cocktail is thought to be the first 'named' cocktail. Prior to this moment, people made do with names like Improved Brandy Cocktail (see page 119) and Fancy Gin Cocktail. Afterwards, the floodgates opened to Slow Comfortable Screws and Irish Car Bombs (terrible cocktails, terrible names). What it had to do with Japan, no one can say (it contains no raw fish) but it was invented around the time that Japan had ended its period of self-imposed isolation and launched its first trade mission to the west, bringing about a wave of bemused Japanophilia (see *The Mikado*, *Madame Butterfly*, etc). Only bother with this if you've homemade orgeat syrup (see page 86), otherwise it's not worth the brandy.

> *50ml brandy*
> *5ml orgeat syrup (page 86)*
> *Dash Angostura bitters*

Stir everything together over a couple of large cubes of ice. Then add some more ice and stir some more. Garnish with a lemon-zest twist.

JAPANESE MARTINI

A lot of the drier styles of saké taste like softer and more approachable dry Martinis in themselves.

> *50ml vodka*
> *25ml saké (dry)*

Stir patiently over ice for a while and then strain into a cold cocktail glass. Garnish with a lime-zest twist – or a yuzu-zest twist if you can track any down.

JOURNALIST

One drizzly afternoon, I wandered into Happiness Forgets in London's Hoxton Square hoping to kill a little time between assignments. I asked for something gin-based and dry and this is what I got. I wonder, if I were a Cabinet Maker or a Titular Councillor and not a member of the press, would the bartender's intuition have nudged him to concoct something completely different?

> *40ml gin*
> *10ml French vermouth*
> *10ml Italian vermouth*
> *5ml orange liqueur*
> *5ml lemon juice*
> *Dash Angostura bitters*

Stir all the ingredients with ice and double-strain into a chilled coupe. Garnish with a cherry.

KANGAROO

The Kangaroo is an old-school name for the Vodka Martini – a useful cover if you ever feel like ordering one in a bar. Vodka remains the world's most popular spirit (thanks in part to the prodigious quantity drunk in Russia), but in certain circles, it is the booze that dare not speak its name. Ask for a Vodka Martini in certain establishments in New York and London and you will be told that a Martini is made from gin and perhaps you'd like to leave? It is a far cry from the 1990s, when vodka reigned supreme and gin was in the ditch.

So why is vodka unhip all of a sudden? Well, in simple terms, it is to do with how it tastes – or rather how it doesn't taste. Vodka is a colourless, flavourless spirit that you can make from pretty much whatever organic matter you choose (wheat, potatoes, beetroots, former members of the Politburo, whatever). While a rum will bear a relation to the sugar used to make it, the only defining characteristic of vodka is how purely it has been distilled. You might think of it as the bottled water of the spirit world; there are differences between the brands, to be sure, but they are mostly to do with the size of their respective marketing budgets and the purity of the filtration process. You can use this neutrality to your advantage, if you want a base for making your own infusions, say, or if you want to tame the sweetness of a complex liqueur without sacrificing its kick. In the old days, however, when people actually liked the taste of spirits, no one bothered with it; there is scarcely a reference to vodka in *The Savoy Cocktail Book*.

Vodka's status as an imposter actually goes deeper than that. The term 'vodka' – literally 'little water' in Russian – has changed meaning many times, so when Russian writers like Pushkin or Gogol mention vodka, they do not mean what a Russian thinks of as vodka today. Up until the late 19th century, Russia's national spirit was generally distilled in small copper stills from rye, spelt, wheat and/or barley and had more in common with unaged whiskey than with modern vodka. It was known as *polugar* or sometimes bread wine. 'Vodka' was bread wine infused with extra ingredients, such as garlic or pepper. Russians often drank this with meals – caraway vodka might accompany fish, for example, while apricot vodka might go with dessert.

Modern vodka, with its very high purity, was made possible only with the advent of the rectification column, which was invented in the French chemicals industry and made it into Russia only in the late-19th century. In 1895, the Russian Tsar issued an imperial decree that all vodka in Russia must be made according to the new process, which had the dual purpose of establishing a state monopoly while claiming the new style was safer for ordinary peasants to drink. Pierre Smirnoff (really, Pyotr Smirnov) saw which way the wind was blowing and moved his business to Paris. Meanwhile, small domestic producers were soon out of business, vodka lost its flavour and by the mid-20th century, on a wave of advertising, it was sweeping the world in the form of Moscow Mules (see table, page 190) and French Martinis (see page 165). It's interesting that a Russian product should prove so wildly popular at the height of the Cold War but that's humanity for you.

Happily, today, there are a few producers reviving the old style of vodka. Vestal, HQ'd on a canal boat in London, makes a lot of the differences between each year's potato crop, while the Russian vodka historian Boris Rodionov has gone to impressive lengths to reproduce 19th-century Russian recipes with his Polugar brand (which comes in rye, wheat and barley forms, and numerous flavours). They are full of earth and field, and are quite a surprise if you're used to modern vodka. There are also smaller producers, such as Pleurat Shabani of Konik's Tail, who makes Polish-style vodkas of great elegance and character. There are far worse ways to appreciate them than in a good clean Kangaroo, which is naked enough for the subtleties to shine through. Despite my habitual preference for 'wet' gin Martinis (see page 58), the essence of vodka lies in its good clean hit, so I'm tempted to dispense with the vermouth altogether and just go with a lemon-zest twist. Shoot me.

> *50ml (good) vodka*
> *10ml French vermouth (optional)*

Stir with plenty of ice, at least half a minute, and strain into a cold cocktail glass. Garnish with a lemon-zest twist or a green olive as you prefer.

LONDON COCKTAIL

'To cure a headache take a little absinthe in the palm of the hand, dry it between the two hands and sniff through the nose', advises Robert Vermeire in *Cocktails: How to Mix Them* (1922). 'After this, have a plain cocktail with a dash of absinthe or a good London Cocktail is generally effective.' A good remedy for London, at times, I find.

> *50ml gin (London Dry)*
> *5ml golden sugar syrup (2:1, see page 44)*
> *5ml absinthe*
> *Dash orange bitters*

Stir with plenty of ice and strain into a cold cocktail glass. Express the oils from a lemon-zest twist, discard the zest, and garnish with a green olive.

LOUISIANA

A rich after-dinner drink in the New Orleans style.

> *25ml rye (or bourbon)*
> *25ml Italian vermouth*
> *25ml Bénédictine*
> *Dash absinthe*
> *Dash Peychaud's bitters*

Stir with plenty of ice and strain into a cold cocktail glass. Garnish with a cherry.

LUCIEN GAUDIN

An orange-scented Negroni (see page 62), served up and named after a dashing French fencer of the 1920s.

> *40ml gin*
> *20ml Campari*
> *20ml orange liqueur*
> *20ml French vermouth*

Stir with plenty of ice and strain into a cold cocktail glass. Garnish with a cherry.

MANHATTAN

See The Classics, page 59.

MARGUERITE

See Obituary, page 128.

MARTIKI

Proof that Tiki drinks can be rather elegant too. Apparently, this was served at the Luau restaurant in Beverly Hills as an exotic alternative to the Martini. The coconut water is my addition – coconut chiming surprisingly well with the caraway in the kummel.

50ml light rum
25ml coconut water (optional)
10ml kummel

Stir over plenty of ice in the manner of a Martini and strain into a cold cocktail glass. Garnish with a lemon-zest twist and/or a slice of coconut.

MARTINEZ

The missing link between the Manhattan and the Martini (see pages 59 and 57), the Martinez dates back at least as far as 1884 when it was listed as a variant on the Manhattan in *The Modern Bartender's Guide* by O.H. Byron. In his 1888 *Bartenders' Manual*, Harry Johnson wrote out the first proper recipe, calling for half Dutch gin and half vermouth with a dash of curaçao and some Angostura bitters. Later versions call for Old Tom gin… but most modern bars make use of regular London Dry. In short, there are plenty of versions of the Martinez to play with. The version I like best is from Jerry Thomas's *Bartender's Guide*, which doubles the vermouth content – essentially making it a vermouth cocktail. With Dutch gin, it's a riot. See also the Gin & It (page 89).

50ml Italian vermouth
25ml genever (or other gin)
5ml maraschino
A good dash of bitters

Stir everything patiently over ice and strain into a cold cocktail glass. Garnish with a cherry.

MARTINI

See The Classics, page 57.

METROPOLITAN

An old variant of the Manhattan (see page 59) made with brandy as opposed to rye. The similar Harvard came along a little later... the difference being that the Harvard should be made with orange bitters and a tiny splash of soda water. I just prefer the name Metropolitan.

>*50ml brandy*
>*25ml Italian vermouth*
>*Dash of Angostura bitters*

Stir all the ingredients over ice and strain into a chill cocktail glass. Garnish with a lemon-zest twist.

MINT JULEP

See The Classics, page 71.

MOONRAKER

A rearranged version of a forgotten drink from *The Savoy Cocktail Book*.

>*25ml brandy*
>*25ml quinquina (e.g. Byrrh or Dubonnet)*
>*25ml crème de pêche*
>*Dash absinthe*

Stir everything up over plenty of ice and strain into a cold cocktail glass. Garnish with a lemon-zest twist.

NEGRONI

See The Classics, page 62.

NYMPH

A fun thing from the *Café Royal Book* (1937).

> *25ml rye (or bourbon)*
> *25ml sweet white vermouth (Lillet Blanc recommended)*
> *25ml apricot brandy*
> *Dash Angostura bitters*

Stir with plenty of ice and strain into a cold cocktail glass. Garnish with a lemon-zest twist.

OAXACA OLD FASHIONED

A modern classic by New York bartending icon Phil Ward. The cleverness lies in using the smoke of the mezcal as a little grace note as opposed to the dominant chord. See the Penicillin too (page 177), which does a similar thing with contrasting Scotch whiskies.

> *50ml tequila (añejo or reposado)*
> *10ml mezcal*
> *2.5ml agave syrup*
> *Dash Angostura bitters*

Make like an Old Fashioned. Stir the tequila, syrup and bitters in an old fashioned glass without ice at first, so as to dissolve the agave syrup properly. Then add the mezcal and a couple of cubes of ice and stir some more. Then add a couple more cubes of ice and stir a little more. At Death & Co, they garnish with a flamed orange-zest twist – though I like grapefruit.

OBITUARY

An old variation on the Martini, made 'wet' (see page 58), with a pleasing 'spot' of absinthe lurking in the middle. It's also known as a Marguerite.

Dash absinthe
35ml gin
35ml French vermouth

Rinse out a cocktail glass with absinthe and place in the freezer to chill. Meanwhile, stir the gin and French vermouth over plenty of ice and then strain into the absinthe-rinsed glass. Mist a lemon peel over the top and discard, garnishing instead with a cherry.

OLD ETONIAN

Apparently London's favourite drink, for a heady spell in the 1920s. Perhaps due a revival now that all things Old Etonian are on the ascendancy again?

35ml gin
35ml sweet white vermouth (Cocchi Americano recommended)
2.5ml crème de noyaux (or any almond liqueur)
Dash orange bitters

Stir with plenty of ice and strain into a cold cocktail glass. Garnish with an orange-zest twist.

OLD FASHIONED

See The Classics, page 63.

PABLO ALVAREZ DE CANAS SPECIAL

An adaptation on an obscure classic from the Floridita bar in Havana, seemingly named after a Cuban journalist, which strikes me as an excellent way to name a cocktail. It is a refreshing pre-dinner slurp with a taste a little like watermelon.

30ml brandy
30ml fino sherry
10ml cherry brandy
Lemon-zest twist

Muddle the lemon-zest twist in the bottom of the mixing vessel, then add the alcohol and ice and stir well. Strain into a cold cocktail glass and garnish with a cherry.

PACIFIC COAST HIGHWAY

An Alaska cocktail (see page 103) given a Mexican twist and named after the great road that links the two locations.

5ml Yellow Chartreuse
Grapefruit
50ml tequila
10ml mezcal (optional)

Pour the Chartreuse into an old fashioned glass with a very large lump of ice and roll it around so that everything is well rinsed. Express the oils from a fat length of grapefruit peel and drop that in too. Now, slowly pour over the tequila (and mezcal) and stir.

PING-PONG

A dash of bitterness sets this off a treat – try rinsing the glass in Fernet-Branca or Cynar first?

> 50ml sloe gin
> 10ml French vermouth
> 10ml Italian vermouth
> Dash orange bitters

Stir over large ice and strain into a cold cocktail class. Garnish with a lemon-zest twist.

PINK GIN

It is the cocktail with the most effeminate name – 'Yeah mine's a pink gin mate' – and yet it is the hardest drink of them all. The version drunk by British sailors would have consisted of Navy-strength gin (*i.e.* 55% ABV) served at room temperature in a glass that had been heavily doused in Angostura bitters. The contemporary landlubber could easily make Pink Gin more palatable by stirring it up with ice, Martini-style, and adding a little sweetness too – but to me this feels like cheating. Sometimes, after a hard day, one likes to be rough-housed by a drink. Colonials used it to ward off dysentery – and it does make an excellent post-jalfrezi digestif.

> 2.5ml Angostura bitters
> 50ml gin (ideally Navy-strength)

Place the bitters in a workaday glass and roll it around until it is thoroughly coated. Then pour in the gin. Serve at room temperature. Down the hatch.

PINK RABBIT

'Am I the one you think about / When you're sitting in your fainting chair / Drinking Pink Rabbits?' sang Matt Berninger of The National on the song 'Pink Rabbits' (2013). Which begs the question: what is a Pink Rabbit? My letters have gone unanswered. The only recipe I have been able to find on the internet consists of strawberry Nesquik and tequila, which sounds gross; Pink Squirrels, which combine equal parts crème de cacao, crème de noyau and cream, are more common. Still, I feel the mood calls for something strong but wistful. Most light or floral liqueurs will work in place of the rose.

50ml pisco
25ml sweet white vermouth
10ml crème de rose
Dash absinthe

Stir over plenty of ice and strain into a cold cocktail glass. Spritz over lemon zest and garnish with a rose petal if you happen to have one.

POET'S DREAM

A lyrical take on the Martini (see page 57), which I first tried at the Varnish bar in Los Angeles.

40ml gin
20ml French vermouth
10ml Bénédictine

Stir over plenty of ice and strain into a cold cocktail glass. Garnish with a lemon-zest twist and a bespoke sonnet for each guest.

REFERENDUM

The obvious pairing for elderflower is something light and floral, but it goes just as well in a brooding brown drink such as this one.

50ml Scotch (blended)
15ml elderflower liqueur
Dash Peychaud's bitters

Stir over large ice in an old fashioned glass and serve just like that, with a lemon-zest twist.

REMEMBER THE MAINE

In his *Gentleman's Companion*, Charles H. Baker claims to have drunk one of these as Havana resounded to bombs during the 1933 revolution. It somehow beats drinking one in a gentrified retro-themed bar as London resounds to the 2015 election. It's a Manhattan riff that caves into the temptation to add some cherry but then recovers its composure with a light mist of absinthe.

> *50ml rye (or bourbon)*
> *20ml Italian vermouth*
> *5ml cherry brandy*
> *Dash absinthe*

Stir over ice and strain into a cold cocktail glass. Garnish with a cherry.

ROB ROY

A Scotch Manhattan (see page 59).

> *50ml Scotch (blended)*
> *25ml Italian vermouth*
> *Dash Peychaud's bitters*

Stir with plenty of ice and strain into a chilled cocktail glass. Spray a fine mist of lemon-zest oil over the top and discard the zest, and garnish with a cherry. Also try rinsing the glass first in a good single malt (particularly Islay) first to add a different accent. You can of course use Angostura bitters but Peychaud's goes better with Scotch.

ROSE

An adaptation of an old French drink.

> *40ml gin*
> *20ml cherry brandy*

20ml French vermouth
Dash rose water

Stir with plenty of ice and strain into a cold cocktail glass. Garnish with a rose petal.

ROSITA

A Negroni (see page 62) with tequila in place of the gin – better, I find, if you up the proportion of tequila. Recommended.

50ml tequila (reposado)
15ml Campari
15ml Italian vermouth

Stir over ice in an old fashioned glass and garnish with a lemon slice.

RUSTY NAIL

Once, the Rusty Nail was pre-eminent among sophisticates – it was the favoured order of the Rat Pack, for example. If you are lucky enough to sample Rat Pack-era Drambuie you will see why: it is a subtle and delightful liqueur, something of the order of alcoholic honey with a wisp of smoke, very much the thing for warming beside the fire after a sodden day on the moor. Today, it has fallen down the ranks and if you sample modern Drambuie, you will also see why. Sweet, aggressive... hopefully a recent change in ownership will restore it to former glory. The old recipes often call for 50–50 ratio. If all you have is the modern stuff, I would use it much more sparingly.

50ml Scotch (blended)
10ml Drambuie

Stir in an old fashioned glass with some large lumps of ice. Mist a lemon-zest twist over the top and drop into the glass.

SARATOGA

A Manhattan (see page 59) in all but name, from Jerry Thomas's *Bon Vivant's Companion* (1862). Saratoga is a delightful racing town in New York State; I tried ordering one of these in a local diner, to no avail.

> *25ml brandy*
> *25ml rye (or bourbon)*
> *25ml Italian vermouth*
> *Dash Angostura bitters*

Stir over ice and strain into a chilled wine glass. Garnish with a lemon slice.

SAZERAC

The Sazerac is a connoisseur's Old Fashioned (see page 63) from New Orleans, where everyone is a connoisseur. We owe its invention to Antoine Peychaud, a 19th-century apothecary who set up shop in the city's French Quarter in 1834 and compounded his own bitter cordial. The keeps at a nearby bar named Sazerac Coffee House soon began to mix Peychaud's Bitters with brandy and sugar in their vogueish 'Cocktails' and in so doing, created a new house drink: the Sazerac. Over time the Sazerac underwent a few mutations. First, rye whiskey began to supplant cognac (these days you can compromise with half of each). Second, it gained a little dash of anis, as the absinthe craze swept the French Quarter in the early 20th century. Three, it became one of the few cocktails to be served in an old fashioned glass without ice. One memorable night in a theme bar in Camden, this instruction confused our bartender so much that he filled our glasses up to the brim with neat spirit – and duly obliterated our entire evening.

> *Dash absinthe*
> *30ml brandy*
> *30ml bourbon (or rye)*
> *2.5ml brown sugar*

Dash Peychaud's bitters
Dash Angostura bitters

An odd method but bear with. Pour a small amount of absinthe into an old fashioned glass and roll it around so as to coat the surface. Place this glass into the freezer. Now make the cocktail. In a second glass, stir together the spirits, sugar and bitters without ice until the sugar is dissolved. Add large ice and stir until very cool. Remove the first glass from the freezer, discard excess absinthe and strain the cocktail into this glass. Express the oils from a lemon-zest twist on top and discard.

SKID ROW

A no-holds-barred genever cocktail from the Varnish Bar, very near the actual Skid Row in Downtown Los Angeles. Nowadays, gentrification means that the bums who used to populate the infamous street are gradually being replaced by artisanal cocktail joints. Does the name of this cocktail, therefore, count as a tribute or a taunt?

50ml genever
15ml apricot brandy
15ml Yellow Chartreuse
Dash Angostura bitters

Stir with plenty of ice and double-strain into a cold cocktail glass.

SPRING GREEN

Chartreuse without the headache – and truly, a sensational lunchtime aperitif. Adapted from a recipe listed by Dinah Sanders in *The Art of the Shim* (2013) and credited to the Nopa restaurant in San Francisco.

45ml fino sherry
15ml Green Chartreuse
15ml elderflower liqueur

Stir everything over large ice and strain into a cold cocktail glass.

STINGER

A superior digestif, in which mint and brandy ally far more sympathetically than you might suppose. I once made an accidental Stinger by dropping a tot of French mint syrup (available in French supermarkets and worth smuggling home) into some very expensive aged Armagnac at a house we were staying at, and I was pleased I did. Truman Capote used to begin each lunch with a Double Martini and conclude it with a Stinger.

> *50ml brandy*
> *15ml crème de menthe*

Stir in an old fashioned glass with large ice. Garnish with a mint leaf if you have one; otherwise leave plain. It's good with gin instead of brandy too. If you want to get all fancy on your Stinger's ass, try rinsing the glass first in Fernet-Branca and/or Green Chartreuse.

STOMACH REVIVER

This is what passed for medicine in the 1920s.

> *25ml brandy*
> *25ml kummel*
> *10ml Fernet-Branca*
> *2.5ml Angostura bitters.*

Stir over plenty of ice, decant into a cocktail glass and sip in front of daytime TV feeling sorry for yourself.

SUBURBAN

From *The Old Waldorf Astoria Bar Book* (1935). I like to think of it as the less sophisticated counterpart to the Metropolitan (see page 126).

40ml bourbon
20ml dark rum
20ml port
Dash Angostura bitters
Dash orange bitters

Stir with large ice in an old fashioned glass. Garnish with an orange-zest twist.

SYLVANIAN MARTINI

Tony Conigliaro of 69 Colebrooke Row in London makes a fancier version of this drink called the Woodland Martini. It's so delicious, it's worth having a go at reproducing even if you don't have time to forage in the lower Alps for ingredients. A rinse of Zirbenz Stone Pine Liqueur (made from Austrian pine cones) will lift it to the sylvan heavens, if you can find it. Try Yellow Chartreuse, Galliano, any pine- or fir-based liqueur or even the dreaded Jägermeister if not.

2.5ml Alpine-style liqueur (if you can find it)
50ml gin
25ml amontillado sherry
Dash Angostura bitters

If you have an appropriate liqueur, pour a teaspoon of it into the glass and gently roll it around to coat the surface. Place in the freezer. Now stir all the other ingredients over large ice, Martini-style (see page 57). Once well chilled, remove the glass from the freezer and strain in the drink. At Colebrooke Row, they garnish with a pickled walnut.

TIPPERARY

Ireland's whiskey industry was the big loser of Prohibition and modernisation in general (around 150 Irish distilleries closed between 1880 and the end of the Second World War). In cocktail terms, Irish whiskey tends to fall between the two stools of Scotch and bourbon but it does so in a very charming, raffish sort of way and it deserves more than its St Patrick's Day outing.

> *50ml Irish whiskey*
> *25ml Italian vermouth*
> *5ml Green Chartreuse*

Stir over plenty of ice and strain into a cold cocktail glass. Garnish with a real four-leaf clover.

TRILBY

The crème de violette lends a certain faraway quality to this ancient aperitif (adapted from *Jack's Manual* of 1910). A Debussy prelude playing in a locked-up house?

> *35ml gin (Old Tom)*
> *35ml Italian vermouth*
> *10ml crème de violette*
> *Dash Angostura bitters*
> *Dash orange bitters*

Stir slowly over large ice and strain into a cold cocktail glass. Express the oil from an orange-zest twist onto the drink, discard the zest and garnish with a cherry instead.

TUXEDO

In the old formulations, the Tuxedo is something of a nonentity. 'Where are you going with this?' you say, barely looking up from the chaise longue. A whisper of fino makes it a pleasant light cocktail.

25ml gin
25ml French vermouth
25ml fino sherry
2.5ml maraschino
Dash absinthe
Dash orange bitters

Stir slowly over large ice and strain into a cold cocktail glass. Garnish with a lemon-zest twist.

VIEUX CARRÉ

If the Sazerac (see page 134) is the New Orleans Old Fashioned, the Vieux Carré is the New Orleans Manhattan (see page 59). It is one of the greatest cocktails yet created.

25ml brandy
25ml bourbon
25ml Italian vermouth
5ml Bénédictine
Dash Peychaud's bitters.

Stir everything slowly over large ice and strain into an old fashioned glass filled with ice.

WHISKY MAC

A simple after-dinner drink, the Whisky Mac is a useful one when visiting relatives. Stone's Original Green Ginger Wine is a favourite of English grandfathers, who often have a bottle of Scotch knocking around somewhere too. It works fine without ice, too, but you can make a fancier version on the rocks with a superior ginger liqueur. Central heating for adults.

> *50ml Scotch*
> *25ml ginger wine (if using ginger liqueur, try 15ml)*

Stir in a glass, over ice if you prefer, and serve just like that.

WIDOW'S KISS

One of the most powerful weapons in the bartender's arsenal, the Widow's Kiss combines a hefty amount of spirit with two strong and potent herbal liqueurs but somehow manages to remain balanced. It's one of a number of 'Widow' cocktails listed in vintage cocktail books (Merry Widow, Widow's Dream, Widow's Kiss, etc). When you bear in mind the amount of husbands left in the trenches, there would probably have been a lot of widows about to kiss.

> *50ml apple brandy*
> *15ml Bénédictine*
> *15ml Chartreuse (Green or Yellow)*
> *Dash Angostura bitters*

Stir over plenty of ice and strain into a cold cocktail glass. Garnish with a mint sprig.

The same drink made with bourbon or rye in place of the apple brandy is called the Purgatory.

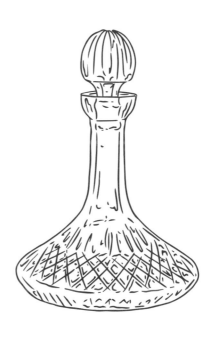

THE SHAKEN

'I expect you would prefer sherry, but, my dear Charles,
you are not going to have sherry. Isn't this a
delicious concoction?'

Anthony Blanche orders Brandy Alexanders in Evelyn Waugh's
Brideshead Revisited (1945)

I THINK OF shaken cocktails as fun cocktails, short, sharp and sweet, to be drunk while they're still laughing at you as Harry Craddock had it. Most of the cocktails in this section are built on a similar formula of spirit, citrus and sweetener (though there are a few that use cream in place of the citrus element too). Many are made to precisely the same ratio as the classic Sour (page 65) though some take their sweetness from liqueurs as opposed to sugar syrup which requires a little rebalancing.

ABSINTHE SUISSESSE

The Swiss present such a neutral face to the world – but who really knows what wickedness lurks in their bank vaults and their cuckoo clocks? Certainly, the Swiss method of serving absinthe (actually, from New Orleans) is as decadent as they come.

> *Handful of mint leaves*
> *50ml absinthe*
> *10ml orgeat syrup (see page 86)*
> *20ml egg white*

Dry shake very hard without ice to froth up the egg – then add ice and shake again to chill. Double-strain into a cold cocktail glass. Garnish with a mint leaf.

AMARETTO SOUR

The combination of almond, sugar and tang is childish but irresistible – and much better with a backbone of spirit. See the Mandorla Sour (page 171) and the Army & Navy (page 86) for slight variations.

> *25ml bourbon (or brandy)*
> *25ml amaretto*
> *15ml lemon juice*
> *5ml golden sugar syrup (2:1, see page 44)*
> *10ml egg white*

Dry shake without ice to froth up the egg – then add ice and shake again to chill. Double-strain into a cold cocktail glass and pour on a few drops of Angostura bitters for a garnish.

APEROL SOUR

Barbie would drink this cocktail if she could drink at all.

25ml gin
25ml Aperol
15ml lemon juice
5ml golden sugar syrup (2:1, see page 44)
10ml egg white

Precisely the same as the Amaretto Sour, page 145: dry shake without ice to froth up the egg, then add ice and shake again to chill. Double-strain into a cold cocktail glass and pour on a few drops of Angostura bitters for a garnish.

APPLETINI

See Abominable Cocktails, page 239.

ARMY & NAVY

See The Classics, page 86.

AVENUE B

See The Classics, page 82.

AVIATION

The Aviation is like a jazz age idol who everyone forgot about. It scratched a living doing dusty cabarets for a while, appreciated by only a few loyal fans. Finally rediscovered by a younger crowd, it now earns a respectable pension playing theatre shows for a hipper audience than it ever really had in the first place.

The lost years were lost mostly due to the difficulty in procuring crème de violette. It's a measure of the cocktail renaissance that there are now at least five decent brands to choose from. In truth, the violette is there more for the distinctive sky-blue tinge than its floral character – you can make it without. It's best think of the Aviation as a Gin Sour, sweetened with maraschino (which is the real star here) and just a drop of violette. I'd like to think this was the last thing Amelia Earhart sipped before climbing into the cockpit.

50ml gin
15ml lemon juice
10ml maraschino
2.5ml violet liqueur (optional)

Shake everything with plenty of ice and double-strain into a cold cocktail glass. Soar! Garnish with a cherry.

By way of variation, add 15ml egg white for an Eagle's Dream. Also try with 20ml added orange juice for a Casino. A King's Jubilee is the same with light rum instead of gin, and rather good.

BACARDI SPECIAL

Back in the 1930s, when the Bacardi family still made their rum in Cuba, the Bacardi Cocktail and Bacardi Special provided pink variations on the Daiquiri (see page 158). The character of Bacardi has changed a lot since then, so I see no reason not to substitute a more flavourful light rum, such as Havana Club (which is still made in Cuba). The original 'Bacardi Cocktail' was basically a Daiquiri with grenadine, but the 'Special' version combines the rum with a bit of gin to create one of the great 'twin-spirit' drinks.

35ml light rum
15ml gin
10ml lime juice
5ml grenadine (see page 83)

Shake up with plenty of ice and double-strain into a cold cocktail glass. Garnish with a lime wedge.

To create a simple Bacardi Cocktail, replace the gin with more rum.

BARBARA WEST

Barbara West was one of the few survivors from the *Titanic*; the vintage cocktail that bears her name has only recently bobbed up to the surface. Amontillado and lemon make a pleasant life raft.

> *25ml gin*
> *25ml amontillado sherry*
> *15ml lemon juice*
> *10ml golden sugar syrup (2:1, see page 44)*
> *Dash Angostura bitters*

Shake up with plenty of ice and double-strain into a cold cocktail glass. Garnish with a lemon-zest twist.

BARNUM WAS RIGHT

How this vintage cocktail acquired its name and who Barnum was, we may never know, but I'll tell you one thing. He was absolutely spot on. As with many cocktails that use liqueurs to sweeten, you may need a drop of sugar syrup for balance.

> *50ml gin*
> *25ml apricot brandy*
> *15ml lemon juice*
> *Dash Angostura bitters*

Shake up with plenty of ice and double-strain into a cold cocktail glass. Garnish with a lemon-zest twist, having first expressed the oils onto the drink.

BATIDA

If the Caipirinha (see page 153) is the Pele of cachaça cocktails, *i.e.* the star player, the Batida is still useful to have on the bench. It works with most tropical fruits (papaya, kiwi, passion fruit, etc) and like all cachaça cocktails, is much better with regular light rum.

½ fresh mango
50ml cachaca
5ml golden sugar syrup (2:1, see page 44)
Squirt of lime juice

Score the mango, peel off the skin and place the fruit pieces into your shaker. Muddle to extract the juices then introduce the cachaça, sugar syrup, a little lime juice and plenty of ice. Shake hard and double-strain into a cold cocktail glass (this may take a little work), and garnish with a lime wedge.

BEE'S KNEES

The Bee's Knees is a Gin Sour sweetened with honey (hence the apiological name). The results are dramatically different depending on the honey you use. The Bee's Knees was a piece of 1920s slang meaning the dog's bollocks. 'Well, that's just the bee's knees!' they used to say, signifying approval. Other variants include: the Cat's Miaow; the Cat's Pyjamas; the Snake's Hips; the Eel's Ankles; the Capybara's Spats; the Elephant's Instep; the Beaver's Dick; the Kookaburra's Yawn; the Trout's Nose and the Hippo's Tail.

50ml gin
15ml lemon juice
10ml honey loosened with 5ml hot water

Introduce everyone in the shaker and make sure that the honey is fully dissolved before adding ice. Shake up hard and double-strain into a cold cocktail glass. Garnish with a lemon-zest twist.

BETWEEN THE SHEETS

If you ever find yourself in an English meat market at 2am, looking up from cocktail menu of Porn Star Martinis and Sex on the Beaches and Slow Comfortable Screws, looking at your fellow humans pawing and clawing at one another and crying out 'What has become of us?', then take comfort. People were just as smutty back in the supposedly more elegant day, with their Bosom Caressers and Maiden's Blushes and How's-Your-Fathers. When Harry MacElhone first mixed this in 1922, the Between the Sheets was liable to deliver on its titillation, too. If you make it as per his instructions with Cointreau (which comes in at 40% ABV), it has a deceptively high alcohol content for something so sweet and may soon have you retiring to bed. A good long shake will help to tame it.

25ml brandy
25ml light rum
25ml orange liqueur (Cointreau)
10ml lemon juice

Shake up with plenty of ice for a little longer than normal, and double-strain into a cold cocktail glass. Garnish with a lemon-zest twist.

BLOOD & SAND

A good Scot will tell you there is only one way to drink Scotch, which is with Irn-Bru. A more discerning one will tell you that it's best neat, with no ice, and that you should flick in a couple of drops of water to open it up. However, should you wish to shake things up a little, a Blood & Sand is a good way to do it. It is an early example of a promotional tie-in, invented in 1922 to honour a film starring the silent heartthrob Rudolph Valentino, whose exotic Italian looks set the style for the era and turned women insane. Blood orange juice is not specified in the original recipe but adds a welcome bitter tang.

40ml Scotch (blended)
20ml cherry brandy
20ml Italian vermouth
20ml (blood) orange juice

Shake with plenty of ice and double-strain into a cold cocktail glass. Garnish with an orange-zest twist.

BRAMBLE

A slightly doctored 'smash' from the 1980s with a taste supposedly reminiscent of an English hedgerow. It was invented by the legendary London bartender Dick Bradsell whose reputation is so great, he could work in any fancy hotel he chooses but prefers to keep a divey Soho tequila bar so he can be with his mates. Cassis is an OK substitute for the crème de mure, otherwise create your own 'instant' crème de mure: muddle a few blackberries in gin (or vodka) and add sugar to taste.

> *50ml gin*
> *25ml lemon juice*
> *10ml golden sugar syrup (2:1, see page 44)*
> *10ml crème de mure (blackberry liqueur)*

Shake the gin, lemon and sugar syup with plenty of ice and strain into an old fashioned glass filled with crushed ice. Pour the liqueur over the top without mixing to create a bleeding effect. Decorate with mint, lemon and/or blackberries and serve with a straw.

BRANDY ALEXANDER

Originally made with gin, the Alexander became popular during Prohibition as the dessert-like elements of cream and cacao disguised the turpentine in the gin. Juniper and chocolate, however, is not an enduring combination and the formula works better with almost any other spirit – especially brandy. If you make it with Irish whiskey, you have Bailey's pretty much. With vodka, you're not a million miles from a White Russian (see page 214).

For such a creamy pleasure, the Alexander has an abominable reputation. In Edward Albee's drama of marital dysfunction, *Who's Afraid of Virginia Woolf?* (1962), George sneers at his wife Martha's former predilection for 'lady-like little drinkies'. 'Back when I was courting Martha she'd order the damnedest things... Brandy Alexanders!' John Lennon was also fond of a Brandy Alexander.

'After one, he was everybody's friend', recalled one drinking companion. 'After three, he was nasty-drunk.' Perhaps what these men feared was not that they wouldn't like it but they would like it too much.

> *50ml brandy*
> *25ml crème de cacao (brown)*
> *25ml single cream*
> *Nutmeg for grating*

Shake hard with ice and double-strain into a fancy glass. Grate fresh nutmeg on top to garnish.

A good dash of Angostura bitters changes the flavour interestingly. The 2:1:1 spirit/liqueur/cream formula is worth playing around with, if you can withstand the derision.

BRANDY FIX

A 'Fix' is an old sweet-and-sour sipper that combines spirit and fruit juice. It often comes out like an unfizzy Fizz. The greatest expression that I've tried is the brandy version prescribed by the 19th-century bartender Harry Johnson, an early approximation of a Tiki drink (see page 214). First, I'm afraid, you'll have to make your own pineapple syrup. It will take 24 hours but there's nothing too complicated and it will save you paying £7.99 for a vile commercial variety.

Pineapple syrup
Chop up half a fresh pineapple into bits, coat with around 100g brown sugar and leave under clingfilm in the fridge overnight. The next day, juice should have leeched out. Set up a sieve over a saucepan, tip in the contents of the bowl and push the pineapple pieces through, extracting as much juice as possible. Gently warm this mixture and stir in an equal amount of additional brown sugar, taking it off the heat as soon as it is all dissolved. Line the sieve with a piece of kitchen roll and strain this syrup into a jug and then transfer to a clean glass bottle. Add a little vodka or rum to act as a preservative. This should make about 250ml and it will keep in the fridge for one month (sniff before use to be sure).

Now you are ready to create a Brandy Fix. As prescribed by Johnson:

50ml brandy
15ml pineapple syrup (you may need to up this
according to taste)
15ml lime juice
5ml Green Chartreuse

Shake hard with plenty of ice and double-strain into a fancy glass filled with ice. Decorate with an extra isosceles of pineapple.

BRONX

See The Classics, page 77.

BROWN DERBY

The Brown Derby was an old Hollywood hangout. The house cocktail paired bourbon and honey, with grapefruit joining in for a pas de trois. It's even better with maple syrup.

45ml bourbon
30ml pink grapefruit juice
10ml honey (loosened with 1 dessertspoon/5ml hot water)
or 10ml maple syrup

Shake hard with plenty of ice and double-strain into a cold cocktail glass. Garnish with a grapefruit-zest twist, taking care to express the oils.

CAIPIRINHA

When made poorly (say, by a time-pressed bartender in a suburban fleshpot c2004), the Caipirinha is an unpleasant cocktail – a sort of lime mash that poorly disguises the kerosene-like qualities of cachaça, and adds a few mouthfuls of undissolved sugar to the mix. When made correctly (say, by the Girl from Ipanema as the sun falls behind Christ the Redeemer), it becomes a sort of favela Daiquiri – which, after all, uses the precise same combination of lime, sugar and sugar-based spirit (see page 158).

The key thing is to take your time, much as if you were crafting an Old Fashioned (see page 63), ensuring that all the sugar is dissolved and all the juice and oils are teased from the lime. You should also expect the results to have a certain streetfighting roughness – you are going for funk, not finesse.

½ lime
2.5ml golden caster sugar
50ml cachaça

Slice the lime half into three wedges and place in the bottom of a sturdy old fashioned glass along with the sugar. Muddle hard – I mean, really pulverise the contents – then taste for balance and add more sugar or a squirt of lime if desired. Only when not a granule of sugar remains undissolved should you introduce the cachaça and enough ice cubes to fill the glass, then stir and garnish with a lime wedge.

CAMPARI SMASH

The Smash was an old category of drink, somewhere between a cobbler and a julep, garnished with fresh berries. I'd sooner lob the berries into the drink. Here, Campari, strawberry, mint and rose marry in an unexpectedly lush way.

40ml vodka
20ml Campari
20ml crème de rose (or a few drops of rose water
 and a dash of sugar syrup)
2 fresh strawberries
5 mint leaves

Muddle the berries and mint in the bottom of the shaker before adding the other ingredients. Add ice and shake hard for a few seconds. Strain into a cocktail glass and decorate with mint.

CHAMPS-ELYSÉES

Chic as a sheik.

50ml brandy
15ml lemon juice
10ml Green Chartreuse
5ml golden sugar syrup (2:1, see page 44)
Dash Angostura bitters

Shake hard with plenty of ice and double-strain into a cold cocktail glass. Garnish with a lemon-zest twist.

CHANTICLEER

A fluffy pre-dinner sipper, named after Edmond Rostand's barnyard drama, in which the main character is a chanticleer rooster.

30ml gin
45ml French vermouth
15ml orange liqueur
15ml egg white

Dry shake everything without ice to froth up the egg, and shake again with ice to chill. Double-strain into a cold cocktail glass.

CHARLIE CHAPLIN

Out of favour for many years, the Charlie Chaplin was revived and much improved by the Discount Suit Company bar in London, where they had the bright idea of adding more gin to the mix. It's now worthy of the great silent star.

40ml gin
20ml sloe gin
20ml apricot brandy
20ml lime juice

Shake hard with plenty of ice, and double-strain into a cold cocktail glass. Garnish with a lime-zest twist.

CHERRY BOMB

I like to think this is the sort of thing cowgirls drink at country fairs.

>50ml bourbon
>20ml cherry brandy
>20ml lemon juice
>10ml golden sugar syrup (2:1, see page 44)
>20ml egg white

Shake hard without ice to froth up the egg white, and again with ice to cool. Double-strain into an old fashioned glass containing ice. Garnish with a cherry and stain the froth with a little of the liquor from the jar.

CORPSE REVIVER #2

While the Corpse Reviver #1 remains obscure, the #2 is one of the most celebrated creations of Harry Craddock, fabled head bartender of the American Bar in London's Savoy Hotel in the 1920s and '30s. Recently, his modern-day successor, Erik Lorincz, let slip that he poured a Corpse Reviver #2 over Craddock's actual grave to see if it did the trick. At the time of writing, it hasn't. For the living, however, the lemon juice purifies, the liqueur adds a sherbety sweetness and the Lillet makes it feel all sophisticated. The absinthe (which you must not overdo) floats above the drink like a wistful phrase in a Ravel piano sonata. The #2 is at once delicate and incredibly powerful. Though as Craddock warned: 'Four of these will swiftly unrevive the corpse again.'

>20ml gin
>20ml orange liqueur
>20ml Lillet Blanc (or sweet white vermouth)
>20ml lemon juice
>2.5ml absinthe

Shake hard with plenty of ice and double-strain into a cold cocktail glass. Garnish with a lemon-zest twist.

COSMOPOLITAN

The quintessential Cosmopolitan recipe comes courtesy of Dale 'King Cocktail' DeGroff from New York, where this was once seen as a sophisticated thing to order. Cointreau is the usual orange liqueur used, though Grand Marnier adds a certain *je ne sais quoi* that would be lost on *Sex and the City*'s Carrie Bradshaw, no doubt. See the Clover Club (page 69) for a slightly more *à la mode* order.

> *45ml vodka (lemon-flavoured vodka to be accurate)*
> *15ml orange liqueur (typically Cointreau, though*
> *Grand Marnier is more interesting)*
> *30ml cranberry juice*
> *1 tablespoon (7.5ml) lime juice*

Shake hard with plenty of ice and double-strain into a cold cocktail glass. Garnish with a flamed orange-zest twist. How do you do that? Easy! Cut a length of orange zest from the side of a pert orange, taking care not to include any pith. Hold it over the glass with a lighter in your hand. Bend the orange peel back to release a fine spray of bitter oils, light the flame and they will catch alight in the air. Sip in a pair of Manolo Blahniks as your internal monologue goes into overdrive.

COTONIAN

I found the Cotonian while leafing through the 1937 *Café Royal Cocktail Book* one day (or, I should say, swiping through the Café Royal e-book). The combination of Scotch, Drambuie, French vermouth and passion fruit struck me as unusual enough to make a note. Oh my! There's a pleasant passion sweetness but the vermouth makes it a little more sophisticated before the whole thing dries out in an enigmatic finish. See Rusty Nail (page 133) for complaints about the modern formulation of Drambuie – suffice to say this is better with homemade (page 282).

40ml Scotch (blended)
20ml Drambuie
20ml French vermouth
20ml passion fruit pulp (one passion fruit usually suffices)

Shake hard with plenty of ice and double-strain into a cold cocktail glass. Garnish with a lime-zest twist.

CUCUMBER GIMLET

A clean summer refresher.

5cm piece cucumber
Handful of fresh mint leaves
50ml vodka (or gin)
10ml lime cordial (see Gimlet, page 84)

Peel the cucumber and chop it into pieces. Place in the shaker along with the mint leaves and muddle for a bit. Add the other ingredients plus plenty of ice, shake well and double-strain into a cold cocktail glass. Garnish with a cucumber slice. By way of variation, try basil, tarragon or dill in place of the mint.

DAIQUIRI (CLASSIC)

There's a memorable double-date scene in John Updike's Rabbit, Run in which our protagonist Harry Angstrom orders a Daiquiri in a Chinese restaurant because both the girls have. He imagines it will taste like limeade... and finds it does sort of taste like limeade, 'riding like oil on a raw transparent taste'. He has a few more and when he emerges, 'the pavement is a shadow of the Daiquiri's luminous transparence; he is light-hearted, and skips once, to get in step with the girl he adores.'

Like Updike's midcentury hero, the Daiquiri (rum, lime, sugar) is simple and direct but capable of the greatest lyricism. When its constituent parts are held in perfect harmony, something amazing happens. The dogs lose their bark; the eels cease to reel; oil paintings come to life. And then everything resets and goes back to normal and everyone forgets that ever happened. There is a luminous transparence around, though, if you care to look.

Since rum is made from sugar and limes grow pretty much everywhere that sugar grows, it's likely that some tropical roustabout or other came up with a prototype Daiquiri on the porch of his plantation. Certainly, many have laid claim to it. Still, the drink had to be christened somewhere, and it took its name from a Cuban mining town named Daiquiri, which was occupied by US troops following the Spanish-American war of 1898. The miners used Bacardi rum to disinfect the local water and added sugar and lime to make it more palatable.

An engineer named Jennings Cox noted down the first recipe in 1898, and it then made its way to Havana, and then, as Charles H. Baker noted: 'Like the Martini, Manhattan, Side Car and other immortals, the Daiquiri marched straight around the world...' Right into small-town Chinese restaurants and small-town discos and all-inclusive resorts where its spoilt offspring the Strawberry Daiquiri (see page 160), the Kiwi Daiquiri, the Blue Bubblegum Daiquiri and so on did their best to corrupt the noble line.

Nothing, however, can detract from a simple, well-balanced handmade Daiquiri. You can spend a long time getting the proportions right (see the Sour, page 65, for a fuller discussion). However, as Baker points out, there are only really two ways you can go wrong: insufficient chilling and too much sugar. In the end, it's about balance. 'A too-sweet Daiquiri is like a lovely lady with too much perfume.'

> *50ml light rum (my choice is El Dorado 3-year)*
> *15ml lime juice*
> *10ml golden sugar syrup (2:1, see page 44)*

Shake hard with plenty of ice and double-strain into a cold cocktail glass. Garnish with a lime wedge. For a simple variant – the Miami – add a few mint leaves to the shaker. It's also worth trying with any number of different syrups: ginger, orgeat and pineapple all good.

DAIQUIRI (FROZEN)

It was at the Florida bar in Havana, Cuba (now known as the Floridita), that the Daiquiri reached its apotheosis. 'We remind our readers that a decent electric mixer is just as necessary on any well equipped bar these days as a horse in a stable', wrote Charles H. Baker. The 'new style Daiquiri', he noted, 'simply cannot be shaped by hand at all.' The head bartender, Constantino Ribalaigua Vert would still hand-squeeze each and every lime to ensure that not one drop of oil escaped from the skin – but he'd then whizz up the drink with ice in the new-fangled blender and strain the ice away so that all you had was ice-cold liquid. If you go to the Floridita bar today and order a Daiquiri, that's more or less what you'll get (ask for Daiquiri-Natural if you want the old style). It makes a whole lot more sense in the tropical heat than it does on a windswept day in London, but its sherbet cool is still pretty delightful in all weathers.

> *50ml light rum*
> *25ml lime juice*
> *10ml golden sugar syrup (2:1, see page 44)*
> *5ml maraschino*

Place all in a blender with 100ml crushed ice and whirr for about five seconds. Pour into a cocktail glass and sip through a short straw.

DAIQUIRI DE FRESA

It's not one for the purist (see Daiquiri, page 158) but fresh strawberries do make for lively sipping on a summer's day. You can adapt the recipe here with any other soft fruits, too, to make Kiwi Daiquris, Melon Daiquiris, Lychee Daiquiris, etc, or simply add 20ml fruit juice to a regular Daquiri to give yourself another kind of spin. Guava juice is heavenly.

> *3 or so fresh strawberries, stalks discarded*
> *50ml light rum*

15ml lime juice
10ml golden sugar syrup (2:1, see page 44)

Muddle the strawberries in the bottom of your shaker. Add the other ingredients and ice, shake and double-strain into a cold cocktail glass. Garnish with a strawberry.

DAIQUIRI DE MARACUJA

My own Tiki-inspired passion fruit Daiquiri.

40ml light rum
20ml dark rum
20ml passion fruit pulp
10ml lime juice
10ml orgeat syrup (see page 86)
2.5ml pimento dram
Dash Angostura bitters
Dash absinthe

Shake hard with plenty of ice and double-strain into a cold cocktail glass. Garnish with a lime wedge.

DAIQUIRI MULATA

A darker take on the Daiquiri for the end of the evening – you can use coffee liqueur or chocolate liqueur with equal success. The current head bartender of Havana's Floridita, Alejandro Bolivar (a proud Communist who speaks fluent Russian), informed me that this is what he drinks when he comes off shift, puffing on a nice fat cigar.

45ml dark rum
30ml lime juice
15ml Kahlua (or dark crème de cacao)
5ml golden sugar syrup (2:1, see page 44)

Either shake very hard with tons of ice and double-strain into a cold cocktail glass. Else place all in a blender with 100ml crushed ice, whirr for about five seconds, pour unstrained into a cocktail glass and sip with a short straw.

DIKI-DIKI

In his perspicacious *Cocktails: How to Mix Them* (1922), Robert Vermeire says that he invented the Diki-Diki at the Embassy Club in London. Apparently the name comes from a Filipino chieftain who, at 37 years old, 'stands only 32 inches tall and weighs 23 pounds'. It seems that our cocktailing forebears were easy to amuse. The cocktail is excellent mind you, a non-obvious combination of calvados, grapefruit juice and Swedish Punsch. To my mind, it's even better with tequila in place of the calvados, a variation I call the Riki-Riki after a man I met in Borneo who was two centimetres wide and as tall as the earth is square.

> *50ml apple brandy*
> *25ml Swedish Punsch*
> *25ml pink grapefruit juice*

Shake everything over lots of ice and double-strain into a cold cocktail glass. Garnish with a grapefruit wedge.

DULCHIN

It's something of a pisco disco in there but as long as you balance it correctly, the subtle combination of fruits (orange, apricot, lime, pomegranate) draws out the equivalent notes in the pisco itself – with the Grand Marnier lending an aged depth. It is strangely reminiscent of a Sex on the Beach but it's much better than that, more like Very Good Sex on a Very Exclusive Beach.

> *50ml pisco*
> *10ml Grand Marnier*

10ml apricot brandy
10ml lime juice
5ml grenadine (see page 83)

Shake up with ice and double-strain into a cold cocktail glass. Garnish with a lime wedge.

ESPRESSO MARTINI

A piece of far-sighted genius invented by Dick Bradsell in Soho in the 1990s. According to legend, he was tending bar when a supermodel asked for something that would 'wake me up then f**k me up'. He came up with the Pharmaceutical Stimulant, a combination of espresso, Kahlua, vodka and sugar that would become a modern phenomenon.

Its reputation suffered for many years at the hands of chain bars, where they tend to pull a bunch of espressos in the morning and leave them sitting around all day, compensating for the stale, bitter taste with extra sugar. Now that people are starting to take their coffee really pointlessly seriously, however, they're also starting to take the Espresso Martini seriously. Take out the Kahlua (why do you need coffee-flavoured liqueur when you have the real thing?), make it fresh and lively and you have a picker-upper-f**ker par excellence. Perhaps even the last great classic.

1 shot espresso
Teaspoon sugar
50ml vodka

Make a fresh espresso, to the most exacting standards you possibly can, and stir in a spoonful of sugar. Fill up the shaker with an unusually large volume of ice to compensate for the heat and pour over the coffee and vodka. Shake hard and double-strain into a cold cocktail glass. Garnish with an arrangement of coffee beans.

FIGARO

I hit upon the Figaro while attempting to make a Fig Cobbler one day. When you pulverise figs and try to sip them through a straw, you just get a horrid mess. Sieve out the goop, however, and you're left with a yummy combination of dry sherry and luscious rich fruit.

> *1 black fig*
> *50ml fino sherry*
> *15ml lemon juice*
> *10ml golden sugar syrup (2:1, see page 44)*

Cut the fig into 8 pieces and place 7 of them in the shaker along with the other ingredients. Shake with plenty of ice. You will now have to patiently edit out the fig husks and seeds – do so in a sieve over a bowl. Decant the resulting liquid into a cold cocktail glass and garnish with the eighth piece of fig.

FLIP

A popular bone-warmer among 18th-century travellers in roadside inns, a flip was originally a mixture of egg, sugar, ale and nutmeg, heated with a poker from the fire. The style just about survives the contemporary aversion to raw egg yolk. A shot of liqueur will lend it a little more intrigue – the sort of fruits you'd use in a crumble work well (pear, apricot, apple, blackberry, sloe gin, rhubarb, etc)

> *50ml brandy, whisky or dark rum*
> *1 egg yolk*
> *10ml golden sugar syrup (2:1, see page 44)*
> *Dash vanilla extract*

Shake everything with plenty of ice, and double-strain into a cold wine glass with a lump of ice in it. Grate fresh nutmeg or cinnamon on top for a garnish.

FLORIDA

One of the signature drinks of the Florida bar (now the Floridita) in Havana from its 1930s heyday. The rum and lime provide a classic tropical hit, before the vermouth and cacao take it somewhere altogether more sophisticated. Well worth a sniff.

45ml light rum
20ml lime juice
15ml Italian vermouth
5ml white crème de cacao
2.5ml orange liqueur
2.5ml grenadine (see page 83)

Shake over plenty of ice and double-strain into a cold cocktail glass. Garnish with an orange-zest twist.

FRENCH MARTINI

A one-night-stand of a drink. It's neither French, nor a Martini, and is a little less appealing than it was in its 1980s heyday. However, in dim lighting, you still would.

40ml vodka
30ml pineapple juice
5ml Chambord or similar berry liqueur

Shake hard with plenty of ice until the juice froths up, and double-strain into a cocktail glass. Garnish with a cherry or a pineapple wedge.

GINGER ALEXANDER

A Christmassy twist on a regular Alexander.

25ml bourbon
25ml ginger liqueur (King's Ginger is good)
25ml crème de cacao (brown)
25ml single cream

Shake over ice and double-strain into a cold cocktail glass. Garnish with a dusting of ginger powder.

GOLDEN DAWN

Nothing to do with any neo-fascist movement, the Golden Dawn is named after its appearance. The grenadine is supposed to sink to the bottom of the glass to create a morning skyscape. The drinking person's Tequila Sunrise? Apparently, it was declared 'The World's Finest Cocktail' in 1930.

20ml gin
20ml calvados
20ml apricot brandy
20ml orange juice
5ml grenadine (page 83)

Shake the first four ingredients over ice and double-strain into a cold cocktail glass. Trickle in the grenadine without mixing.

GRASSHOPPER

A liquidised after-dinner mint, by no means sophisticated but indecently yum. It was invented in New Orleans in the 1910s, most likely as a Pousse-Café (see page 235) and takes its name from the greenish tinge that the crème de menthe gives it... but a more respectable version can be made with brown cacao and white menthe.

25ml crème de cacao (white)
25ml crème de menthe (green)
25ml single cream

Shake with plenty of ice and double-strain into a cocktail glass. Garnish with a mint leaf or, if you prefer, a dusting of cocoa.

GREEN PARK

See The Classics, page 67.

HEMINGWAY DAIQUIRI

Also known as the 'Papa Doble Daiquiri', this is what Ernest Hemingway used to drink at La Floridita in Havana... Except that isn't strictly true. He certainly took his Daiquiris with an extra shot of rum (because Hemingway was hard) and no sugar (because Hemingway was diabetic). The maraschino and grapefruit juice were later additions. Maraschino is full of sugar and Cuban grapefruits are much sweeter than Asda ones, the drink that now takes his name would have played havoc with his fragile constitution. One wonders how Hemingway's diabetes must have sat with his general bullfighting image? One sympathises, of course, hereditary condition and all that, but forgoing all sugar really is one step away from being constantly on the two bit of the 5:2 diet. I suppose he made up for it by drinking 15 of his Daiquiris in one sitting – the equivalent of drinking 1.25 litres of rum.

If you want to make what he drank, blend 75ml light rum and 15ml lime juice in an electric mixer with a scoop of crushed ice. It's not as delicious as this, however:

50ml light rum
15ml lime juice
10ml maraschino
10ml grapefruit juice

Shake up with ice and double-strain into a cold cocktail glass. Garnish with a lime wedge.

By way of variation, a Lima Sour is the same thing with a pisco base.

HOLLAND HOUSE

Before Harry Craddock came to London to take up work at the Savoy Hotel during American Prohibition, he was the head bartender at the Holland House Hotel in New York. This was the house drink. Craddock's recipe calls for English gin but the Dutch connection pushes me towards genever.

> *40ml genever (or gin)*
> *20ml French vermouth*
> *5ml maraschino*
> *10ml lemon juice*
> *10ml pineapple juice*

Shake hard with plenty of ice and double-strain into a cold cocktail glass. Garnish with a lemon-zest twist.

IDEAL

A Martinez (see page 125) with a tart squirt of grapefruit.

> *50ml gin*
> *25ml Italian vermouth*
> *10ml grapefruit juice*
> *5ml maraschino*

Shake hard with plenty of ice and double-strain into a cold cocktail glass. Garnish with a lime-zest twist.

JACK ROSE

The autumn profile of the Jack Rose always puts me in mind of Bonfire Night. If you rinse the glass first with a good smoky Scotch, such as Laphroaig, the effect is still more pronounced. This was one of David Embury's seven essential cocktails from his *Fine Art of Mixing Drinks* (1948) and though applejack is classic, it's best with English cider brandy.

50ml apple brandy
15ml lemon juice
10ml grenadine (page 83)

Shake with ice and double-strain into a cold cocktail glass. A lemon garnish is traditional, but I would go for an apple slice rammed onto the side of the glass. If you moisten the apple with lemon juice, it will not go brown.

KINGSTON COCKTAIL

This curio prompts one of Harry Craddock's few authorly interjections into the *Savoy Cocktail Book*: 'The unique taste of this cocktail is due to the Kummel mixed with a liqueur known as Pimento Dram (a Jamaican liqueur) without which it would lose all distinction.' The combination is caraway and cloves and it is surprisingly good; Pimento Dram also makes a good addition to an Old Fashioned (see page 63) made with aquavit (see page 273).

50ml dark rum (light works well too)
15ml kummel
15ml orange juice
2.5ml pimento dram

Shake with plenty of ice and strain into a cold cocktail glass.

KNICKERBOCKER

How can you not fall for a cocktail called the Knickerbocker? This recipe is adapted from Thomas Stuart's *Fancy Mixed Drinks* (1904) – Stuart most likely got it from the Chicago hotel of the same name.

50ml dark rum
15ml lemon juice
10ml orange liqueur
5ml golden sugar syrup (2:1, see page 44)
Two fresh raspberries

Shake hard over ice (until the raspberries are nicely pulverised) and double-strain into a tall glass filled with ice. Decorate prettily with more raspberries, orange and pineapple... 'and imbibe through a straw'.

LAST WORD

The Last Word occupies a hallowed position in the pantheon of modern mixed drinks. It was first cited in Ted Saucier's 1951 volume *Bottoms Up!* as the favoured drink of the Detroit Athletics Club, made with equal parts gin, lime, Green Chartreuse and maraschino. However, it was only after its rediscovery in 2005 at the Pegu Club in New York that it became a standard bearer for the craft cocktail movement. Why? It's a goddam crazy drink that's why! The Chartreuse and the maraschino go wild in each other's company, rutting on the lawn, while the lime swings from the chandelier and the gin starts a fight with the glass. To my palate, it is way too sweet in the 'equal parts' proportions (half the drink consists of liqueurs) so I would suggest doubling the gin content (and possibly halving the maraschino), even if it is less easy to remember.

> *40ml gin*
> *20ml Green Chartreuse*
> *20ml maraschino*
> *20ml lime juice*

Shake up with plenty of ice and double-strain into a cocktail glass. Garnish with a lime wedge. If you think of it as 2x spirit, 1x herbal liqueur, 1x sweetener and 1x citrus, you can play with the formula to your heart's content. Strong flavours work particularly well here – try an Islay Scotch base? Tequila/yellow Chartreuse/Cointreau/lemon? Aquavit/Pimento Dram/Falernum/lime? See also Naked & Famous, page 173.

MANDORLA SOUR

The heavenly house cocktail at Russell Norman and Florence Knight's Polpetto in London's Soho is built on Nardini Mandorla, an almond-infused grappa, and Amarena cocktail cherries. It is a slightly more grown up Amaretto Sour and *almost* a rival to the house Spritz.

> *50ml Mandorla Grappa by Nardini*
> *25ml lemon juice*
> *15ml golden sugar syrup (2:1, see page 44)*
> *10ml egg white*

Dry shake all the ingredients without ice to froth up the egg, then again with ice to cool. Double-strain into an old fashioned glass containing large ice cubes. Garnish with a cherry and spoon a decent amount of juice from the jar into the cocktail so it falls to the bottom and looks really pretty.

MARGARITA

On a parched afternoon, an ice-cold Margarita (plus homemade guacamole and tortilla chips) is one of the greatest pleasures known to man. Its origins lie in a classic cocktail called the Picador, which uses the same ingredients; the name Margarita caught on only once it became the money-spinner of choice in Tex-Mex restaurants across the United States. The standard method for serving Margaritas in such establishments involves pre-made 'Margarita Mix' and tequila that isn't really fit to disinfect a wound. Once you taste a proper one, made with 100% agave tequila, you will be very careful about where you order one in future.

The essential formula is tequila soured with lime, sweetened with orange liqueur and sipped through a 'salt rim', which forms a crust around half or all of the top of the glass. The salt not only helps to rehydrate thirsty Mexicans, it also binds the sweet and sour elements of the drink together and as such covers over your mistakes.

Flaked sea salt
50ml tequila (100% agave)
20ml orange liqueur
15ml lime juice

First, you need to do some rimming. (Why are you laughing?) Cut a wedge of lime and wipe the flesh around the edge of a martini or margarita glass to moisten it. (You may choose to wipe it round half the glass only if you like.) Then dip the glass rim into a plate of salt. Shake off the excess salt, dabbing with some kitchen roll if you've made a mess, and leave it to encrust while you mix the drink.

Shake the tequila, orange liqueur and lime juice over plenty of ice and double-strain into the salted glass. Garnish with a lime wedge on the rim of the glass. See also Tommy's Margarita (see page 183).

MARY PICKFORD

A chirpy bit of rum fun, named after the silent movie star.

40ml light rum
40ml pineapple juice
5ml grenadine (page 83)
Dash maraschino

Shake over plenty of ice and double-strain into a chilled glass. Garnish with a cherry.

MEXICAN JUMPING BEAN

One afternoon, I ran into my friends Cleo and Stewart in a bar near my work. They make AquaRiva tequila for a living and I get the impression that they also drink it for a living – it's impossible to spend more than three minutes in their company without a tray of Tommy's Margaritas (see page 183) arriving. After five or six of them, we were all pleasantly pixelated but that amount of citrus does begin to feel astringent. So I asked the bartender if he could make one with fresh espresso in place

of lime. The result was a Mexican take on the Espresso Martini
(see page 163). I really can't remember much else other than the fact
it was divine.

50ml tequila reposado
25ml freshly made espresso
10ml agave syrup

Shake up over even more ice than usual and double-strain into a chilled
coupe. Garnish with a coffee bean or three.

MONKEY GLAND

In Mikhail Bulgakov's novel *Heart of a Dog* (1925), a satire on life in
the early years of the Soviet Union, a Moscow professor decides to
transplant the testicles of a dog onto a human criminal. As a result, he
accidentally creates the model Bolshevik. Bulgakov may have had in
mind the real-life Dr Serge Voronoff, who tried to do perform a similar
procedure with monkey bollocks, believing them to have anti-ageing
properties. Harry MacElhone of Harry's Bar, Paris, was amused enough
by the story to create a liquid satire in Voronov's honour. I like to think
that the absinthe plays the part of the monkey.

50ml gin
30ml orange juice
5ml absinthe
5ml grenadine (see page 83)

Shake everything up with plenty of ice and double-strain into a cold
cocktail glass. An orange-zest twist is the traditional garnish, but I feel
MacElhone missed a trick by not going for a pair of cherries.

NAKED AND FAMOUS

A love-it-or-hate-it variant on the Last Word (see page 170), from
Death & Co, with a three-way collision of super-strong flavours.

20ml mezcal
20ml Yellow Chartreuse
20ml Aperol
20ml lime juice

Shake over plenty of ice and double-strain into a cold cocktail glass.
No garnish.

NUCLEAR DAIQUIRI

Nuclear, in a cocktailing context, refers to the addition of Chartreuse
(Chemical symbol Ch; atomic mass 55; half-life five centuries). It lends
a radioactive note to rum and lime drinks. In London, they do a
Nuclear Hurricane at Nola's (Shoreditch) and you will find a Nuclear
Banana Daiquiri at Hawksmoor (Spitalfields). Use Wray & Nephew's
Overproof Rum if you possibly can.

50ml light rum
15ml lime juice
10ml falernum
10ml Green Chartreuse

Shake everything over plenty of ice and double-strain into a cold
cocktail glass. Garnish with a lime wedge. If you have spare overproof
rum, float a dessertspoon's worth on top and set on fire for effect.

NURSERY PLUSH

An alcoholic version of a childhood bedtime drink (warm milk in a
saucepan with a few cardamom pods, and sweeten with honey). You
can use something more interesting than the vodka (*e.g.* rum) but this
way, the fragrant richness of the cardamom and Bénédictine dominate.

5–6 green cardamom pods
25ml vodka
25ml Bénédictine
25ml single cream (or whole milk)

Bash the cardamom pods a bit with a muddle. Add the other ingredients, shake with plenty of ice and double-strain into a cold cocktail glass.

OH GOSH!

I've upped the rum content in Tony Conigliaro's famous triple-citrus Daiquiri, which he invented for a brain surgeon on the spot at Dick's Bar at London's former Atlantic Bar and Grill in the 1990s. 'Oh Gosh!' was what the brain surgeon said when he tried it.

50ml light rum
20ml orange liqueur
15ml lime juice

Shake over plenty of ice and double-strain into a cold cocktail glass. Garnish with a lemon-zest twist.

ONE WAY

Another curio from the *Café Royal Cocktail Book*. As usual, I've upped the gin.

40ml gin
20ml crème de peche (apricot brandy will do)
20ml Swedish Punsch
20ml lemon juice

Shake over plenty of ice and double-strain into a cold cocktail glass. Garnish with a lemon-zest twist.

OPAL

Orange x 4. I just hope you like orange. With a squirt of lemon and some sparkling water, you can lengthen this into a pleasing fizz too.

40ml gin
10ml orange liqueur

30ml orange juice
Drop orange blossom water
Dash orange bitters

Shake with plenty of ice and double-strain into a cold cocktail glass.
Garnish with an orange-zest twist to take the orange elements to five.

PAN-AMERICAN CLIPPER

Another *Gentleman's Companion* drink – a Jack Rose (see page 168)
viewed through green-tinted specs.

Dash absinthe
50ml apple brandy
15ml lime juice
10ml grenadine (see page 83)

Mist or rinse a cocktail glass with absinthe and freeze. Shake up the
other ingredients with large ice and double-strain into the absinthe-
rinsed glass.

PAPER PLANE

Created a few years ago by the New York bartender Sam Ross, the
Paper Plane has flown far and wide. The cleverness is in the two types
of amari, sweet and becoming Aperol and dark and broody Amaro
Nonino in the original, though Averna and Amaro di Montenegro
also work well.

40ml bourbon
20ml Aperol
20ml Amaro Nonino (or other dark amaro)
20ml lemon juice

Shake with plenty of ice and double-strain into a cold cocktail glass.
Garnish with a lemon-zest twist.

PEGU CLUB

The Pegu Club was once a colonial outpost in Rangoon, Burma (now Yangon and Myanmar), but the fame of its house cocktail seems to have transcended it. Now, the Pegu Club is an influential bar in New York City.

50ml gin
20ml orange liqueur
15ml lime juice
Dash Angostura bitters
Dash orange bitters

Shake over plenty of ice and double-strain in to a cold cocktail glass.

PENICILLIN

The prolific Sam Ross (see Paper Plane across the page) created this cure-all in 2005 and it has proved effective at fighting modern afflictions (ennui... Weltschmerz... FOMO...). It combines the Hot Toddy standbys of Scotch, ginger and honey (see page 199) into a Sour formula, but the cleverness lies in the combination of smooth blended whisky and the smoky single malt. You only need a soupçon of the expensive stuff to impart huge complexity. If you have no ginger liqueur, either buy a decent ginger cordial – Bellvoir makes a good one – or make your own ginger syrup (see Gin Cocktail, page 117).

40ml Scotch (blended)
10ml smoky single malt (e.g. Laphroaig or Talisker)
10ml ginger liqueur
15ml lemon juice
10ml honey loosened with 5ml hot water

Shake everything over plenty of ice and double-strain into an old fashioned glass filled with large lumps of ice. Garnish with a piece of ginger.

PINK LADY

A Prohibition favourite, ideally made with bathtub gin and sipped through the fronds of a newly bobbed hairdo.

Before the 18th amendment to the American Constitution came into force in 1919, American saloons were pretty much all-male affairs. However, the speakeasies where people flocked instead were open to all – and the fact that bartenders mixed bootleg liquor with fruits and sugar to disguise the burn only increased their appeal to women, it seems. Zelda Fitzgerald, the archetypal liberated woman of the day, was fond of Orange Blossoms (gin, orange juice, sugar syrup) and Pink Ladies (gin, apple brandy, grenadine, lemon and egg white) and wrote spirited defences of a woman's right to flirt and drink as men do. Her attitude proved to be widely influential and so were her drinking habits: soon, women across America were having all sorts of fun with gin. Needless to say these drinks were reviled by male drinkers – *Esquire* magazine listed both Pink Ladies and Orange Blossoms among the 'Ten Worst Drinks of the Decade' in 1934, along with such 'girly' classics as the Clover Club (see page 69), the Bronx (see page 77) and the Brandy Alexander (see page 151). The disdain is weirdly reminiscent of the way that contemporary males turn their nose up at Cosmopolitans (see page 157). Is it the drink or the drinking that inspires such disapproval? Do we not think that she can handle a nice Martini?

> *25ml gin*
> *25ml apple brandy*
> *15ml lemon juice*
> *10ml grenadine (page 83)*
> *10ml egg white*

Reverse double shake: pour all the ingredients into the shaker with plenty of ice and shake hard. Double-strain into a spare vessel, empty the shaker of ice, and return the cocktail to the shaker and shake hard again to froth up the egg. Pour into a cold cocktail glass and garnish with a cherry.

PISCO SOUR

Among the greatest sours of them all. A good pisco has so much fruity depth (apricot... lime... cherry... lavender...) that it stands up to more lime and sugar than I'd normally use in a simple sour. Hardly anyone will dislike this cocktail.

50ml pisco
25ml lime juice
15ml golden sugar syrup (2:1, see page 44)
10ml egg white
Dash Angostura bitters

Shake up the pisco, lime juice, sugar syrup and egg white hard without ice, so that the egg froths up. Then add ice and shake some more to cool. Double-strain into an old fashioned glass filled with ice, and shake a few drops of bitters onto the foam on top by way of garnish.

PORN STAR MARTINI

See Abominable Cocktails, page 240.

RED LION

Like Christmas in a tropical time zone.

50ml gin
10ml Grand Marnier
15ml lime juice
5ml grenadine (page 83)

Shake with plenty of ice and double-strain into a cold cocktail glass. Garnish with an orange-zest twist.

SANGRE DE AGAVA

An excellent invention by the cocktail historian David Wondrich, who noted the wonderful affinities of tequila and blackcurrant. It may need a dash of sugar syrup.

45ml tequila reposado
15ml dark rum (heavy Jamaican if possible)
20ml lime juice
15ml crème de cassis

Shake with plenty of ice and double-strain into a cold cocktail glass. No garnish.

SANTIAGO

A minor spin on the Daiquiri (see page 158), which I occasionally make when I'm out of limes.

50ml light rum
15ml lemon juice
10ml grenadine (page 83)

Shake with plenty of ice and double-strain into a cold cocktail glass. Garnish with a cherry.

SCOFFLAW

A Prohibition classic, created at Harry's Bar in Paris. The word 'scofflaw' was the winning entry in an American newspaper's competition to come up with a term for an illegal drink.

30ml bourbon
30ml French vermouth
15ml lemon juice
10ml grenadine (page 83)
Dash orange bitters

Shake over plenty of ice and double-strain into a chilled cocktail glass. Garnish with a lemon-zest twist.

SIDECAR

Whether it was invented in Paris or not, it is hard to tell, but the Sidecar is synonymous with the city and particularly the era when Picasso and Cocteau and Stein and Hemingway and the Fitzgeralds would have been mooching about. When made well, it captures some of the dash of that gilded age... however, it is not often made well. It doesn't help that the two most influential recipes for it are both quite wrong. Harry MacElhone presided over the great Parisian bar of the period – but his formula from 1922 has equal measures of brandy, orange liqueur and lemon juice. Way too sweet! David Embury pooh-poohed this in 1944, calling it 'the most perfect example of a magnificent drink gone wrong', but his recipe went way too far the other way. His favoured ratio of 8:2:1 brandy/orange liqueur/lemon is so dry you could use it in place of a bath towel. It works with rich sugar syrup, but not with liqueurs. All you have to do is taste it, guys!

I've come out somewhere in between. You can spend a while playing with the orange liqueur too. Grand Marnier, with its brandy base, might seem a logical choice, but it's too moody on its own. The tangy sharpness of Cointreau is far better, but a dash of something deeper, like Grand Marnier or Amer Picon, does help lend depth.

50ml brandy
20ml orange liqueur (15ml Cointreau/5ml Grand Marnier if you can)
15ml lemon juice

Shake everything hard over plenty of ice and double-strain into an ice-cold cocktail glass. Garnish with a lemon-zest twist.

SILVER BULLET

A good recipe for the now highly unfashionable kummel – improved no end by egg white and celery bitters if you happen to have any.

50ml gin
25ml kummel
25ml lemon juice
15ml egg white
Celery bitters (optional)

Shake everything hard over plenty of ice and double-strain into an ice-cold cocktail glass. Garnish with a lemon-zest twist.

SOUR

See The Classics, page 65.

TERESA

A wild and weird combination of flavours from Gaz Regan's *The Joy of Mixology* (2003) – he attributes it to his Spanish amigo Rafael Ballesteros and wonders at how he came up with the combination. The original calls for a full double shot of Campari, which I've tamed with some vodka to lend some oomph while the other flavours shine.

25ml vodka
25ml Campari
25ml lime juice
10ml crème de cassis

Shake over plenty of ice and double-strain into a cold cocktail glass. Garnish with a mint sprig.

TI' PUNCH

In the French Caribbean, Ti' Punch is the traditional way to serve rhum agricole. The unique flavour comes not only from the rhum but a local syrup made from raw cane sugar. It sounds an awful hassle to source until you realise that Tate & Lyle's Golden Syrup is pretty much the same thing.

50ml rhum agricole (light)
½ lime cut into wedges
10ml golden syrup loosened with 5ml hot water

Muddle the rhum, lime and syrup in the bottom of a sturdy old fashioned glass until well combined and full with ice cubes. Garnish with a lime wedge.

TOMMY'S MARGARITA

A variation that almost eclipses the original (see page 171), Tommy's Margarita uses agave syrup as a sweetener instead of the traditional orange liqueur. Agave not only vamps up the fresh cactus flavour of the tequila, it also scores very low on the old Glycaemic Index. So it's healthy! In practical terms, it also means that you can get through a few more of these without having a sugar crash. My friend Cleo Rocos, who makes AquaRiva tequila, calls this her 'No Hangover Margarita'. If you miss the orange flavour, you can always squirt in some fresh orange.

50ml tequila
15ml lime juice
10ml agave syrup
Sea salt

These, I prefer served 'down', or 'on the rocks'. Rim half an old fashioned glass with salt (see Margarita, page 171, for method) and fill with ice cubes. In your shaker, shake up everything with plenty of ice and double-strain into the prepared glass. Garnish with a lime wedge.

TOREADOR

One of a number of early tequila drinks from the 1937 *Café Royal Cocktail Book.*

> 50ml tequila
> 20ml apricot brandy
> 20ml lime juice

Shake over plenty of ice and double-strain into a cold cocktail glass. Garnish with a lime wedge.

TRINIDAD SOUR

Adapted from a paradigm-shifter invented by Giuseppe Gonzalez of New York calling for a phenomenal amount of bitters. The full shot of Angostura listed in the original recipe actually presents less of a problem than the full shot of orgeat, which imparts a soupy texture but also makes it unbearably sweet. I've halved the quantity here. The high-proof rye is crucial – try overproof rum too.

> 30ml Angostura bitters (yes)
> 15ml orgeat syrup (see page 86)
> 15ml rye (100 proof)
> 20ml lemon juice

Shake with plenty of ice and double-strain into a cold cocktail glass. No garnish.

TWENTIETH CENTURY

See Abominable Cocktails, page 241.

TWO-ONE-TWO

Named for the proportions of its ingredients, the Harlem area phone code, and the ode to girl-on-girl with which Azealia Banks once charmed the world. Now get that tongue deep in.

40ml tequila reposado
20ml Aperol
40ml grapefruit juice

Shake with plenty of ice and double-strain into a cocktail glass. Garnish with a grapefruit-zest twist.

You can omit the grapefruit juice, if you like, and simply stir up the tequila with Aperol: this creates a Restraining Order.

VESPER

'Just a moment', James Bond instructs the barman in the famous scene in *Casino Royale*. 'Three measures of Gordon's, one of vodka, half a measure of Kina Lillet. Shake it very well until it's ice-cold, then add a large thin slice of lemon peel. Got it?' And that is how the famous spy liked his Martinis. It's not how his creator, Ian Fleming, liked his Martinis – and he drank a lot of them. Fleming was no fool and he had his stirred, with gin. The vodka is there to show that Bond was modern and the shaking to show he was a brute; all the shaking does is add air bubbles and dilution making for a cloudier, weaker, colder drink. You can't get Kina Lillet anymore (bottles go for a fortune at auction). Lillet Blanc is its legitimate heir, though connoisseurs claim Cocchi Americano is closer in flavour.

45ml gin
15ml vodka
7.5ml sweet white vermouth (Lillet Blanc or Cocchi Americano)

Shake. Strain. Lemon-zest twist.

VOWEL

A strange and spicy vintage cocktail.

30ml Scotch (blended)
30ml Italian vermouth
15ml orange juice
15ml kummel
Dash Angostura bitters

Shake everything over large ice and double-strain into a cold cocktail glass. Garnish with an orange-zest twist.

WAH-WAH

A good-time girl with hidden depths. From Range, San Francisco.

40ml pisco
30ml elderflower liqueur
20ml Aperol
20ml grapefruit juice
Dash Angostura bitters

Shake everything over large ice and double-strain into a cold cocktail glass. Garnish with a grapefruit-zest twist.

WARD EIGHT

A fruitier Whiskey Sour (see page 67) named after an electoral district in Boston.

40ml bourbon
20ml lemon juice
20ml orange juice
2.5ml grenadine (see page 83)

Shake everything with plenty of ice and double-strain into a cocktail glass. Garnish with an orange slice.

WHISKEY SOUR

See The Classics, page 67.

WHITE LADY

A filigree classic, the White Lady was one of the most popular drinks in the golden age of cocktails – so popular indeed, that they used to sell bottles of it pre-mixed. Harry Craddock's original recipe did not call for egg white, but they serve it that way now at the American Bar in London's Savoy Hotel, where they use this recipe.

50ml gin
25ml lemon juice
20ml orange liqueur (Cointreau by preference)
15ml egg white

Dry shake with no ice to froth up the egg white, then add ice and shake again to cool. Double-strain into a cold cocktail glass and leave naked.

THE LONG

'We have no excuse for self-satisfaction while we allow
the atrocity of the Piña Colada to flourish unchecked
in our midst.'

Kingsley Amis, Everyday Drinking (1983)

IN THIS SECTION, you will find numerous punches and coolers, plushes and slings and various other insinuating sippers. They tend to be built to the basic architecture of the Americano (see page 61) – a stirred style of long drink – or the Gin Fizz (see page 74), which requires you to shake up a sour first and then dilute it. Some long drinks become fearsomely complicated (see Zombie, page 214). However, there are many combinations that are so simple – spirit, mixer, boom – they're barely worth a recipe at all. These are collectively known as Highballs. The Tom Collins (see page 74) is basically a Highball – spirit plus lemonade – and so its lime cousin, the Rickey. Rather than list a recipe for each possible iteration, I've collected them all here with in handy table form.

	LEMON, SUGAR, SODA	LIME, SUGAR, SODA	GINGER BEER (+ LIME)	COCA-COLA (+ LIME)
GIN	TOM COLLINS / GIN FIZZ 1	GIN RICKEY 2	GIN MULE OR BUCK 3	SUCH A THING HAS NEVER BEEN DONE
RUM	ASSES' MILK / RUM COLLINS	RUM RICKEY	DARK 'N' STORMY 4	CUBA LIBRE 5
WHISKEY	WHISKEY COLLINS	WHISKEY RICKEY	WHISKEY MULE OR BUCK	JD & COKE
TEQUILA	JUAN COLLINS	MARGARITA FIZZ	TEQUILA MULE	BATANGA 6
VODKA	IVAN COLLINS	LONG VODKA (WITH BITTERS)	MOSCOW MULE 7	VODKA & COKE
BRANDY	BRANDY FIZZ	BRANDY RICKEY	STIFF HORSE'S NECK 8	DON'T WASTE THE BRANDY
APPLE BRANDY	HARVARD COOLER	APPLEJACK RICKEY	HALLOWEEN FIZZ (I MADE THAT UP)	HARDLY WORTH IT

1 See page 74 for the recipes.

2 The Rickey has associations with Washington DC, but it makes me think more of India, where the Fresh Lime Soda is a popular non-alcoholic option. If you order one, they will ask: 'Salt or sweet?' The correct answer is 'half-half' – which finds a hydrating balance between the two. A pinch of salt works wonders in the alcohol variety too.

3 Bucks traditionally take lemon, Mules lime. Bitters improve both.

4 The Dark'n'Stormy is to be made with dark rum, properly Gosling's from Bermuda, and spicy Caribbean-style ginger beer. Light rum makes a pleasant Mule too.

5 The Cuba Libre is traditionally made with Bacardi Light Rum, about the best use for it.

6 The Batanga is to be stirred with a large knife, as per Don Javier Delgado Corona who formulated this at his Mexico City bar, La Capilla, in 1961.

7 Invented in 1940s Hollywood, the Moscow Mule was the drink that 'broke' Smirnoff in the USA thanks to a marketing campaign worthy of *Mad Men*'s Don Draper. People were encouraged to take Polaroids of themselves drinking Moscow Mule in special branded mugs and take them to the next bar and ask why they didn't serve Moscow Mules.

8 A length of lemon peel should hang over the edge of the glass like a horse's neck, and Angostura bitters should be involved.

APRICOT RICKEY

A mellow summer cooler, the Apricot Rickey is a simple way to highlight the affinity of apricot and lime ('such a great couple...'). Sweeten to taste.

30ml gin
30ml apricot brandy
15ml lime juice
60ml fizzy water

Shake the gin, apricot brandy and lime juice with ice, add the fizzy water and strain into a tall glass filled with ice. A lime peel coiled around the glass looks pleasing, but a lime wedge will do.

BABY

An august pool of refreshment, inspired by a (considerably more complex) drink called the Baby Bias served by Ryan Chetiyawardana at his White Lyan bar in London. Consider it a pale cousin of the Americano (see page 61) or a modern Sherry Cobbler (see page 210), good for summer-afternoon sipping. Apricot brandy will do in place of the peach; do play with the sherry too.

30ml fino sherry
30ml crème de pêche
30ml fizzy water

Stir everything in a tall glass with plenty of ice. Garnish with a mint sprig or slice of lemon.

BIERE PICON

The French invented this aperitif to disguise the taste of poor-quality beer. It is useful to this day, turning a 99p tinny into a Trappist brew.

25ml Amer Picon

Top up with beer.

BLACK G&T

A good way to reward yourself after a summertime forage. Sweeter blackberries work best here – so if you're doing the picking, go for the plumper, darker fruits that leave stains on your fingers.

Few fresh blackberries
Squeeze of lime
50ml gin
Tonic water

Muddle the blackberries and the lime at the bottom of your shaker, introduce them to the gin and shake hard with ice. Double-strain into your preferred vessel, fill with ice and top with tonic water. Garnish with a blackberry if you fancy.

BLACK RUSSIAN

See Abominable Cocktails, page 239.

BLOODY MARY

The thing to remember about a Bloody Mary is that it is not a drink, as such, more of an alcoholic soup. Also, it is not a recipe, so much as a set of ideas. The central architecture is spirit, tomato juice, squeeze of lemon and spice, usually provided by Tabasco sauce. The crucial element, however, is not heat but a deep savouriness. Worcestershire sauce and celery salt are the traditional ways of incorporating this element, but Thai fish sauce, fresh clam juice and even fresh beef stock have all been known. The alcohol element may stray into port, sherry, Guinness, red wine and Italian amari such as Punt e Mes or Fernet-Branca.

Whatever, it should be prepared tenderly and tasted at all stages for balance.

The finest I ever tasted was the response to an innocent request during the interval of a play at London's Old Vic. Clearly, the bartender had been waiting for someone to ask for a Bloody Mary, since he duly spent the entire 15-minute interlude adjusting the levels of port, dash of sherry, even at one point nipping to the shops for Worcestershire Sauce. 'It's no trouble...' I cannot recall what the play was, but I do remember that Bloody Mary. The below is my approximation of what he did, with fino sherry for its savoury bite, Punt e Mes and my own addition, Thai sriracha, the fermented chilli sauce that has a sizeable hipster cult.

50ml vodka
100ml tomato juice
Dash port
Dash fino sherry
Dash Italian vermouth (Punt e Mes)
Dash sriracha
Lemon
Salt and pepper
Celery stick

Place the vodka and tomato juice in the cocktail shaker without ice and stir. Add the other ingredients in stages, tasting as you go. Freshen with a squeeze of lemon, season with salt and pepper, then add ice cubes and roll it around gently to chill. Pour into a tall glass, garnish with celery and a lemon wedge.

Housepersonly tip! If you are preparing for one or two people, a tin of plum tomatoes ought to provide ample juice and save a trip to the shops. Turn out the tomatoes into a sieve over a bowl and press down until all the juice is separated from the flesh. (Conserve the flesh for a pasta sauce.) As with most vodka cocktails, it's better made with other spirits. Tequila is divine; this gives you a Bloody Maria. Also good are the Red Snapper (with gin base) and the Valhalla (with aquavit).

BRANDY DAISY

The Daisy is an old-school category of long drink – here's Harry Johnson's brandy iteration from 1888.

50ml brandy
15ml lemon juice
10ml Yellow Chartreuse
10ml golden sugar syrup (page 44)
Fizzy water

Stir the first four ingredients in a tall glass over ice and add a splash of fizzy water to finish. Garnish with berries and mint.

CHARTREUSE SWIZZLE

If you think of Chartreuse as a sophisticated, devotional liqueur, its double life in exotic-style drinks comes as a surprise – like finding a vicar at a pool party. I like to imagine that it went out to the tropics as a missionary, fell in love with a local girl and went native. There are few better expressions of its lively character than the Chartreuse Swizzle, a fearsomely sweet, pungent and flavoursome combination that is at once ridiculous and irresistible.

40ml Green Chartreuse
15ml falernum
30ml pineapple juice
15ml lime juice

Fill a large wine glass with crushed ice. Add the liquids and swizzle – ideally with a real swizzle stick, but more likely with a spoon. The ice needs to melt a fair bit to temper the sugar content. Garnish with a mint sprig, heap a little more crushed ice on top and grate a load of nutmeg on that. Serve with a straw.

BUCK

See table, page 190.

DELICIOUS

A simple summer fizz from *The Flowing Bowl* (1891), so harmonious it's almost a little one-note. Good for a tennis party.

> *50ml apple brandy*
> *25ml peach liqueur*
> *25ml lemon juice*
> *5ml golden sugar syrup (2:1, see page 44)*
> *20ml egg white (optional)*
> *Fizzy water*

Place everything except the fizzy water in the shaker without ice and shake very hard until the egg has frothed. Add the ice and shake some more to cool. Then pour into an ice-filled tumbler, top up with water, stir, and garnish with a lemon slice and/or a cherry.

FERNET SLING

Adapted from a piece of mad genius in Beta Cocktails by Maks Pazunia, who describes it as a weird soda from a country you've never been to. 'I'm sure to the locals it's totally normal, but to you, you're like, "what is this, pine-tree-grasshopper-toothpaste soda?' I want to visit this country.

> *40ml Fernet-Branca*
> *20ml Italian vermouth*
> *10ml lemon juice*
> *5ml golden sugar syrup (2:1, see page 44)*
> *Fizzy water*

Shake everything (except the fizzy water) hard over ice, and double-strain into a tall glass filled with ice cubes. Top with (not too much) water and garnish with an orange-zest twist.

FOG CUTTER

A weird but good Trader Vic combination. Of its mist-dispelling qualities, he wrote: 'Hell, after two of these, you won't even see the stuff.'

30ml light rum
20ml brandy
10ml gin
15ml lemon juice
30ml orange juice
15ml orgeat (see page 86)
15ml amontillado sherry

Shake up everything except the sherry with plenty of crushed ice and pour unstrained into a tall glass. Carefully layer the sherry on top by holding a dessertspoon to the rim of the glass and letting it trickle. It should form a float through which you now sip the drink. Garnish with an orange wheel.

G&T

See The Classics, page 90.

GIN FIZZ

See The Classics, page 74.

GINGER ROGERS PUNCH

See The Classics, page 81.

GREEN ISAACS SPECIAL

As prescribed in Ernest Hemingway's semi-memoir, *Islands in the Stream*. 'Thomas Hudson tasted, took a swallow and felt the cold that had the sharpness of the lime, the aromatic varnish taste of the Angostura and the gin stiffening the lightness of the ice-cold coconut water.' Presumably straight from the nut, rather than a £3.50 carton.

> *50ml gin*
> *Squeeze of lime*
> *Dash Angostura bitters*
> *Coconut water*

Build the gin, lime squeeze and bitters in a tall glass filled with ice, and top with coconut water.

GREEN WING

A digestive remedy par excellence, invented by me one sleepless night at 4am after a fat platter at a fashionable London burger restaurant had given me appalling meat dreams. It cuts through most stuff.

> *30ml Green Chartreuse*

Top with peppermint tea.

HOT BUTTERED RUM

There are a few recipes that simply do not work, no matter how many times they are copied from book to book. Hot Buttered Rum is one of them. Oil and water do not mix, so all you really get if you put a pat of butter into some warm rum is the Deepwater Horizon disaster in a mug. Still, it's such a lovely idea, butter and rum – and if you had the foresight to fat-wash your rum in butter 24 hours in advance, you will get a much more pleasing result.

Butter rum
Melt a pat of butter (50g) and pour into a jar with 250ml of dark rum.
Agitate a little and leave in the fridge overnight. In the morning, strain
away the butter with a coffee filter (spread it on toast?) and decant the
rum. Also makes a mean Old fashioned (see page 63)

> *Hot dry cider*
> *50ml butter-washed rum*
> *10ml honey*

Warm the cider in a pan or the microwave. Stir into the butter-washed
rum and honey, and garnish with grated nutmeg.

HOT TODDY

The term 'toddy' once referred to both hot and cold drinks, but
nowadays conjures a warming brew of alcohol and spice such as
you might consume by an open fire while chortling over a volume of
P. G. Wodehouse. It may not cure the common cold but it does make it
more bearable, sort of a halfway house between being ill and being
well. It's a staple in my house in wintertime. I usually riff on the recipe
below with occasional additions/substitutions of dark rum, lime,
orange, cloves, cinnamon, golden syrup and brown sugar.

> *Thumb-sized piece of ginger*
> *25ml Scotch*
> *Spoonful of honey*
> *Lemon wedge*
> *Dash Angostura bitters*
> *Hot water*

Peel the ginger (or use the edge of a good knife to rub the skin away)
and chop it into slices. In the bottom of a mug, muddle all the
ingredients except the water. Top up with hot water from the kettle,
stir and serve.

HURRICANE

The Hurricane was invented at Pat O'Brian's bar in New Orleans (established in 1933). It was served in a hurricane lamp and that's why it's called a Hurricane. Apparently, they needed a way of using up old rum (did they not realise rum keeps?) but I suspect they actually had a surfeit of passion fruit syrup, since the original recipe calls for a ridiculous amount of the stuff. A far better recipe comes from the London bar NOLA, courtesy of Dan Priseman.

30ml light rum
30ml dark rum
30ml lime juice
20ml passion fruit pulp (i.e., the flesh and seeds of 1 fruit)
15ml golden sugar syrup (2:1, see page 44)
15ml overproof rum (to float)

Shake up everything minus the overproof rum with crushed ice and pour unstrained into a large vessel – hopefully a hurricane glass? Carefully float the overproof rum on top and garnish with an orange slice and an inside-out umbrella (it's windy in hurricane season!).

JUNGLE BIRD

Believed to have been created at the Kuala Lumpur Hilton in 1978, the Jungle Bird is a) one of the few magnificent 1970s inventions and b) a rare Tiki drink that finds room for Campari. It is nothing short of inspired.

45ml dark rum (the strong stuff)
15ml Campari
15ml lime juice
15ml golden sugar syrup (2:1, see page 44)
60ml pineapple juice

Shake everything with plenty of crushed ice, and pour unstrained into an old-fashioned glass. Garnish with a pineapple wedge.

LONG ISLAND ICED TEA

Ah, the Long Island Iced Tea. From what heady heights hast thou fallen! For a long time, 'Tea was king. 'Tea was boss. 'Tea was a child's idea of what a cocktail should be and since (in the UK at least) we begin drinking as children, 'Tea was the default order whenever one happened to be chirpsing girls at one of the fancier places in town. You know the sort of place: they don't let you in if you're wearing Reebok Classics and offer 2-for-1 cocktails if you get there before any girls bother to get there.

The appeal of the Long Island Iced Tea was simple. It had LOTS of alcohol in it. You could tell even from a cursory glance of a menu: vodka, gin, tequila, rum, triple sec, is this for real? Truthfully of course, it contained little more spirit than a Cuba Libre (see table, page 190), and any intrigue it might have had was lost in a tussle with the Coca-Cola and an industrial potion they used to term 'sour mix'. (You can make your own sour mix by heading to Sellafield with a spade... or alternatively, simply squeeze some citrus fruit.) All the same, for old times' sake:

15ml vodka
15ml gin
15ml light rum
15ml tequila
15ml orange liqueur
15ml lemon juice
15ml lime juice
90ml Coca-Cola

Shake up everything except the Coke; strain over ice into a tall glass, add the Coke, stick a straw in it and garnish with a lemon and/or lime wedge. By way of variation, you might try the Long Beach Iced Tea, which uses cranberry juice in place of the Coke. Or my personal take, the Long Bitch Iced Tea, which subs the normcore white spirits with all the trendy white spirits prized by the sort of people who wouldn't be seen dead ordering a Long Island Iced Tea: pisco, mescal, genever, grappa, maraschino, lemon juice, lime juice and Pepsi.

MAI TAI

One of my first ever jobs involved mixing cocktails at a Thai theme
restaurant in Enfield, north London, having received no training at all.
Fortunately I was kept out of view of the diners, meaning I could follow
my laminated instructions and sip surreptitious Mai Tais in peace.
When you go to a Thai theme restaurant in the suburbs and order a
cocktail with your food, do bear in mind it will probably be made by a
tipsy 16-year-old with poor hygiene and no clue what he is doing.
The Mai Tai's origins are a matter of a tedious dispute between Don the
Beachcomber and Trader Vic. Whoever thought of it first, it was Vic's
version from 1943 that caused the sensation. It was built on twin rums,
heavy Jamaican and aged rhum agricole from Martinique, with a
surprising almond note against tropical lime. Not all of the elements
remained in place as the Mai Tai mutated and spawned. The original is
pale gold. The version I served was red. If you use blue curaçao in place
of the orange liqueur it comes out a beautiful aquamarine colour,
though I'm sure the Tiki gods would frown.

> *30ml dark rum (ideally Jamaican)*
> *30ml golden rum (ideally rhum agricole from Martinique)*
> *10ml orgeat syrup (homemade; see page 86)*
> *15ml orange liqueur*
> *5ml golden sugar syrup (2:1, see page 44;*
>   *but I don't think it needs this)*
> *30ml lime juice*

Shake up with crushed ice and pour, unstrained, into a silly glass.
Garnish with a mint sprig and whatever other garnish material you
have available. Sip with a straw.

MIZUWARI

In an age when bartenders feel the need to shake up half the periodic
table into your glass, there is something compelling about a cocktail
with only two ingredients, one of which is water. The Mizuwari

(literally 'mixed with water' in Japanese) may not leap off the cocktail menu quite like your Liquid Nitrogen Martini or your Dry Ice Daiquiris but that is not its style. In Japan, the mania for novelty is balanced with a respect for doing simple things well. You will find chefs who have spent 50 years making sushi and are never tempted to mix it up with a bit of sashimi. You will find farmers who treat their vegetables with the care that most devote to their loved ones. And you will find bartenders who mix water into whisky with the ritualistic fervour of a monk.

50ml Japanese whisky (or Scotch)
100ml still water

Fill a highball glass with large ice cubes. Pour over the whisky. Slowly stir the contents no fewer than 13-and-a-half times in a clockwise direction. Add another ice cube. Add two measures of still water. Stir no more than three-and-a-half times, slowly. Only now is the drink ready.

MOJITO

Ask your average punter which cocktail they most like drinking, they're likely to say a Mojito. Ask a bartender which drink they least like making, they'll probably say a Mojito too. The same reasoning applies to both answers. Mojitos are fiddly and sticky and you can't really take any shortcuts or substitute any of the fresh ingredients for pre-made ones. The punter feels like they've got their money's worth – a long sweet thing that fairly zings with freshness. The bartender feels like she's kept everyone else waiting for ages and wishes she'd get the chance to try out her Chartreuse Swizzle (see page 195) once in a while. Blame Charles H. Baker, who first listed the drink in his *Gentleman's Companion*, naming it the Sloppy Joe's Mojito (after a Cuban bar), describing it as a Rum Collins and advising, helpfully: 'If for a lady, use grenadine instead of sugar.'

10 or so fresh mint leaves
50ml light rum
15ml lime juice

10ml golden sugar syrup (2:1, see page 44)
Fizzy water

In the bottom of a tall glass, muddle the mint with the rum, lime juice
and sugar syrup. Go easy – you don't want to pulverise the stuff, merely
tease out the flavours. Fill the glass with crushed ice and then churn it
up and down, so the minty liquor is evenly distributed. Then top up
with fizzy water and churn again. Arrange a mint posy on top and serve
with a straw.

MULE

See table, page 190.

NAVY GROG

Grog was the name that British sailors gave to the simple mixture they'd
make from their daily rum and lime rations. The name comes, or so
legend has it, from Admiral 'Old Grog' Vernon, who made the sailors
water down their rum rations; most Grog recipes honour this tradition by
adding a boring amount of water. I much prefer the recipe by Don the
Beachcomber, which turns it into a symphony worthy of the high seas.

30ml light rum (Spanish)
30ml gold rum (English)
30ml dark rum (Jamaican)
20ml lime juice
20ml grapefruit juice
20ml honey loosened with 10ml hot water
20ml fizzy water

Shake everything except the fizzy water with plenty of ice. Strain into
an old fashioned glass filled with ice cubes and top with the fizzy water.
Stir. Garnish with a lime wedge.

PALOMA

A popular roadside cooler in Mexico and increasingly, anywhere where they've taste buds, the Paloma is a Margarita (see page 171) lengthened with grapefruit soda. You can either make it the laborious way (by actually making a Margarita first), or you can do it the sloppy way (by treating it as a sort of grapefruit mule). Life is short, so I favour the sloppy way. At Rita's in Hackney, London, they add a shot of Campari to their Paloma and call it a Palermo.

50ml tequila
¼ lime
Grapefruit soda (Squirt, Ting, San Pellegrino
Pompelmo... maybe Lilt?)

Pour the tequila into a tall glass filled with ice, squirt in the juice from the lime wedge and lob in the husk too, then top up with your grapefruit soda.

You might consider a salt rim on your glass. You can make your own grapefruit soda with grapefruit, sugar and fizzy water.

PAPA GHIRADELLI

Apparently named after a popular Californian chocolatier from Italy by way of Peru, this was chosen as the official drink of San Francisco Cocktail Week in 2010. It's a complicated but transcendentally good cooler.

30ml pisco
20ml Italian vermouth
10ml Campari
10ml Bénédictine
10ml lemon juice
30ml fizzy water

Shake everything except the fizzy water with plenty of ice, then strain into a tall glass filled with ice. Top with fizzy water (not too much).

'PIN'

See The Classics, page 92.

PINA COLADA #1

The classic beachside Pina Colada, the sort you might sip on a hammock 'twixt palm trees in the Caribbean, is made with rum, pineapple juice and a sickly confection known as Coco Lopez coconut cream. It can be hard to source this can of kitsch in drizzlier climes, but you can do just as well by combining the easier-to-find coconut milk (the kind you'd use for a Thai curry or rice'n'peas) and sugar syrup. Otherwise, the art of the Colada lies in judging the right amount of ice to introduce to the blender and resisting the temptation to mess with the formula by adding limes or cream or anything. Never mind its detractors; sometimes a traditional Pina Colada is precisely what is required. And when it isn't? See Pina Colada #2.

> *50ml light rum*
> *125ml pineapple juice*
> *25ml coconut milk*
> *10ml sugar syrup (2:1, see page 44)*

Place everything in a hardy high-speed blender (the Nutri-Bullet comes into its own here) with about 200ml of crushed ice and whizz it up for about ten seconds. Pour the mixture out into a tall glass and garnish Del Boy-style with parasols, luminous cherries, pineapple wedges, etc.

PINA COLADA #2

An elegant, cream-free version of the gaudy abomination (see above), for self-hating lactose-intolerant cocktail pseuds.

> *40ml dark rum*
> *20ml coconut rum (note: the proper stuff, like Koko Kanu, not Malibu)*

40ml pineapple juice
20ml coconut water

Shake all the ingredients very vigorously over plenty of ice and double-strain into a chilled wine glass containing large lumps of ice. The pineapple should have created froth – grate nutmeg on this, or else administer a drop of bitters.

If you have no coconut rum, just use light rum (fat-wash a little in coconut oil, see Bacon Old Fashioned, page 95, for a DIY version).

PISCO PUNCH

These days, the Pisco Sour (see page 179) gets all the girls, but once upon a time they went wild for the punch. For Rudyard Kipling, no less, it was 'compounded of the shavings of cherubs' wings, the glory of a tropical dawn, the red clouds of sunset and the fragments of lost epics by dead masters'. The most famous PP came from the Bank Exchange in San Francisco in the late 19th century, where the secret was finally revealed to be pineapple marinated with cloves. It's easy enough to replicate that by lobbing a few clove seeds into the shaker, or making a little clove tincture: simply leave a few cloves to steep in strong booze (overproof rum or Navy-strength gin are best) for a day or two, then strain and keep in a small dropper bottle or a diffuser.

50ml pisco
15ml lemon juice
10ml golden sugar syrup (2:1, see page 44)
30ml pineapple juice
Drop of clove tincture
Fizzy water

Shake up everything except the fizzy water with plenty of ice, and double-strain into a tall glass filled with ice cubes. Top with a minimal amount of fizzy water (<25ml) and stir well. Garnish with pineapple or lemon.

PLUSH

Apparently, Plush was the invention of a couple of New York salesmen who slipped whiskey into an abstemious client's milk to mollify him for a deal. The term deserves reviving; essentially, it's a milkshake.

150ml whole milk
50ml bourbon
10ml maple syrup
Drop vanilla extract

Shake just the milk, in the carton if that's easier. It should froth up. Build the drink in a tall glass over ice and stir. Garnish with a dusting of cinnamon and serve with a cookie.

RAMOS GIN FIZZ

See The Classics, page 87.

RICKEY

See table, page 190.

RUM PUNCH

In the famous 'Spoonful of Sugar' scene in *Mary Poppins*, the umbrella-borne childminder tells the children that if they close their eyes and think hard enough, their medicine will taste of whatever they want it to. When Mary herself takes her own spoonful, she closes her eyes and says: 'Rum Punch!' For there is something magical about Rum Punch. It can be taken to the heights of complexity: you can split the base chord with various rums; you can add a rainforest of fruits; you can switch the sugar syrup with orgeat or grenadine or falernum or all three. Or it can be done very simply in the glass, just like this single-serve take on Planter's Punch (see page 227). It's what you still get in innumerable Caribbean hostelries and it's how I would imagine Mary liked it.

50ml dark rum (Jamaican works best)
10ml sugar syrup (2:1, see page 43)
Dash Angostura bitters
75ml still water

Stir it up well in a tall glass with ice and garnish with a lime wedge and a really generous grating of nutmeg.

RUM'N'TING

A simple and lethal Jamaican highball.

50ml overproof rum (Wray & Nephew)
Lime wedge
Ting grapefruit soda

Pour the rum over ice in a tall glass, spritz over a lime wedge and top up with the Ting. Alternatively, simply drink a bit of the Ting and pour the rum into the can.

SANGAREE

The Spanish-style Sangria served at all good pool parties is distantly derived from an old concoction called Sangaree: wine, sugar, water and nutmeg. Here's my all-weather hybrid with a postmodern twist of grapefruit. Multiply all quantities by ten to make an obliging party punch.

25ml brandy
10ml lime juice
10ml golden sugar syrup (see page 44)
75ml red wine (Rioja appropriate)
25ml grapefruit juice
25ml fizzy water

Stir everything in a tall glass with plenty of ice. Garnish with berries and grate over some nutmeg to finish.

SHAKY PETE'S GINGER BREW

An ever-present on the menu at the Hawksmoor chain of British steak houses, where it is termed an 'anti-fogmatic'. It's like an 18th-century English drink reimagined for a Tiki bar.

25ml gin
25ml ginger syrup (see page 117)
25ml lemon juice
100ml London Pride beer

Shake the gin, ginger syrup and lemon juice with crushed ice and pour unstrained, ice and all, into a cold beer mug. Top with the London Pride, give a quick stir and serve.

SHERRY COBBLER

'This drink is without doubt the most popular beverage in the country, with ladies as well as gentlemen', wrote Harry Johnson in 1882. 'It is a very refreshing drink for young and old.' I guess that made it the Mojito (see page 203) of its day. It certainly left an impression on Charles Dickens, who toured the USA in the 1840s and wrote in rapturous terms about the American use of ice in drinks – notably the cobbler, which he endorsed in *Martin Chuzzlewit* (1844): '"This wonderful invention, sir," said Mark tenderly patting the empty glass, "is called a cobbler"'.

The simple definition of a cobbler is sherry shaken with fruit and sweetened. You don't have to be too particular about your fruit – think of it as a Pimm's – just keep within the general ballpark of lemon, orange, raspberries and whatnot. Pineapple is particularly good.

3 slices of orange
3 slices of lemon
1 slice pineapple
50ml fino sherry
5ml golden sugar syrup (2:1, see page 44)

Shake up the fruits, sherry and sugar syrup with plenty of crushed ice.
Pour unstrained into a tall glass, ice and all. Imbibe through a straw,
which was said to have been invented for the cobbler. See also the
Figaro, page 164.

SILVER FIZZ

See Gin Fizz in The Classics, page 74.

SINGAPORE SLING

'We sail tonight for Singapore... Wash your mouth out by the door',
sang Tom Waits on 'Rain Dogs', perhaps with the eponymous Sling in
mind. By all accounts the original Straits Sling, served at Raffles Hotel
in Singapore, was utterly divine. By the account of everyone I know
who has been through Singapore and paid handsomely to 'experience'
the modern version, it is a rank confection of E-numbers and attitude.
The original recipe has been lost to time, but this mid-century
compromise is pretty goddam tasty. Do not overdo the fizzy water.

>   *50ml gin*
>   *25ml cherry brandy*
>   *15ml Bénédictine*
>   *25ml lime juice*
>   *40ml fizzy water*

Shake everything except the fizzy water with plenty of ice. Add the fizzy
water to the shaker, stir, and double-strain into a tall glass filled with
ice. Garnish with a mint sprig.

SLOE GIN FIZZ

Sloe Gin seems to be one of those things that people never know what
to do with. THIS!

>   *50ml sloe gin*

25ml lemon juice
10ml golden sugar syrup (2:1, see page 44)
Fizzy water

Shake up the sloe gin, lemon juice and sugar syrup with ice. Double-strain into a tall glass filled with more ice and top up with fizzy water. Stir, garnish with a lemon slice and serve.

SOUTHSIDE FIZZ

A precursor to the Mojito (see page 203) in its combination of spirit, citrus, mint and carbonation, the Southside Fizz was named after the South Side of Chicago, where it was popular with Al Capone's gang. It seems a slightly girly drink for mobsters, but don't tell Capone I said that.

10 or so fresh mint leaves
50ml gin
20ml lemon juice
10ml golden sugar syrup (2:1, see page 44)
Fizzy water

Shake everything except the fizzy water with plenty of ice, and then double-strain into a tall glass filled with ice.

You can also serve it 'down' as a mere Southside, in a cocktail glass without the fizzy water.

SPREZZAMATURA

One of those untranslatable Italian words that deserves a cocktail… I lend it the heavenly combination of Campari and grapefruit.

50ml Campari
50ml grapefruit juice
Dash fizzy water

Build in a tall glass with plenty of ice. Garnish with a lemon slice.

SWIZZLE

A swizzle is a West Indian style of rum sour, served over crushed ice and ideally swizzled with a swizzle stick. Traditionally fashioned from the base of a woody plant, a swizzle stick consists of a long handle (to be rolled between the palms) and a claw-like head, which churns the drink. One dreads to think what would happen if Snoop Dogg ever laid his hands on one. All parts of the Swizzle are open to negotiation except the swizzling – but here's a good version to start with.

50ml golden rum
15ml lime juice
10ml orgeat syrup (see page 86)
5ml pimento dram liqueur

Pour the ingredients into an old fashioned glass and fill nearly to the top with crushed ice. Swizzle! Once everything is well combined, top with more ice and garnish with a grating of nutmeg, a mint sprig and a lime wedge.

TATANKA

A simple and reliable way to serve Zubrowka. If you make it with good cloudy English apple juice, no one will refuse.

50ml Zubrowka
50ml cloudy apple juice

Don't bother shaking – just stir together in a glass with ice cubes. Garnish with an apple slice (remember to wet the apple with lemon juice otherwise it will turn brown).

TEQUILA SUNRISE

See Abominable Cocktails, page 240.

TOM COLLINS

See The Classics, page 74.

WHITE RUSSIAN

Alcoholic frappuccino, as drunk by the 'Dude' in the Coen Brothers' *The Big Lebowski* (1998). It is improved if you use fresh espresso instead of the traditional coffee liqueur and treat it more as the latte version of the Espresso Martini (see page 163).

> *1 shot espresso*
> *Teaspoon brown sugar*
> *50ml vodka*
> *50ml whole milk*

Combine the espresso and brown sugar in the shaker and stir to dissolve. Add the vodka and plenty of ice, shake hard and double-strain into an old fashioned glass with a few ice cubes in it. Now empty the shaker, add the milk and shake very hard for a while, so that the milk froths up (you can do this within the milk carton itself if you like). Add the milk to the glass, give a little stir and dust cocoa on top to garnish.

ZOMBIE

The Zombie is pre-eminent among 'Tiki drinks', the rum-based exotics that became popular in post-war America and formed a category and a culture all of their own. We have a man named Ernest Gantt, aka Don the Beachcomber, a Californian bootlegger-turned-restaurateur, to thank for them. As such, he is perhaps the single most influential creator of cocktails of all time. Essentially, what we now call Tiki drinks are Caribbean punches pretending to be Polynesian drinks served with Cantonese food to Californians who craved a little escapism and found it in Don's restaurants – and those of his rivals, such as 'Trader' Vic Bergstrom. They're authentic relics of an inauthentic age.

The first wave of Tiki restaurants (a few of which survive today) were lavish affairs, with interiors designed by Hollywood set designers, faux-rainstorms, girls in grass skirts, bartenders with lipstick kisses on their lapels, blue curaçao-stained menus, kitsch before kitsch was kitsch. They were the sorts of places Fred Flinstone and Barney Rubble would have taken Wilma and Betty on a double date and they were, by all accounts, a lot of fun. Still, if it weren't for the drinks, it's unlikely they would be remembered quite so fondly today.

Perhaps the first thing to learn about Tiki drinks is that when made properly, they are terrifying. In genre terms, they fall somewhere between punches and shaken drinks so large that they end up becoming long drinks. The Zombie alone (if you follow Don the Beachcomber's 1956 recipe) contains a phenomenal amount of rum, much of it 151 proof Demerara, which is nigh on double the strength of a sane spirit. For good measure, you have three sweeteners (falernum, maraschino, grenadine) to get the blood sugar whoomphing, an inscrutable combination of fruits (lime, pineapple, grapefruit) and the classic Tiki combination of Angostura bitters plus Pernod to add another layer of complexity. Oh, it slips down easy enough – but if you are used to discreet little Manhattans, it will kill your face off.

As complex as the recipes are, if you divide the ingredients into categories, they are all variations on a theme – basically, Planter's Punch+++. Some of them are Jimi Hendrix-style variations on a theme but even so, we come back to the simple melody of one of sour, two of sweet, three of strong, four of weak surprisingly often.

And then there are a few tricks. Don rarely used one kind of rum when two or three would do (a light, a dark and a little overproof is a good start). The 'secret' ingredients were often almond (whether it comes in orgeat, falernum or almond essence) and cloves (Don's Spice Syrup was grapefruit syrup with cloves in it, and he used a fair bit of pimento dram, an allspice/clove liqueur too). If a recipe calls for curaçao, make it blue. If you can 'split' any element of the drink (say, by using three different syrups), do. Don the Beachcomber often used Angostura bitters and Pernod to finish his drinks. Garnishes should be ridiculous.

David Embury, the author of *The Fine Art of Mixing Drinks* (1948) wrote: 'The Zombie is undoubtedly the most over-advertised, over-emphasised, over-exalted and foolishly feared drink whose claims to glory ever assaulted the American public.' Still not tempted? This is the first known recipe from 1934, and it is easily enough for two.

> *45ml gold rum (ideally Spanisho)*
> *45ml dark rum (ideally Jamaican)*
> *30ml overproof dark rum (ideally Demerara)*
> *20ml lime juice*
> *10ml grapefruit juice**
> *5ml golden sugar syrup (2:1, see page 44)**
> *5ml grenadine (page 83)*
> *15ml falernum*
> *Dash Angostura bitters*
> *Dash absinthe*
> *Pinch ground cinnamon**

Place everything in the blender and blend for about 5 seconds with 175ml scoop of crushed ice. Pour, unstrained, into a capacious and silly-looking glass and garnish with a mint sprig.

*The recipe actually called for 15ml 'Don's Mix #2', which was two parts grapefruit juice to one part cinnamon-infused sugar syrup, but this way you don't need to worry about making that separately.

THE OCCASIONAL

'With a bottle of champagne one can again drift into the
merriest carnival mood in the world!'

Friedrich Engels, Journals (1844)

SPARKLERS

The French region of Champagne is responsible for the single most effective marketing campaign in history. Its winemakers are the only ones in the world to turn their particular grape juice into a byword for celebration and glamour. They have been so successful that people routinely spend £25 on an OK bottle whereas it wouldn't cross their mind to spend £25 on any other wine, even though they could get something sensational for that kind of money. Surely even the most carefree champagne drinker realises that? And yet we still purchase champagne all the same. Such is the power of an idea.

As for champagne cocktails, well, they are decadence squared, but since the bottle's open… What it provides here is bubbles and a touch of acidity. Of course really good champagne should be drunk on its own and champagne cocktails can (and probably should) be made with something like cava, prosecco or crémant de Bourgogne. If you're making drinks for many people (as is likely) it's a good idea to make the base on a larger scale in advance so as not to have to fiddle around in each individual glass as the champagne warms.

AIRMAIL

A honeyed affair, where the tropical rum and lime blend with the subtler acid of the champagne.

> *25ml dark rum*
> *15ml lime juice*
> *10ml honey loosened with 5ml hot water*
> *Champagne*

Shake the first three ingredients over ice and double-strain into a cold flute. Top with champagne.

APEROL SPRITZ

Personally, I prefer Campari to Aperol (see Spritz in The Classics, page 75, for the full recipe) but goshdarnit, you've got to hand it to Aperol – she has done well. In a matter of a few years, the Aperol Spritz has come from nowhere to become the pre-eminent cocktail of the hipster classes. The proportions listed on the Aperol bottle (three parts prosecco, two parts Aperol, one part soda) make for a too-sweet drink for me, if sweeter sales for Aperol. Also good with Cynar.

> *25ml Aperol*
> *25ml fizzy water*
> *75ml prosecco*

Combine all the ingredients in a wine glass or tumbler with a few lumps of ice and give it a stir. Ideally, you should garnish this with one of those amazingly green olives on a stick, plus an orange or lemon slice.

BELLINI

A classic Venetian celebration drink – and a popular alternative to Buck's Fizz among the chattering classes. You can purchase good peach nectar in many grocers, otherwise you will have to purée some peaches, either by pressing them through a sieve or by peeling them, removing the stones and whizzing up in the blender. Depending on the sweetness of your peaches, you may need to add a dash of sugar syrup or a drop of peach liqueur.

> *25ml peach nectar*
> *5ml golden sugar syrup (2:1, see page 44)*
> *100ml prosecco*

Prepare the peach nectar on a grand plan, adding sugar syrup if you like, and then stir up with plenty of ice. Pour a drop in the bottom of each flute and top up with ice-cold prosecco.

BRIT SPRITZ

Alex Kammerling came up with this spin on the classic Venetian aperitif as a showcase for his ginseng spirit. It's like a post-modern Pimms.

> *35ml Kamm & Sons*
> *15ml elderflower cordial*
> *50ml sparkling wine (English please)*
> *50ml fizzy water*

Stir over plenty of ice in a wine glass with a slice of cucumber and a wedge of grapefruit.

CHAMPAGNE COCKTAIL

No classic is quite so poorly designed as this. When made according to the traditional method, the agitating sugar cube at the bottom of the glass looks pretty, but it doesn't do its job of sweetening and results in a harsh drink and a mouthful of granules when you reach the end. It's far better to use golden sugar syrup and include the sugar cube as a bubble machine if at all. A dash of lemon peel is standard but lime is an improvement in my opinion.

> *25ml brandy*
> *2.5ml Green Chartreuse or Grand Marnier (optional)*
> *2.5ml golden sugar syrup (2:1, see page 44)*
> *Brown sugar cube (optional)*
> *Angostura bitters*
> *Lime/lemon peel*
> *Champagne*

Chill the brandy, liqueur and sugar syrup with some ice cubes. If you're using a sugar cube, place it in the bottom of a chilled flute and saturate in bitters. Pour the cold brandy mixture and the champagne into the flute and garnish with a length of peel.

JALISCO FLOWER

Delicate and fair, this is one of the finest champagne cocktails I've tried.

15ml tequila reposado
20ml elderflower liqueur
30ml pink grapefruit juice
Champagne

Stir the tequila, elderflower liqueur and grapefruit juice with a couple of ice cubes in a flute and fill with champagne. Garnish with a grapefruit-zest twist.

KIR ROYALE

The Kir was once known quite simply as the Cassis-Blanc but took on the name of the Resistance hero Félix Kir after the Second World War. A proper Kir is made with Aligoté, an unoaked Chardonnay from Burgundy – but most French cafés use whatever dry white happens to be to hand. I've also seen the cassis subbed with peach, raspberry or strawberry liqueur. The fizzy version is a Kir Royale, classically made with Crémant de Bourgogne, but champagne, cava, prosecco, etc, will do.

20ml crème de cassis
100ml sparkling wine (ideally Crémant de Bourgogne)

Combine in a wine glass. *C'est tout.*

SBAGLIATO

Sbagliato is Italian for 'wrong', and what-a-mistake-a-to-make-a! It refers to a Negroni (see page 62) into which someone accidentally put champagne instead of the usual gin. It's like a posh Spritz (see page 75).

25ml Italian vermouth
25ml Campari
75ml champagne

It is advisable to build this Negroni-style (see page 62) over ice in an old fashioned glass. If you insist on a champagne flute, it is advisable to chill the vermouth and Campari beforehand else the drink will be too warm.

SGROPPINO

A Venetian after-dinner tradition, the Sgroppino is more of a dessert than a drink but it's a pleasant treat all the same. It's usually made with vodka, but gin or grappa would work just as well. By all means, vary the flavour of the sorbet too.

> *100ml prosecco*
> *25ml vodka*
> *Small scoop of lemon sorbet*

Pour the prosecco into a cold flute. Shake up the vodka with the sorbet and a few ice cubes and double-strain over the prosecco. Quick stir and serve.

TWINKLE

An undislikable sparkler from Tony Conigliaro's laboratory. You can also make it with elderflower liqueur in place of the cordial/vodka combination.

> *10ml elderflower cordial*
> *25ml vodka*
> *Champagne*

Stir the cordial and vodka with plenty of ice and strain into a chilled flute. Top up with champagne and garnish with a lemon twist.

See also the French 75 (page 72).

COMMUNAL BOWLS

In Charles Dickens's *David Copperfield*, you will find a description of Mr Micawber that could serve as an advertisement for punch-making in itself. 'I never saw a man so thoroughly enjoy himself amid the fragrance of lemon-peel and sugar, the odour of burning rum, and the steam of boiling water, as Mr Micawber did that afternoon', says our narrator. 'It was wonderful to see his face shining out at us of a thin cloud of these delicate fumes, as he stirred, and mixed, and tasted, and looked as if he were making, instead of a punch, a fortune for his family down to the latest posterity.'

If you're entertaining many people and would like to make them a fortune for posterity – and to give them happy memories through delicate fumes – then punch is the only sensible option. Do be sure to drink up though. '"Punch, my dear Copperfield," said Mr Micawber, tasting it, "like time and tide, waits for no man. Ah! It is at the present moment in high flavour."'

DICKENS'S FLAMING PUNCH

What Busta Rhymes was to Courvoisier and Snoop Dogg was to Gin'n'Juice, Charles Dickens was to punch. His characters are constantly compounding Smoking Bishops and Dog's Noses, while Dickens himself made a grand ceremony of igniting his own punch with a wax taper. This is very much like the punch Mr Micawber would have made, modelled on the punch that Dickens learned from his own father.

For 10 people
4 lemons
100g brown sugar
1 litre boiling water, or 500ml very cold water
*   plus a 500ml lump of ice*
200ml brandy
500ml dark rum
Nutmeg, for grating

Peel the lemons, taking care to remove as little white pith as possible, and pound up the zest with the sugar in your punch bowl. This is your oleo-saccharum, your sherbert, you key to deliciousness. Now squeeze the lemons and set aside the juice. If you would like a hot punch, set the water to boil in a capacious pan and once it is bubbling, turn off the heat. If you would like cold punch, refrigerate your water so it is very cold and ensure you have enough ice to hand.

Now comes the tricky bit. Pour the spirits into the punch bowl on top of the lemon sherbert and set carefully alight – the safest way to do this is by setting a small spoon of rum alight on a ladle and then pouring that in to ignite the rest. Stir the blue flaming liquid for about three minutes until the sugar is completely dissolved. Marvel at it! Then extinguish by covering with a tray. Now add the lemon juice, tasting as you go so you can adjust the proportions if need be. If you want to serve the punch hot, pour in the hot water and that's that. If you want to serve it cold, add the cold water, stir and then add your ice. Grate fresh nutmeg over the top and distribute among your friends.

FISH HOUSE PUNCH

A Philadelphia fishing club was responsible for one of most enduring punch recipes, said to date back to the 18th century. It would originally have been made with aged peach brandy, which sounds delicious but is hard to source these days, so peach liqueur is generally used. The below is a rough transliteration of the recipe that Jerry Thomas says was passed to him by the American humourist Charles G. Leland – I've switched the water for cold black tea.

> *For 10 people*
> *300ml brandy*
> *150ml dark rum*
> *150ml peach liqueur (peach brandy)*
> *200ml lemon juice*
> *150ml golden sugar syrup (2:1, see page 44)*
> *750ml cold black tea (the original recipe calls for water)*

Stir everything in a punch bowl in advance of the party. Just prior to serving, add a single huge lump of ice and a garnish of fresh lemon slices, mint leaves and berries.

For an individual serving, divide the quantities by ten and build in a glass.

PLANTER'S PUNCH (OLD STYLE)

Planter's Punch would eventually evolve into all manner of silly exotic drinks, but it began as a tasty way for Caribbean sugar plantation owners to make use of their rum and sugar, as well as the copious limes. Sometimes, this would be trusted to the houseboys, but more often, the master of the house would have taken care of punch duty himself. There's an account of a West India Planter's Punch in William Terrington's *Cooling Cups and Dainty Drinks* (1869) where the 'grand compounder' takes enormous pains and pride in his labour. He withdraws from his secret store a 'matchless rum' and a small pot of guava jelly ('without this confection no punch can be pronounced perfect'). He also pours in brandy and a little Madeira and makes it clear that only his 'experienced palate' is good enough to judge the lime sherbert. The below is an adaptation of the recipe, only served cold. By all means, add a tot of Madeira and brandy if you have some, and if you can't find any guava jelly, try another tropical-style jam such as pineapple or kiwi, or some guava juice (e.g. Rubicon).

> *For 10 people*
> *8 limes*
> *100g golden caster sugar*
> *500ml pot of green tea*
> *50ml guava jelly (optional)*
> *500ml dark rum*
> *Ice*

Peel the limes, taking care not to remove the white pith, and place the zest in a bowl with the sugar. Pound until the sugar turns greenish. Brew the tea (proper green tea leaves please!). Use a little of this tea to dissolve the lime sherbert and remove the lime skins. Use a little more tea to dissolve your guava jelly into a cordial so it's easy to incorporate. Now squeeze the juice from the limes. You now have the sweet, weak and sour elements of your punch (sherbert, tea and lime juice respectively). Balance all elements carefully in a punch bowl according to the above proportions, but ensuring that no single one overpowers the others – then introduce the rum. Garnish with tropical fruit slices and 'the merest dusting of nutmeg'.

PURL

Purl is an old English drink that became a popular cockle-warmer among Thames boatmen in the 18th and 19th centuries. Classically, it's gin and stout, sweetened with sugar, with optional batter of egg yolks, warmed with a poker from the fire. (Why don't we have these in modern homes?) When made on a large scale, it forms a pleasing alternative to mulled wine at a winter gathering.

For 10 people
2 litres stout or ale
2.5ml ground ginger
1 cinnamon stick
Nutmeg, for grating
1–2 star anise (optional)
6 egg yolks
200g sugar (preferably golden caster sugar)
250ml gin
Angostura bitters

Set the beer to heat on the hob with the ginger, cinnamon, a good grating of nutmeg and star anise and let it warm through, then leave to infuse for about 15 minutes. Meanwhile, in a separate bowl whisk the eggs with the sugar until the consistency becomes lighter. Gradually, very gradually, add a trickle of warmed beer to this batter, whisking all the while, until it becomes liquid. Then pour it back into the pan along with the gin and the bitters. Apply a little more heat and keep whisking.

Taste (add more sugar is desired) before dividing between cups for your amazed guests.

WASSAIL PUNCH

I'm just going to give you the recipe for 'Sir Walter Scott's Wassail Bowl' so you can see how the gentry used to roll in the 19th century. Don't try this at home: 'Place 1lb of sponge cake, 1lb of ratafias and macaroons in a bowl; add wine-glass of sherry, 2 bottles of raisin wine, bottle of champagne, bottle of Chablis and a little lemon juice if desired.' While dousing 500g of macaroons in champagne sounds implausibly decadent, the Wassail Bowl is a much humbler tradition. *Waes heil!* is Old English for 'To your health!' Wassailing was an old Twelfth Night ritual in apple-producing regions, when everyone would get together and sing songs about apples. A traditional wassail bowl was made with hot ale, roast apples and spices, with toast floating around on the top, which may be where Scott got his unholy designs on cake. I think we can live without the soggy toast but we can certainly get into the Wassailing spirit with a contemporary apple punch. My friends Pete and Nell compound this particular punch once a year at their Christmas party, which very often ends up with people getting a bit pagan. It's delicious – and they very kindly passed me the recipe.

For 10 people
3 apples
3 pears
300ml dark rum
400ml apple brandy
150ml lemon juice (3–4 lemons)
100ml golden sugar syrup (2:1, see page 44)
Lemons and limes for decoration
Cinnamon and nutmeg (optional)

A punchy punch, this one. A few hours before your party create a large lump of ice by freezing a bowl of water. Dice up the apples and pears into centimetre cubes and douse them in all the lemon juice and booze in your punch bowl, adding the sugar syrup to taste. Once it is well balanced, leave the mixture to get to know itself for a while in the fridge.

Add the ice lump along with slices of lemon and lime and a grating of nutmeg and/or cinnamon (if you like) just prior to serving.

TEMPERENCE DRINKS

The problem with non-alcoholic cocktails is not that they don't contain alcohol. After all, there are many excellent beverages that do not contain alcohol. They include: flat whites, Diet Coca-Cola, freshly squeezed orange juice, Earl Grey tea, San Pellegrino Pompelmo, apricot nectar, breast-milk, horchata, raspberry shrub, coconut water, Badoit, *kvass*, matcha green tea, birch-sap, Strawberry Frappuccinos, lingonberry juice, cherryade, *agua fresca*, dandelion and burdock, kombucha tea, chamomile tea, chocolate milk, Irn-Bru, fresh lime soda, Ribena, double espressos, beef tea, aloe vera juice, sasparilla, blue bubblegum-flavoured Slush Puppies, cold-pressed kale juice, purefied well-water, Ovaltine and mango lassis.

The problem with non-alcoholic cocktails is the term itself (and don't get me started on 'Mocktail'). A cocktail is alcoholic. Therefore a non-alcoholic cocktail isn't a cocktail. It's a liar. You might as well have a sausageless hot dog or a boiled roast.

This is not to dismiss the pleasant drinks that can be made without alcohol – though I prefer the old-school term 'temperance drinks', which doesn't raise false expectations. The thoughtful host always has a couple in the locker, since you never know when you might be visited by pregnant ladies, designated drivers, devout Muslims, recovering alcoholics or people who have myriad sensible reasons not to consume alcohol. These people need as much love and attention as your other guests and should not simply be fobbed off with tap water. In fact, they need more love and attention than your other guests, since they will retain a sober eye over proceedings.

The key thing to keep in mind is that you shouldn't try to replicate the taste of alcohol, but rather draw on the universe of flavours available to you from nature. (When my wife was pregnant, I attempted to make her a non-alcoholic Martini, reckoning that chilli might give the thing an alcoholic 'kick' and it actually gave her a nosebleed.) There are plenty of milkshakes and smoothies and lassis and coolers and juices that will do the trick – find them in some other book. However, here are five pleasing temperance drinks that draw on cocktailing principles. Almost all are improved by a little dash of bitters by the way; they provide negligible alcohol, but may offend certain abstainers so do check.

COBRA'S BREATH

Here's a variant on a lethal Don the Beachcomber drink called the Cobra's Fang only with the original overproof rum subbed for fizzy water. If you use fiery ginger syrup and Don's classic finish of bitters and a drop of absinthe, you get the sensation of alcohol with a scintilla of proof.

20ml passion fruit pulp
20ml lime juice
20ml orange juice
10ml ginger syrup (see page 117)
10ml grenadine (see page 83)
Dash Angostura bitters
Dash absinthe
50ml fizzy water

Shake up everything except the fizzy water with crushed ice and pour unstrained into an outlandish glass. Top with a little fizzy water and churn a little. Garnish with fresh mint and grate a little fresh cinnamon on top.

CUCUMBER SODA

One of the problems with non-alcoholic drinks is that they're usually so sweet. I tried to remedy that problem with this delicate sipper. It works best with those small, firm cucumbers that are less juicy but provide much more flavour than the supermarket standard.

15cm cucumber
½ lemon
Dash agave syrup
Few leaves of mint (or dill, basil, tarragon, etc)
Fizzy water

Peel and grate the cucumber. Zest the lemon. Transfer both into a shaker with spritz of lemon juice, a scant amount of agave syrup and a few herbs (mint, dill, basil or tarragon), add ice and shake hard. Strain into a sieve held over a jug and press down to extract all the juice. Pour into a tall glass filled with ice cubes and top with fizzy water.

GREEN LEMONADE

Lemon and basil get along famously in both sweet and savoury contexts (lemon and basil spaghetti is one of the dinners I make most often). Here, they create a mood-enhancing summer sipper.

Handful of torn basil leaves
25ml lemon juice
10ml golden sugar syrup (2:1, see page 44)
Fizzy water
Celery bitters (optional)

Lightly muddle the basil in the bottom of your shaker. Add the lemon juice, sugar syrup, celery bitters, if using, and plenty of ice and shake. Double-strain into a tall glass filled with ice cubes, top with fizzy water and stir. Garnish with more basil.

KERALA FIZZ

The cardamom lends a touch of the bazaar to this simple pineapple fizz... which is excellent with a dash of dark rum too.

Few green cardamom pods
50ml pineapple juice
20ml lime juice
10ml golden sugar syrup (2:1, see page 44)
Fizzy water
Dash Angostura bitters (optional)

Bash the cardamom around a bit in the bottom of the shaker, then add the pineapple juice, lime juice, sugar syrup and some ice cubes. Shake hard until the pineapple juice is nice and frothy. Double-strain into a tall glass filled with ice cubes and top up with fizzy water. Stir. Garnish with a lime wedge and if you don't mind a miniscule amount of alcohol, shake some bitters over the top.

SHIRLEY TEMPLE

Named after the 1930s child actress who later became the American ambassador to Czechoslovakia, the Shirley Temple is the quintessential midcentury guilt-trip, the sort of thing that Humbert Humbert would have ordered for Lolita in a Milwaukee drugstore. Apparently Lana Del Rey drinks them to this day. If you make them with proper grenadine (and maybe a dash of bitters?) it's a fine non-alcoholic option, though I feel the essence of the drink lies in its garish fakery. The quintessential Shirley Temple is made with a luminous red syrup and sipped at the counter, as the bartender tells you what a cutie you are and Daddy makes an anxious call out back.

Dash grenadine (see page 83)
Squeeze of lemon
Dash Angostura bitters (optional)
Ginger Beer

Build in a tall glass filled with ice. Garnish with a luminous cherry.

POUSSE-CAFÉS

A Pousse-Café is a 19th-century effeminacy and an ancestor of the 'shooter' that is generally deemed not worth the effort today. ('More of a test of patience than a drink', notes Simon Difford in his *Bartender's Bible*). It is a sweetie, essentially, one that requires the bartender to layer a number of multicoloured liqueurs one over the other to create a stripy drink. Apparently, in fin de siècle Paris, they were all the rage among *flaneurs* and *flaneuses*, who would order a Pousse-Café to 'push' their afternoon coffee down as they discussed Huysmans novels and surrealist manifestos and the merits of the Eiffel Tower. Every drink has its moment. Think of a pousse as an afternoon rainbow, to be consumed at the moment you might have a macaroon.

The principle of layering drinks is simple. Different liquids have different densities, largely dependent on both sugar and alcohol content. As a general rule, sugar sinks and alcohol floats – so if you put, say, grenadine (0% alcohol; tons of sugar); blue curaçao (25% alcohol; plenty of sugar); and gin (40% alcohol; no sugar) in a glass without mixing them, they would arrange themselves in that order (resulting in a sort of Russian flag). With a little experimentation you should begin to intuit a liqueur's *poussété*. Proceed carefully, however, as the layers will bleed into one another with the merest encouragement. The old dudes recommend using an old-style sherry glass (the thin kind that tapers inwards), which does make a more pleasing alternative to the shot glass.

Either way, the best way to proceed is to pour the desired liquid onto a dessertspoon (5ml) or tablespoon (7.5ml) and bring the shot glass up to it at an angle until the lip of the spoon is just touching the inside of the rim. The surface tension will then break and the liquid will seep slowly down the sides of the glass. You will notice that sometimes, even if you pour them in the wrong order, the liquids often rearrange themselves quite neatly. Other times, they create a weird mess. This is why people outside New Orleans theme bars do not bother making Pousse-Cafés very much.

Some tips, though:

- As a rough guide, you should pour liquids in the following order (though different brands will vary): grenadine; cassis; maraschino; curaçao; crème de cacao; Kahlua; Cherry Heering; Chambord; Cuaranta y Tres; Campari; Bénédictine; Amaretto; Yellow Chartreuse; Baileys; violet liqueur; Green Chartreuse; Grand Marnier; neat spirits; absinthe; overproof spirits.

- You cannot choose which liquid will come out where, but you can encourage them in the right direction: if you mix violette and gin together on your spoon, for example, you can retain the violet hue but be fairly sure it will come closer to the top.

- Absinthe or overproof rum will float to the top, where they may be set aflame. Just saying.

- If you intend to delight your guests with a tray of pousses, make them well in advance and store in the fridge. If there's anything worse than a random assortment of liqueurs in the same glass, it's a random assortment of room-temperature liqueurs in the same glass.

- Cream makes everything taste a lot nicer, but it doesn't look pretty when it runs. It will generally sit over the liqueurs and under the spirits. If you store your pousses in the fridge, then apply cream just before serving and it should remain on top.

- Keep it simple. Three well-chosen liquids is plenty.

Here are some classic and invented Pousses. Pour carefully, in the order listed:

PARISIAN POUSSE-CAFÉ NO.1

5ml raspberry syrup
5ml maraschino
5ml (orange) curaçao
5ml Green Chartreuse
5ml brandy

RAINBOW POUSSE

5ml grenadine (page 83)
5ml blue curaçao
5ml green crème de menthe
5ml Yellow Chartreuse
5ml violet liqueur/gin mix

BUMBLEBEE

5ml Cherry Heering
5ml Cuarenta y Tres (Licor 43)
5ml Averna Amaro
5ml tequila reposado
5ml overproof rum (set aflame)

JERSEY LILY

10ml Green Chartreuse
10ml brandy
5ml Angostura bitters

ABOMINABLE COCKTAILS

Of course, not all cocktail experiments go as planned – some cocktails are abominable. This is no terrible thing if it happens in a private home. It's not even necessarily a disaster if it happens in a public bar either. As long as it remains in one neon fleshpot, where its ill effects may be contained, and the customer is happy and the bartender is happy and everyone gets laid/paid as appropriate, fine. Like the Macarena or the norovirus, however, occasionally an abominable cocktail catches and soon everyone is humming it from Aberdeen to Aberystwyth. I don't simply mean Jagerbombs and Cement Mixers, which are deliberately disgusting. I mean cocktails that someone somewhere thought were a good idea but are not.

Still, the perception of what constitutes an abomination changes over time. The Bronx (see page 77) was once deemed an abomination, but is now an innocuous part of the canon. Later, purists railed against the Zombie (see page 214), which is now seen as a kitsch classic. There is no period more reviled in cocktail circles than the 1970s, the era of the Pina Colada (underrated; see page 206) and the Havey Wallbanger(look it up in a less *à la mode* volume). However, you could just as easily peer back into the supposed golden era and wonder how anyone ever thought the Curzon (1934) a good idea: brandy, grapefruit, crème de cacao?

Most abominable cocktails that you encounter today will be hangovers from the 1990s: sticky, synthetic, garish, faintly pretentious and most likely served in a small-town club with a name like Buddah Bar or Legends. They are usually based on vodka or (Bacardi) rum. They frequently contain peach schnapps, Midori melon liqueur, Malibu, Kahlua, blue curaçao and/or Chambord too. Approach a menu listing too many of these with caution – and certainly watch out for 'Sour Mix', lychee purée and unfunny sexual puns. Also steer clear of anything that calls itself a Martini but doesn't contain vermouth.

Having said that, I have a weakness for a few abominable cocktails – not least the Long Island Iced Tea (see page 201). There's not a whole lot wrong with a Sex on the Beach, either, if you happen to be on the pull in Ipswich town centre. I've tasted far more execrable efforts from some of London's most cutting-edge bartenders, not least a Blue Cheese and Chocolate Martini and a Salt Beef-flavoured Sazerac. These are too esoteric to ever be canonised as true abominable cocktails (which is actually a secret honour), but truly, No. In the meantime, here are five lingering infections.

APPLETINI

Popular among Silicon Valley types, this is what Jesse Eisenberg and Justin Timberlake drink in *The Social Network* when they're vowing to make Facebook a billion-dollar business. It is the most enduring of the non-Martini Martinis, its immediate appeal masking a disturbing undertone. (A Tatanka, page 213, is a much classier version of the same.)

25ml vodka
25ml sour apple schnapps
25ml fresh apple juice

Shake with plenty of ice and double-strain into a chilled cocktail glass. Garnish with a little slice of apple, unmoistened with lemon juice so it goes brown and yucky.

BLACK RUSSIAN

The White Russian (see page 214) has a certain insouciant charm, but the Black Russian? You may as well pour Nescafé into a can of Coke. It's the classic example of a pointless vodka drink and the Espresso Martini (see page 163) should really have made it obsolete.

50ml vodka
25ml coffee liqueur
75ml Coca-Cola

Stir in a tall glass over ice. No garnish.

PORN STAR MARTINI

Ludicrous... but to be fair have any of the artisanal moustaches in their craft speakeasies crafted anything that has given so much pleasure to so many? The original comes from 1990s London (where else?), where the bartender Douglas Ankhra shrewdly surmised that his customers would find the lascivious name and promise of 'free' champagne irresistible. Apparently Prince William wooed Catherine Middleton with one.

50ml vodka
20ml passion fruit pulp (one whole fruit)
10ml lime juice
10ml golden sugar syrup (2:1, see page 44)
Vanilla pod
Champagne

Combine the vodka, passion fruit, lime and sugar syrup in a shaker. Split the vanilla pod and scrape in about half of the seeds. Muddle awhile to allow the vanilla to infuse then ice, shake, and double-strain into a cold cocktail glass. Garnish with half a passion fruit and serve alongside a shot of chilled champagne.

TEQUILA SUNRISE

You can tell the Tequila Sunrise is going to be terrible because the Eagles had a song called 'Tequila Sunrise' and the Eagles were a terrible band. Orange juice and tequila simply aren't very nice together (especially if it's inferior tequila), while a mouthful of grenadine at the end of the drink is a horrible surprise. If you would like the same sunrise prettiness but a better drink, replace the orange with grapefruit and the grenadine with Campari.

50ml tequila reposado
100ml fresh orange juice
15ml grenadine (see page 83)

Stir the tequila and orange juice together in a tall glass with plenty of ice, then pour the grenadine down the side so it settles on the bottom. Garnish with an orange wheel. Pretty! Now throw it down the sink.

TWENTIETH CENTURY

The success of golden-era revivals such as the Last Word (see page 170) and the Aviation (see page 146) has inspired many contemporary bartenders to unearth lost classics from the old cocktail books. I've seen many attempts at the Twentieth Century (invented by someone called C.A. Tuck and first listed in 1934), but none that mask the horrible collision that is lemon, juniper and chocolate. Bleurgh.

40ml gin
20ml crème de cacao
20ml Lillet (or sweet white vermouth)
20ml lemon juice

Shake over plenty of ice and double-strain into a chilled cocktail glass. Garnish with a lemon-zest twist.

THE INVENTED

'After two of those babies, the dullest, most by-the-book Vogon will be up on the bar in stilettos, yodelling mountain shanties and swearing he's the king of the Gray Binding Fiefdoms of Saxaquine!'

Zaphod Beeblebrox hymns his Pan-Galactic Gargle Blaster in Douglas Adams's *Hitchhiker's Guide to the Galaxy* (1978)

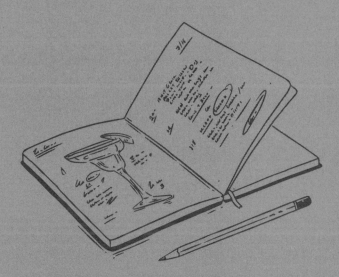

MOVING BEYOND RECIPES

After trying a certain amount of cocktail recipes, you may feel the desire to go your own way. For many, however, going recipe-free is not easy to do. Recipes are everywhere. Weekend newspapers contain whole supplements full of them. The internet contains almost as many recipes as it does pornographic videos. We live in the golden age of the recipe. But recipes – and I say this as someone who has just laid about 250 of them in front of you – are a bit of a tyranny.

For while all these recipes suggest that we spend every waking minute trying out new things with celeriac, actually the opposite is true. People who cook, in an everyday kind of way, rarely use recipes. Once the fundamentals of a tomato sauce or a roast chicken are in place, there is simply no need to consult your Nigella each time you make it. I bet if you think of the dish you make best – even if it is just a toasted cheese sandwich – you never use a recipe. You use your judgment and your experience.

Recipes are useful for providing pointers and guidelines and inspiration and exactitudes (in the few dishes where that particularly matters). If you adhere to them too rigidly, however, you will not make delicious food. You will end up being one of those people who says: 'But Jamie/Lorraine/Yotam says NO!' and refusing to add salt when salt is required, or lemon when lemon is required. Sticking too closely to the guidelines and not trusting your instincts, as we know, leads to bank failure, aeroplane crashes, medical negligence, etc.

Now, cocktails are a little different from food but not that different. You can inch towards a perfect Daiquiri (see page 158) and once you've made 20 or so, you might have strong opinions about them too. However, it is only really professional bartenders who need to get their recipe 'perfect' every single time. The reputation of London's Artesian Bar or New York's Attaboy depends on their products being consistently exquisite. But that's their problem. At home, your guests aren't going to ask for a refund. Here, the pleasure lies more in the attempt, the revision, the randomly perfect attempt. There's a precept in *Beta Cocktails* that applies equally well to the home as to the bar:

'Transcendent cocktails are the product of circumstances beyond your control. Embrace this.'

The first couple of times you make a cocktail – particularly a 'special-occasion' cocktail like a Ramos Gin Fizz (see page 87) – I'd recommend that you go down to the millilitre. That way, you know roughly what you're aiming for (also, I've taken great pains to get these measurements right for you). After a couple of tries the proportions of spirit, citrus, sweetener, etc, should become more intuitive. At this point, your little Oxo measuring jug may be replaced with a jigger. Before long you may even pour straight from the bottle, relying on judicious eye, steady hand and telltale tongue. Preparing your cocktails will feel less like making Heston Blumenthal's snail porridge, and more like making *lunch*. What, you may ask yourself, do I fancy today?

Creating your own cocktails

The most delightful thing about having a reasonable selection of spirits is the scope it allows you to experiment. The transient occupants of your cupboards and fridge can also suggest new combinations. You bought some maple syrup for pancakes... well why not use it in a Brown Derby (see page 153)? Your basil plant has come good. Green Park (see page 67)! However, even the base ingredients themselves can be combined in interesting ways if you know what you're doing.

I see the process as a bit like improvising a tune on the piano. You might begin with one spirit you particularly like, say tequila reposado, and the dim memory that crème de cassis goes well with it. I'd lob a shot or so of tequila in the bottom of an ordinary glass and then introduce just a trickle of cassis, bearing in mind that the tequila – as the base spirit – needs to remain dominant. The cassis will sink stroppily to the bottom, so swirl it around, taste it neat... The blackcurrant brings a graceful bloodiness to the wild desert notes of the tequila (bullet wound in the noonday sun..? Flamenco dancer walks into a bar..?). You might simply leave it there, adjusting the proportions a little. You might take it in a lime direction. Or you might want to keep it as an aromatic-style drink, and throw in a couple of drops of Angostura bitters to bind the two flavours together.

Angostura certainly sews it up, but now the agave seems less pronounced and the Spaghetti Western quality is gone. A touch more tequila? Or how about something else to dry it out, like French vermouth or, even better... sherry? (The Hispanic connection!) A lick of fino immediately adds a widescreen quality, taut violin strings... but it brings a certain nuttiness too, which hints at another direction the drink might go. Next time, try amontillado sherry? But never mind – at this point you have something drinkable and delicious. Add a large lump of ice, look at the fruitbowl, notice a fat yellow grapefruit and use a little grapefruit-zest twist as the garnish, because why not? And wow: the oils from the grapefruit lighten it up like something else... Make a little scribble; work on it next time; give it a fancy name – Charco de Sangre ('pool of blood') – and put it on page 110.

The key here is being able to intuit what each ingredient will do – tequila will form the canvas, cassis will sweeten, sherry will lengthen, bitters will bind, grapefruit zest will lighten. You might also keep the general idea in your repertoire for the next time you're at a house party and you notice some Ribena, tequila and someone's gran's sherry. This is probably the most fun you have making cocktails, the secret to the whole thing, like sitting at a piano and just... playing.

A general guide to subsitutions

The population of your home bar will likely depend on your budget. Bear in mind, however, that substitutions can always be made – in fact, substitutions *should* be made. Evolution progresses through mutant genes and a Margarita, after all, is just a Mutant Sidecar with lime where the lemon should be and tequila where the brandy once went. To make an effective substitution (either through necessity or design), you simply need to intuit function. Lemons work in place of limes, since both provide sourness. Grenadine works for sugar syrup, since both provide sweetness. Cointreau does the same for maraschino. Spirits stand in for other spirits, since all provide strength – and don't assume that you need to sub dark spirits with dark or light with light either. The same goes for fortified wines such as port, vermouth, sherry, marsala, quinquina which will ably deputise for one another.

When it comes to flavouring agents, you should think of weight and texture as much as flavour. Peach liqueur and apricot liqueur work almost interchangeably, since they both provide soft, bright fruit. However, pear liqueur and elderflower liqueur and Aperol and crème de framboise and that peculiar bilberry liqueur you bought back from Scandinavia may also bring a complimentary lightness. The main thing to watch out for is sweetness. If you're using sweet Madeira in place of Italian vermouth, you will need a little less of it. Likewise, if you want a dry liqueur – say, crème de menthe – to perform the sweetening function that Cointreau normally plays, you may need a little syrup for balance.

You can always sub in half an ingredient too, a reliable way of adding complexity to a drink. Replace the 10ml sugar syrup in a Daiquiri with 5ml ginger syrup, 5ml orgeat? (This is the principle behind a lot of Don the Beachcomber's punches). Divvy up the base of an Old Fashioned between rum, bourbon, brandy and calvados? (Death & Co have a drink along these lines called the Conference). You can see why bartenders rarely get bored.

Some ideas for flavour combinations

There are certain flavour combinations that appear so often in cocktails, they're almost like base ingredients themselves – gin and vermouth, bourbon and bitters, rum and lime. There are others that you'll notice come up time and again – apricot brandy and lime, Campari and grapefruit, Scotch and honey. A cook will be able to supplement these with some classic one-twos from the kitchen – lemon and basil, pear and almond, apple and cinamon. Then there are certain little secrets that might need a little teasing out – tequila and fino, Italian vermouth and coffee beans, Cocchi Americano and chocolate, kummel and coconut, pineapple and cardamom, pisco and flowers, grapefruit and cinnamon (one of Don the Beachcomber's secret mixes, see page 216).

The chart below is a loose guide to what works well with the main base spirits (I have left out vodka, which has no flavour and so works well with everything.) Feel free to interpret as wilfully as you like.

	Fresh citrus	Other fruits
GIN	LEMON, LIME, GRAPEFRUIT, ORANGE	RASPBERRY, BLACKBERRY, POMEGRANATE, APRICOT, PEACH, PLUM, PEAR, PINEAPPLE , RHUBARB
AMERICAN WHISKEY	LEMON, GRAPEFRUIT	CHERRY, POMEGRANATE, APRICOT, PEACH, FIG, APPLE, PUMPKIN
SCOTCH WHISKY	LEMON	PLUM, APPLE, PEAR, GOOSEBERRY, RHUBARB, PINEAPPLE, PASSION FRUIT
LIGHT RUM	LIME, LEMON	PINEAPPLE, POMEGRANATE, PASSION FRUIT, COCONUT, TROPICAL FRUIT, BANANA
DARK RUM	LIME, LEMON, ORANGE	PINEAPPLE, POMEGRANATE, PASSION FRUIT, COCONUT, TROPICAL FRUIT
BRANDY	LEMON, LIME, ORANGE	PINEAPPLE, RASPBERRY, POMEGRANATE, BLACK GRAPE
TEQUILA	LIME, GRAPEFRUIT	BLACKCURRANT, STRAWBERRY, TOMATO, PEPPERS
APPLE BRANDY	LEMON, ORANGE	POMEGRANATE, BLUEBERRY, ORCHARD FRUIT
PISCO	LIME, LEMON	POMEGRANATE, PINEAPPLE, APRICOT, BLUEBERRIES
ZUBROWKA	LEMON	PEAR, APPLE, RASPBERRY, BLUEBERRY

Herbs/spices	Alcohol	Others
MINT, THYME, BASIL, ANISE, CARDAMOM, NUTMEG, CLOVE, CINNAMON, SAFFRON, GINGER, CARAWAY	ANGOSTURA, ANY APERITIF WINE, SHERRY, ORANGE LIQUEUR, MARASCHINO, AMARI, GREEN AND YELLOW CHARTREUSE, BÉNÉDICTINE, LIGHT RUM	ELDERFLOWER, ROSE, VIOLET, HONEY, ALMOND, OLIVE, SALT, PICKLES, QUININE, PINE
MINT, VANILLA, CINNAMON	ANGOSTURA, BRANDY, ITALIAN VERMOUTH, MARASCHINO, BÉNÉDICTINE, AMARI, CHERRY BRANDY, CRÈME DE CACAO	MAPLE SYRUP, HONEY, CHOCOLATE, ALMOST ANY NUT, BACON, COKE, ROOT BEER
GINGER, ROSEMARY, SAGE, LIQUORICE, CINNAMON	FRENCH/ITALIAN VERMOUTH, PEYCHAUD'S, DRAMBUIE, ABSINTHE, OTHER WHISKIES, SWEET SHERRY	HONEY, TOFFEE, CREAM, ELDERFLOWER, IRN-BRU
GINGER, CARDAMOM, VANILLA, MINT, BASIL	DARK RUM, GIN, ANGOSTURA, FALERNUM, ORANGE LIQUEUR, MARASCHINO	ALMOND, CASHEW, WHITE CHOCOLATE, DARK SUGAR, COKE
VANILLA, GINGER, CLOVE, ALLSPICE, CINNAMON	LIGHT RUM, FALERNUM, PIMENTO DRAM, ORANGE LIQUEUR, COFFEE LIQUEUR, CRÈME DE CACAO, PUNSCH	TEA, CREAM, CHOCOLATE, BUTTER, COFFEE, WALNUT
CLOVE, ALLSPICE, NUTMEG	CHAMPAGNE, ANGOSTURA, ORANGE LIQUEUR, GREEN CHARTREUSE, BÉNÉDICTINE, DARK RUM, BOURBON	CHOCOLATE, HONEY, CREAM, COFFEE, WALNUT
CHILLI, BLACK PEPPER, CORIANDER	MEZCAL, ORANGE LIQUEUR, AMARI, DRY SHERRY, YELLOW CHARTREUSE	AGAVE, ROSE, CACAO
VANILLA, CINNAMON, ALLSPICE	ZUBROWKA, APERITIF WINES, SCOTCH	ELDERFLOWER, BEER
CARDAMOM, CLOVES	ORANGE LIQUEUR, ITALIAN VERMOUTH	LAVENDER, ROSE
VANILLA, CINNAMON, MINT, THYME, CARDAMOM	APPLE BRANDY	ELDERFLOWER, BIRCH SAP, PINE

TEN BASIC RATIOS

Here's some formulae that you'll use time and again.

1. The Sour ratio (sugar)

Used for Daiquiris, Pisco Sours, etc. Works with orgeat syrup (see page 86) or grenadine (page 83) in place of sugar syrup too.

50ml spirit, 15ml citrus, 10ml golden sugar syrup (2:1, see page 44).

2. The Sour ratio (liqueur)

Liqueurs are less intensely sweet than sugar syrup, so you will need to up the proportion in White Ladies, Margaritas, Sidecars, etc. With dryer liqueurs, you may need 5ml sugar syrup to help things along.

50ml spirit, 20ml citrus, 20ml liqueur.

3. The Old Fashioned ratio

The original 'Cocktail' is highly adaptable. By way of variation, try a 'split base', using two different spirits, or take your sweetness from a small amount of orange liqueur/maraschino.

50ml spirit, 2.5ml golden sugar syrup (2:1, see page 44), dash bitters.

4. The A+B ratio

Useful for dark after-dinner drinks such as B&Bs and Stingers.

50ml spirit, 10–20ml liqueur.

5. The Manhattan ratio

The simplest aromatic ratio, as used in the Gin & It, the Chopin , etc.

50ml spirit, 25ml aperitif wine, dash bitters.

6. The Manhattan Plus ratio

An easy way to add intrigue to a Manhattan-style drink is to lob in a spoon of liqueur (Trilby, Pink Rabbit etc).

50ml spirit, 25ml aperitif wine, 5–10ml liqueur, dash bitters.

7. The Fizz ratio

A Fizz is a Sour with length. To account for the extra dilution, I'd up the citrus-sugar quantities from a regular Sour. If your 'fizz' element is sweet (e.g. lemonade) drop the sugar quantity.

50ml spirit, 25ml lemon juice, 15ml golden sugar syrup (2:1, see page 44), 50ml fizz.

8. The Negroni ratio

A cinch to remember, 1:1:1, no fuss, build in a glass. Sherry works well as the aperitif element.

25ml spirit, 25ml bitter liqueur, 25ml aperitif wine.

9. The Last Corpse ratio

Inspired by both the Last Word and the Corpse Reviver, which have a similar architecture, this is a way of making a sour more interesting.

40ml spirit, 20ml herbal liqueur/aperitif wine, 20ml citrus, 10ml sweet liqueur.

10. The Tiki Punch ratio

When you break down Don the Beachcomber's mammoth frozen rum punches, they usually end up something like this.

75ml spirit, 25ml syrups/liqueurs, 25ml citrus, 25ml fruit juice, 150ml crushed ice, bitters/spices.

THE PHILOSOPHY

'Water? Never touch the stuff. Fish fuck in it.'

W.C. Fields (1880–1956)

COCKTAILONOMICS

'I wish I'd drunk more champagne.'
John Maynard Keynes (1883–1946) on his deathbed

If I were to tell you that cocktails are a highly economical way of drinking, you would probably tell me to get out of town. After all, the main reason people do not consume more cocktails is the idea that they are expensive. It may be reassuring (or not) to know that they have always been expensive. Even back in the Golden Age, speakeasies charged as much as 20 times the pre-Prohibition price for a simple highball. F. Scott Fitzgerald, with his $36,000 a year, found it hard to fund his Gin Rickey habit.

It would be easy to lay the blame at the modern bartender for present prices – he or she doesn't have to negotiate with Al Capone's gang to procure liquor, only Diageo and friends – but hear them out. It costs money to pay rent, renovate a premises, train staff, pay them respectable wage, stock a bar. Rents are not getting any cheaper either.

Typically, bars will set the price of a cocktail at GP x 4. That's 'gross product' (the cost of the raw materials) multiplied by four, so a drink that costs a bar £2 to make ought to go on the menu at £8. However, they also tend to price all cocktails more or less the same – so both a Manhattan (see page 59) and a Hurricane (see page 200) might come in at £8, even though the Hurricane contains more ingredients and costs more to make. Some drinks subsidise the other drinks, in other words. As long as the average is GP x 4, everyone will get paid.

For the customer, however, this isn't always a great deal. You can end up paying a lot for a simple drink. Take the Americano (see page 61), comprising equal parts Campari and Italian vermouth (neither of which are particularly expensive) plus soda water (which in most bars is free). It requires no special technique or bespoke equipment, and is considerably less effort to make than pulling a pint of Guinness. 'That'll be £9.50 sir,' says the bartender. (Across the bar, a Midwestern tourist with a bum-bag sips a Mai Tai that you helped pay for.)

In large cities, as least, there is enough competition to keep prices down – sometimes, you can find a Negroni for as little as £6. Still, make yourself a Negroni at home (see page 62) and you discover that not only is it as easy as 1-2-3, but all you have to pay is GP x 1, too. You may have to pay a little more for your booze than a bar does... but not *much* more. Moreover, unlike a bar, you don't have to stock stuff you don't like on the off-chance someone comes and orders it.

So a 700ml bottle of Campari is around £15. A 750ml bottle of Martini Rosso is £10. A 700ml bottle of Beefeater gin is £15. Each bottle contains 28 shots of 25ml (with 50ml leftover Martini Rosso for use in spaghetti sauces). A Negroni comprises a shot of each, which means you can make 28 Negronis for an outlay of £40, or £1.43 per Negroni. That's only a little more than a bottle of Stella Artois from the off-licence round the corner – and far less per glass than a crap bottle of wine would be.

Moreover, unlike wine, spirits keep. Once you unscrew your £5.99 Pinot Grigio, you're under pressure to finish it. An ice-cold Negroni is usually all you need. There is no need to wake up the next day and pour half a bottle of wine (that's like two Negronis!) down the sink because it sent you to sleep in front of *Call the Midwife*.

Now let's say your tastes are little more elevated. You're particular about your Martinis. The connoisseur's choice of vermouth, Dolin Dry, is £10.25 for 750ml in Waitrose. Sipsmith gin, delectable stuff, is £28 for 700ml. If you make your Martinis, for the sake of argument, with a ratio of 50ml gin to 15ml vermouth, it will average out over time to £2.18 per drink (plus the negligible expense of a few olives or lemons). That is clearly more than a bottle of Stella. It is still less than an individual 'gin in a tin' from Marks & Spencers and roughly equivalent to a stinging £7.99 New Zealand Sauvignon Blanc between four of you.

Now let's say you have developed a proper pash for cocktails. A Last Word (see page 170) requires you to invest £25 on 500ml of Chartreuse and £25 on 500ml Luxardo maraschino in addition to the gin of your choice – let's say the ultra chic Tanqueray 10, £32 for 700ml, though it's unnecessarily posh for these purposes – plus a few limes (30p each). That's an initial outlay of £82 and if you make it according to the recipe I give, it's about £4 per drink. Not cheap! But look at it this way. Champagne costs about £24 per 750ml bottle standard. People buy champagne regularly. Between six people, that's also £4 per drink. The difference is, champagne is overrated and Last Words are amazing. Moreover, you need so little of the expensive liqueurs, little more than a dash of each a time, that they will see you through a lot of cocktails. The first bottle of maraschino I ever purchased lasted me a couple of years and I felt as if I were using it constantly.

Of course, you could go much lower too. Sainsbury's own Dry London Gin recently won the IWSC Silver Outstanding medal, which means that, to the palates of the best judges, it is more delectable than Gordon's and better in its class than Sipsmith's. At the time of writing, it is £15.50 for 1 litre. If you use it to make a platoon of Gin Sours, each containing 50ml of gin, you're looking at just over 75 pence per drink, rising to as much as £1 if you factor in the cost of the eggs, lemons and sugar. It's not a bad idea to keep two bottles of gin, one super-chic one for Martini purposes and another less elite bottle for your fruitier mixes. The equation for price per measure, by the way, is bottle price (£) divided by bottle volume (ml) multiplied by the size of the measure (ml).

Still, gin has always been good value. Vodka too, as long as you don't fall for the marketing nonsense. Rum is also economical if you don't develop the taste for the 25-year-old stuff. Your other base spirits will prove more of an expense. Good brandy has always been dear – but if you're using it for Sidecars (see page 181), you don't need the *very* best brandy, you merely need a decent one. (Save your best stuff for sipping.) American whiskeys are hard to find for less than £25 a bottle but there are still bargains to be had. Aldi stock remarkably good premium spirits for pretty cheap. Online, Whisky Exchange and Master of Malt have huge ranges. If you're travelling, mainland Europe often turns up what are considered 'premium' products here for dirt cheap (1 litre of Averna Amaro for €8 in Milan Airport? *Grazie*!). There's always duty-free – use your bottle allowance for the stuff that's prohibitively expensive on land, like bourbon and cognac, rather than bottles that are frequently discounted, like gin and vodka.

As a general rule, you get what you pay for, but do bear in mind that as far as big brands go, 'what you pay for' will usually incorporate a considerable marketing budget. With a small producer, a larger percentage of your outlay will go on what's in the bottle. Choose your purchases carefully. You don't want to buy a bottle on a whim only to find you never use it – more likely to happen with liqueurs than base spirits, I find. If you are unsure, you can always order in miniature form. A 50ml sampler of Bitter Truth's Violet Liqueur, for example, is £3.50 and will provide you with enough for ten Aviations (see page 146). If you like them that much, go back for the full half-litre.

By this point, you can class it as a hobby. You should also have saved so much money on disappointing wine that you have a little left over at the end of the month for a night out on the Zombies (see page 214), leaving a nice tip at the end.

COCKTAILS AND FOOD

'Let's get something to eat – I'm thirsty!'
Nick, *After The Thin Man* (1934)

There is a simple rule when it comes to food and cocktails. It's fine to have food with cocktails. But it's appalling to have cocktails with food. I have had 'cocktail pairing' attempted on me in pretentious restaurants and it never works. 'But chef specifically…' No! 'But our mixologist has matched each of his …' No! Fetch me the wine list! Remember wine? That's what it's for. Eating.

There are various reasons why civilised people don't take their Paper Planes (see page 176) to dinner. Cocktails are typically 25% ABV, and that amount of alcohol will kill off all but the most strident flavours (even the most aggressive New World reds wimp out at 15% ABV). They should be about 3°C if they are made correctly, which is tongue-numbingly cold (white wine should be served at around 8°C). They are, for the most part, too sweet, and sugar has a dulling effect on the appetite. This is why we don't serve the raspberry trifle with the roast beef, but after it. There are few dishes that can stand up to this assault and they tend to be the ones that fight back. I quite like a G&T (see page 90) with curry. Burritos plus Margaritas (see page 171) makes sense. Freshly BBQ'd jerk chicken plus some sort of Planter's Punch (see page 227), fine. American trash cooking (dirty burgers, pulled pork, meat fries, etc) would appear to demand a Whiskey Sour (see page 67), albeit a bit like how a backed-up drain demands bleach.

In ordinary circumstances though, the cocktails should be served before dinner, when they will whet the appetite, stimulate conversation and make you anticipate pleasure to come. They shouldn't be rushed. The pregnant pause before dinner is known as 'cocktail hour' rather than 'cocktail few minutes' for a reason. In civilised countries, they call it *l'aperitivo* or *l'apéritif* and make an unfussy ceremony of it.

The no-pairing rule does not mean that cocktails should be served without nibbles. Far from it. My mother-in-law once declared that aperitif was her favourite meal of the day (she recently called her solicitor to arrange for her best friend, a Campari-and-Orange drinker, to be left aperitif money in her will). There should always be a few salted things around (*i.e.* olives, a few nuts, radishes, superior crisps – plain – and perhaps even something to dip them in). You may stretch to slightly more elaborate antipasti, as long as it does not interfere with dinner (cheese things, a few bits of charcuterie, sausages-wrapped-in-bacon, marinated artichokes). Once the proper food is ready, however, that's when the wine should emerge.

When eating out, it can be hard to ensure the sanctity of the aperitif – particularly if you're in one of those rude places where they want your table back at 9.30pm. It's not a bad idea to order two G&Ts and a few nibbly things immediately, without even looking at the menu or cocktail list. Not only will this mark you out as the sort of customer who knows what they want; it will spare you the danger of ordering some drink that on paper looked like a pleasant aperitif but made by the bartender's (unseen) hands turns out to be Calpol. It will also leave you more time to flirt, anticipate, peruse the wine list, get lost and go 'Oh God we haven't even looked yet!' when the waiter comes past to take your order, which is always a sign a meal is going well.

As for what to order, aperitif-wise, go for bitter and dry (appetite-whetting) as opposed to sweet and sour (appetite-suppressing) and err towards light spirits (as with wine, you should go darker as the evening progresses). The Negroni (see page 62) is an excellent aperitif. The Spritz (see page 75) even better. An Adonis (see page 103), a Kir (see page 223), an El Presidente (see page 115), a Tuxedo (see page 139), a Martini (wet; see page 57), a Gin & It (see page 89), a Gin & Tonic (see page 90), an Elderflower Martini (see page 115), an Alaska (see page 103), a Spring Green (see page 135), a Bijou (see page 107), a Chopin (see page 111) – these are all very fine choices. If you time it correctly, you will be sipping the last drop just as the waiter hoves into view with a nice bottle of *Vino Nobile de Montepulciano* and your starters. There now follows an interlude while you eat.

Interlude.

Once the mains are cleared away, and you've done whatever you want to do vis-à-vis cheese, and the wine bottle is drained and the waiter interrupts your mutual reverie with a shy smile to ask whether you would like to see the dessert menu... *now* is the time to call for the cocktail list. Fuck dessert. The danger of sweet cocktails ruining your appetite is passed. If you go for something sugary now, you can write it off as dessert. If you go for something dry – or even a simple Armagnac or Scotch – you simply reset.

HANGOVER MANAGEMENT

'It was one of those midsummer Sundays when everyone sits around saying, "I drank too much last night."'
John Cheever, *The Swimmer* (1964)

Hangovers, I'm afraid, are an occupational hazard of cocktailing. Much as a CIA agent may expect to get shot in the ribs once in a while, and the England footballer will miss a penalty, so the proficient consumer of cocktails will wake up, some mornings, with a dirty protest in the skull. The average British person, apparently, spends a year of their life hungover. Even the most sensible drinker will find it hard to legislate against the occasional booze-hole opening up on a work night – but if you are sensible, you needn't watch the whole week spiral into it.

Kingsley Amis, who conducted really groundbreaking research in his seminal essay on hangovers, collected in *Everyday Drinking* (1983), usefully divided the hangover into two parts: the physical and the metaphysical. The physical part refers to the parlous situation of the body (mostly caused by dehydration and exhaustion); the metaphysical part refers to what's going on in your mind (the concomitant feelings of despair and self-loathing). However, if we consider the hangover holistically, we can subdivide it into phases too.

The aftermath

the first thing to do is remind yourself how lucky you are to feel so awful, Amis says. The hangover is the receipt for your ribaldry. Then: 'If your wife or other partner is beside you, and (of course) is willing, perform the sexual act as vigorously as you can', he advises. 'The exercise will do you good, and – on the assumption that you enjoy sex – you will feel toned up emotionally, thus delivering a hit-and-run raid on your metaphysical hangover before you formally declare war on it.'

There is good science behind Amis's suggestion. As a by-product of making clammy love to your partner, you will be doing something called 'exercise'. Scientists believe that this, sometimes called a 'work-out', is beneficial. If you have no lover, Amis cautions strongly against performing the act alone (which will make the inevitable feelings of self-loathing much worse). However, I would recommend the counter-intuitive trick of going for a short run or a swim. I'm not saying that this will be easy. There will be moments when each cell in your body taps you on the shoulder and asks you in a high-pitched voice, '*Daddy, why?*' At a certain point, as you are coursing through the fresh air and the blood remembers how to flow again, they will understand. Don't overdo it though. Once round the block, or two lengths of breaststroke will do it. Remember, you are an invalid.

When you return, make a simple preparation of two tablets of Alka-Seltzer and one of Berocca, dropped into a large glass of water. I call this the Sun and Moon cure, after the appearance of the white and yellow discs, which provide most of what is needed to combat a physical hangover, namely salts, vitamins and water.

There often follows a period known as the 'false dawn', when you feel surprisingly OK. 'I feel surprisingly OK!' you will say, thoughts turning to a full English, or an Egg McMuffin. I cannot advise this. Your system may be craving salt and sugar (that's dehydration) and your stomach may be asking you please to fill it with something other than gin, but the idea that animal fat should cement that void is a pernicious myth. It may provide momentary satisfaction, but the meat-sweats will make the Inevitable Dawn far, far worse.

The same goes, I'm afraid, for the Bloody Mary, the Corpse Reviver #2, the English Breakfast Martini, the Eye-Opener, the Espresso Martini or any number of 'morning' cocktails you may be tempted to prepare. The 'hair-of-the-dog' principle is not so much a cure as a delaying tactic. What you are doing is nothing more complicated than getting pissed again. In certain situations (Ibiza, Glastonbury, the World Economic Forum, Paris Fashion Week, university, Saturday) this may be precisely what is required. However, assuming you want to be vaguely functional, fruit sugars are most effective, and banana on (wholemeal) toast is the advised breakfast (banana has the added advantage of potassium, which will help to improve your mood). Otherwise, you should become Japanese: miso soup, sushi, green tea. As a general rule, err towards brown grains, green plants and as little fat as possible. Take another Alka-Seltzer at 11am, salve your hunger with unsalted almonds, use tea (not coffee) to meet your caffeine needs, treat yourself to some of that overpriced coconut water stuff and you should be good for the noon meeting.

I'm aware that it may sound like I am punishing you further. I realise that these wholesome strictures may sound like something from a Hollywood actress's lifestyle website. However, you will thank me in the afternoon when you actually feel like a reasonable person.

If you lack the heart for the fight, however, the best thing to do is sleep. Drink water and sleep. Water and sleep.

The trauma phase

Occasionally, you manage to catch a hangover just as it's forming. You extricated yourself just before things got really messy but now you are in a double-bind. You are missing out on high jinks. However, the alcohol heretofore consumed still risks skull-fucking you in the morning. Your Physical Hangover will be a little better, but your Metaphysical Hangover will be far worse. As an A&E doctor will tell you, however, the first 60 minutes of a patient's care are the most crucial to the outcome, so you should take this moment seriously.

In these scenarios, I would recommend you take yourself firmly by the scruff of the neck, march to the kitchen tap and consume at least one pint of water. Ensure that your stomach is well-lined – not with any of the traditional 2am food groups but with bananas and brown toast. Have a shower now. It will not only leave you feeling cleaner, but also the steam will open your pores and allow your sin to evaporate. Clear away any debris. Throw away any cigarettes. Create an environment in which you will not be ashamed to wake up. If you have been hosting, do the washing up *now* if you can bear it. Leave two pints of water by your bedside, plus two Alka Seltzers and one Berocca so that you can make a Sun and Moon from a supine position in the morning.

The crash scene

Even more occasionally, you can play Paramedic, actually performing surgery on yourself at the crash scene. Assuming alcohol is a constant, eliminate everything else that will make you feel bad. Sugar is the worst offender: a night on Mojitos, champagne, Blue Raspberry WKD, cider or similar will leave you with a horrible crash. So err towards dry, clean cocktails. Likewise, cheap wine and spirits will poison you with pesticides. So drink only fine wines and spirits. Avoid beer altogether – it gives hangovers far harsher than they really deserve to be.

Prevention

It should really go without saying but you should never drink on an empty stomach. Britain is about the only country in the world where people routinely do (unless you count the odd packet of Salt and Vinegar). There is no surer way to disaster. Before you go out, I recommend two bananas and a spoonful of olive oil, which will line your stomach and prevent you from ingesting alcohol too fast.

Metaphysics

The rest is metaphysical. 'You are not sickening for anything, you have not suffered a minor brain lesion, you are not all that bad at your job, your family and friends are not leagued in a conspiracy of barely maintained silence about what a shit you are', Amis reminds you to remind yourself.

I favour one of two tactics here: the 'wallow' or the 'anti-wallow'. If you are fortunate enough to time your hangover for the weekend, try to spend your hangover lolling among people you got drunk with, who will feel exactly the same as you do. These are the moments that you will watch bad films and play Super Mario World and rip the piss out of George and fondly remember times past and occasionally go, 'Oh God I feel *terrible*...' To which everyone will reply, 'Me too!' These are the moments in which friendships are set in stone.

If you must go to work, do the precise opposite to the above: do not mention your hangover to a soul. I've a friend, Jim, who works in music festivals and so works with a bunch of headcases. He has controversially installed the policy in his workplace. Only at home time are you allowed to inform your colleagues that you were out until 4am drinking Drambuie with the Croatian women's basketball team. Moaning alone only increases the pain and makes you annoying. Take pride in sweating it out. You have earned it.

ON HOSTING

'I want to give a really bad party. I mean it. I want to give a party where there's a brawl and seductions and people going home with their feelings hurt and women passed out in the cabinet de toilette. You wait and see.'
Dick Diver in F. Scott Fitzgerald's *Tender Is the Night* (1934)

Making drinks isn't really an art, as we have discussed. Hosting is, however. It takes talent, charm and tact to be a good host. It also takes forethought, preparation and a careful application of knowledge. F. Scott Fitzgerald clearly put a lot of thought into the art of hosting. Jay Gatsby is famously the perfect host – floating rounds of cocktails; a magical Bronx machine; an orchestra playing 'yellow cocktail music'; copious pre-Prohibition liqueurs; everyone who is everyone. For my money, however, Dick Diver in *Tender Is the Night* is even more considerate. At his French Riviera parties, the happiness of every single person present seems to matter to him deeply:

> '...to be included in Dick Diver's world for a while was a remarkable experience: people believed he made special reservations about them, recognising the proud uniqueness of their destinies, buried under the compromises of how many years. He won everyone quickly with an exquisite consideration and a politeness that moved so fast and intuitively that it could be examined only in its effect. Then, without caution, lest the first bloom of the relation wither, he opened the gate to his amusing world. So long as they subscribed to it completely, their happiness was his preoccupation, but at the first flicker of doubt as to its all-inclusiveness he evaporated before their eyes, leaving little communicable memory of what he had said or done.'

So this is what you're aiming at. (Don't worry for now about the fact that Dick Diver ended up a resentful alcoholic who cheated on his wife.) In practical terms, being able to tend to each and every person does not mean prepping each person a bespoke cocktail of their choice. It's more to do with ensuring that within five minutes of entering, everyone has a drink in hand, nibbles within reach, music to listen to, someone interesting to talk to, the promise of intrigue/flirtation/sphallolalia to come and an unstressed host (*you*) who will intervene should any of these fail. How you achieve this depends on a few factors, mainly the size of your party.

For a large party, don't bother with cocktails of any complexity unless – like Gatsby – you have a platoon of staff and a mechanised cocktail kitchen. Actually, even if you do have a platoon of staff, it's still not a great idea to let them serve complex cocktails. 'If there are guests who appreciate decent cocktails, let's do the mixing ourselves', as Charles H. Baker warned. 'The amateur will always take infinitely more pains than any houseboy or butler. Trust him for such usual fare as whisky and soda, the Tom Collins and so on.'

The thing to remember, whatever your domestic situation, is that you will lose control of the serving of drinks quickly. Soon, people will be serving themselves whether you like it or not. Therefore the mainstays of your party will be beer and wine. That's fine. A flock of Highballs (see page 190) will help too. (Al Capone coined the collective noun.) It may seem obvious, but it takes people longer to drink a longer drink, which will keep them happy and you unrushed. Leave people to serve themselves. Gin and rum are cheap, ginger beer is a fine all-purpose mixer, wedges of lemon and lime cut in advance make handy garnishes, Angostura should be available for seasoning, and there should also be plenty of ice. For a serious party, the ice manufacturing process should begin about three days in advance.

If you do want to serve spirits in a fancier way, make a pretty punch well in advance, but add ice and garnish only five minutes before your first guests arrive. Nothing too thumpingly alcoholic. You might serve it from jugs; you might serve it from a bowl; you might entrust a guest to do this for you. Whichever you choose, just be sure that there's enough accessible ingredients in reserve to top it up and that it's freezing cold. If it's a winter party, a good Dickens-style hot punch will fill the house with inviting aroma and make a change from bloody mulled wine.

If you're flush, make a batch of base mix for something like a French 75 (see page 72) or a Jalisco Flower (see page 223). If you have this in a well-iced jug, you can make a Champagne Cocktail (see page 222) for each person on arrival, without too much fuss. (I'm sure they won't mind if it's only prosecco either.) A bottle of liqueur is a good shortcut to this effect. Preferred choices: crème de peche, elderflower liqueur, Aperol. Chill the liqueur bottle in advance, as you would your fizz itself.

For a medium-sized party, you may have time to make cocktails, but only if you offer one solitary option. ('Hey guys, come in, we're drinking Aviations, want one?') This way, you won't need to keep washing the shaker, and can easily top people up. I'd keep an ice bowl and a slops bowl somewhere discreet, so you can empty spent ice without too much fuss. If you're using fresh fruit juice, squeeze it an hour or so in advance and store in the fridge until ready to use. The model here, as so often, is Nick and Nora in *The Thin Man* movie. At their Christmas party, a silver tray does the rounds containing nothing but a shimmer of Martinis.

For a small party, the same general rule applies: minimise choice. You wouldn't offer a dinner guest a choice of three mains, so there's no need to offer three cocktails. Simply choose an appropriate one for an aperitif. Negronis (see page 62) before Italian; Margaritas (see page 171) before Mexican; etc. Match to season, too. A Spring Green (see page 135) in the spring; an El Presidente (see page 115) in the summer; a Jack Rose (see page 168) in the autumn; a Suburban (see page 136) in the winter?

For a genuine 'cocktail party' where you make a large range of cocktails, I'd keep the numbers of people fairly low, make sure everyone knows that there'll be a certain amount of botched attempts, and restrict yourself to a theme. Tiki Night! That way, you will have an idea of the general direction of travel and can bookmark recipes, squeeze limes, purchase garnishes, etc, well in advance. You can also choose appropriate playlists and dress in a silly hat.

In all cases, ensure there's a ready supply of water and of food to soak up the alcohol. Then you too can float around, all charm and tact, armed with bons-mots and a ready shaker, and allow your guests to entertain you. It's your party, after all.

THE INGREDIENTS

'And after dinner sweet Arabian coffee and the tray
of liqueurs; Drambuie – our favourite of all – Chartreuse, green
and yellow; Cordial Medoc, which is made from peach pits;
brandy fine; Bénédictine, Curacao, Kirschwasser and
Cointreau; and kummel in a bottle like a bear.'

Charles H. Baker, *The Gentleman's Companion* (1939)

ALCOHOLIC

The following list is not an encyclopaedia – if you want to know precisely how cognac is made and what VSOP means, I'm sure you have the wherewithal to find out. It is intended as an overview of how the most prominent varieties of booze are used in mixed drinks so the amateur cocktaileur can work out what to buy and what to make with it when they decide: 'Yes! Punt e Mes!' I've included a few ingredients not included in the recipes in this book but which make interesting additions and substitutions. Spirits vary, so I've mentioned favourite (and unfavourite) brands here and there, but make no claim to have tried them all. As ever, don't just settle for the cheapest, mistrust marketing, err towards small independent producers and never ever buy celebrity vodka.

Absinthe

Abominator of poets, destroyer of painters, deranger of teenage tourists in Prague... there is no spirit with quite so much mystique as absinthe, nor one that lives up to it so well. It's so strong – both in flavour (anise-heavy herbal) and alcohol (70 per cent ABV) – there are two ways to use it. Either you bend over and say: 'Over to you absinthe!' and allow it to have its wicked way with you in the form of an Abinsthe Suissesse (page 145) or a simple Abinsthe Drip (with sugar and water). Or you use just a few drops to impart a dry finish to anything from Martinis to Zombies. I keep a small diffuser of La Fontaine to spray a fine mist on top of cocktails – it also doubles as a mace spray for getting rid of unwanted guests. See: Arsenic and Old Lace (page 105), Bobby Burns (page 108), Chrysanthemum (page 111), Eye-Opener (page 116), Harry's Cocktail (page 118), Improved Brandy Cocktail (page 119), London Cocktail (page 123), Louisiana (page 124), Moonraker (page 126), Obituary (page 128), Remember the Maine (page 132), Sazerac (page 134), Tuxedo (page 139), Corpse Reviver #2 (page 156), Monkey Gland (page 173), Pan-American Clipper (page 176), Zombie (page 214).

Advocaat
Gloopy Dutch liqueur made from egg yolk with a brandy base. Limited use in cocktails unless you count the Christmas favourite, the Snowball (mix with lemonade).

Amaretto
An Italian almond liqueur with a taste like marzipan. Disaronno is the bestselling brand but look out for smaller producers too. It's best for after-dinner sipping (ideally with a few biscotti to dunk) but the Amaretto Sour (page 145) will please a sweet palate. Also good in milky coffee drinks, over ice cream, etc.

Amaro
Amaro is Italian for 'bitter' and refers to a category of herbal liqueurs that draw out the bitter notes from verbena, wormwood, orange peel, gentian, rhubarb – all sorts really. **Campari, Aperol** and **Cynar** are varieties of amari – but others tend to be dark in colour and tarry in texture. Averna, Amaro di Montenegro, Nonino and Rammazzotti are common brands, much cheaper in Italy than they are here. Use in place of Campari in Negroni-style drinks, add 5–10ml to any aromatic after-dinner cocktail, use in place of the Amer Picon in the Brooklyn (page 109) and see also Paper Plane (page 176) and Bumblebee (page 237).

Amber rum
Another term for **gold rum**.

Amer Picon
A bitter French orange aperitif somewhere between **Grand Marnier** and an **amaro**, sadly no longer made to the vintage recipe but still worth a sniff (it's cheap in French supermarkets). The French used to use it to make poor quality beer palatable: see Biere Picon (page 192). It also works in concert with a lighter **orange liqueur** in a Sidecar (page 181) and as a minor seventh in Manhattan-style drunks such as the Brooklyn (page 109).

Amontillado

A mid-dry style of **sherry** with a rich flavour that often calls to mind hazelnuts. It can be luscious as a substitute for vermouth. See Charco di Sangre (page 110), Consolation (page 111) Dunaway (page 113), Sylvanian Martini (page 137) Barbara West (page 148), and Fogcutter (page 197).

Angostura bitters

The AK-47 of the cocktail cabinet, used as a seasoning in too many recipes to list but more prominently in the Angostura Sour (page 96), Trinidad Sour (page 184) and Pink Gin (page 130). See Preliminaries, page 40, for full explanation.

Anisette

The generic term for any sweet anis-flavoured liqueur (not to be confused with absinthe, which is an anis-flavoured spirit). Most Mediterranean countries have a version: **ouzo, pastis, raki, sambuca,** etc. Keep away from cocktails.

Aperol

In the last few years, Aperol has gone from unhip European exchange student with an embarrassing bumbag to everyone's best friend. It's so obliging! It's the gentlest style of **amaro,** brighter and more orangey than the similar **Campari** and as such tends to work better in sours. The Aperol Spritz (page 221) is the classic expression. See also the Aperol Sour (page 146), Naked & Famous (page 173), Paper Plane (page 176), Two-One-Two (page 185) and Wah-Wah (page 186).

Apple brandy

Aged spirit distilled from cider apples. Used as a base in many cocktails, it brings a rustic influence to the urban business of mixing and works well in both heavy aromatic drinks and sours. There are three main styles: French **calvados** (which can reach cognac-like levels of refinement); American **applejack** (which is usually cut with neutral spirit, leaving it bland); and English **cider brandy** (crisp and subtly acidic). I've used the generic term apple brandy throughout this book though the provenance of the apples obviously makes a huge difference. Somerset Royal Cider Brandy is my pick of them all. See Avenue B (variation, page 82), Consolation (page 111), Corpse Reviver #1 (page 112), Jack Rose (page 168), Pan-American Clipper (page 176), Widow's Kiss (page 140), Diki-Diki (page 162), Golden Dawn (166), Pink Lady (page 178), Delicious (page 196) and Wassail Bowl (page 229).

Applejack

See Apple Brandy (opposite). Laird's is feted though no match for a good calvados or cider brandy in my opinion.

Apple liqueur

The Basque styles (Manzana Verde) can be excellent. Try a splash in an Elderflower Martini? Avoid the ones with names like Sourz Apple unless you fancy making a round of Appletinis (page 239).

Apricot brandy

Apricots are erratic little things in fruit form but delicious steeped in alcohol – and apricot brandy is among the most useful liqueurs you can buy. Its softness chimes well with the sharpness of citrus (particularly limes), the melancholia of gin, the tropical fun of rums and the moodiness of dark spirits. It's worth paying a little more for a good brand as the cheaper ones can by cloying: Gabriel Boudier's Abricot de Roussillon is heavenly, while Rothman & Winter's Orchard Apricot Liqueur is beautifully fresh. Nymph (page 127), Skid Row (135), Barnum Was Right (page 148), Charlie Chaplin (page 155), Dulchin (page 162), Golden Dawn (page 166), Toreador (page 184), Apricot Rickey (page 192).

Aquavit

The Scandinavian cousin of gin. It's distilled from grain spirit or potatoes, introduced to a range of botanicals – predominantly caraway, dill and anise – and often aged. Traditionally drunk ice-cold with bits of pickled fish, its strong flavour and savoury profile is winning favour among the cocktail cognoscenti. It works in place of gin in vegetal creations such such as the Celery Cocktail (page 109) but also in tequila and rum contexts (try splitting the base of a Margarita to half aquavit). The aged Linie brand makes a mean Old Fashioned (page 63) with a dash of **pimento dram** too.

Armagnac
A superior *appellation* of aged French brandy, lighter than cognac and best appreciated *au naturel* due to its price. If you are feeling decadent, use in place of **brandy** in your cocktails.

Arrack
Love-it-or-hate-it Indonesian rice spirit. It's hard to find nowadays but was once commonplace as an ingredient in early punch recipes. It is also the principal ingredient in **Swedish Punsch.**

Aromatic bitters
The generic term for cocktail bitters in the traditional style. **Angostura** dominates the market but look out too for alternatives such as the Bitter Truth's Jerry Thomas Decanter Bitters and the revived Boker's Bitters.

Baiju
Unforgivable Chinese hell-juice distilled from fermented rice. The sheer size of the Chinese population ensures that this is the third bestselling spirit in the world, after vodka and Scotch. It doesn't, however, make it any less rank.

Batavia arrack
See **arrack**

Beer
I'm not a fan of beer cocktails, more on ideological than taste grounds; I just think we need to keep a few things back as an unponcy alternative to cocktails. Still, it can be an interesting ingredient to use in

long drinks in place of fizzy water. Biere Picon (page 192), Shaky Pete's Ginger Brew (page 210), Purl (page 228).

Becherovka
A cult Czech herbal and honey liqueur – use like **Bénédictine** in aromatic drinks.

Bénédictine
One of the world's great secret recipes and a benchmark for herbal liqueurs. Bénédictine has been made by happy monks since the 16th century and combines spice, warmth and honey. It's lovely on its own or paired with brandy in a B&B (page 106), the classic 'throw-together' drink. It also finds its way into numerous cocktails, from tropical slings and aromatic aperitifs but mostly hefty digestifs. Bobby Burns (page 108), Chrysanthemum (page 111), Louisiana (page 124), Poet's Dream (page 131), Vieux Carré (page 139), Widow's Kiss (page 140), Nursery Plush (page 174), Papa Ghiradelli (page 205), Singapore Sling (page 211).

Blue curacao
Almost exclusively used in 'tiki' drinks, blue curacao is essentially regular **curacao** with blue food colouring. Why? Because why not! Plus it's fun to wind up vintage cocktail types by subbing it in recipes that call for regular **orange liqueur**, serving them Blue Sidecars (page 181) and Blue Corpse Revivers (page 156).

Bourbon
Sweet, toothsome American whiskey from the South, generally more approachable than **rye**. See Preliminaries (page 36) for a fuller paean. Used in Manhattan (page 59), Old Fashioned (page 63), Sour (page 65), Mint Julep (page 71), Avenue B (page 82), Bacon Old Fashioned (page 95), Algonquin (page 104), Boulevardier (page 108), Brooklyn (page 109), Louisiana (page 124), Nymph (page 127), Saratoga (page 134), Sazerac (page 134), Suburban (page 136), Vieux Carré (page 139), Purgatory (see Widow's Kiss, page 140), Amaretto Sour (page 145),

Brown Derby (page 153), Cherry Bomb (page 156), Paper Plane (page 176), Scofflaw (page 180), Ward Eight (page 186), Ginger Alexander (page 165), Plush (page 208).

Brandy

Brandy is the generic term for spirit distilled from fruits – but it's usually used to mean fermented grape juice (ie wine) that has been distilled and aged. French cognac is the most distinguished form. A decent one such as Courvoisier VSOP or Hennessey will do wonders for serious after-dinner drinks such as the Sazerac (page 134) but if you're shaking it around in Sidecar (page 181), you can get away with a less elevated variety such as Three Barrels. The Spanish, Americans and South Africans also make perfectly respectable (and cheaper) varieties and there's usually more value in small producers. See also Ampersand (page 105), B&B (page 106), BCC (page 107), Corpse Reviver #1 (page 112), East India (page 114), Eye-Opener (page 116), Improved Brandy Cocktail (page 119), Japanese Cocktail (page 120), Metropolitan (page 126), Moonraker (page 126), Pablo Alvarez de Canas Special (page 129), Saratoga (page 134), Sazerac (page 134), Stinger (page 136), Stomach Reviver (page 136), Vieux Carré (page 139), Brandy Daisy (page 195), Fog Cutter (page 197), Sangaree (page 209), Dickens's Flaming Punch (page 225), Fish House Punch (page 226), Champagne Cocktail (page 222), Between the Sheets (page 149), Brandy Fix (page 152), Flip (page 164), Brandy Alexander (page 151), Pousse Café (page 237).

Byrrh

A splendid variety of **quinquina.**

Cachaça

Brazilian rum, made from fermented sugar cane juice as opposed to molasses. Almost always inferior to **rhum agricole** but it's fine in a Caipirinha (page 153) or a Batida (page 148).

Calvados
The superior French style of **apple brandy** from Normandy.

Campari
A bright red bitter Italian liqueur of the first rank – see Preliminaries
(page 39). Recipes: Americano (page 61), Negroni (page 62), Spritz
(page 75), Boulevardier (page 108), Lucien Gaudian (page 124), Rosita
(page 133), Sbagliato (page 223), Campari Smash (page 154), Teresa
(page 182), Jungle Bird (page 200), Papa Ghirardelli (page 205),
Sprezzamatura (page 212).

Chambord
A kitsch French black raspberry liqueur with a slight vanilla nose and a
bottle shaped like a holy hand grenade. Sub **crème de cassis** or **cherry
brandy** if you're lacking. See French Martini (page 165).

Champagne
See **Sparkling wine.**

Chartreuse (green)
Heavenly herbal liqueur made, for reasons best known to themselves,
by silent Carthusian monks in Voirons, south-east France. The green
variety is made to a hefty 55% ABV with dominant notes of menthol,
thyme and 100 other inscrutable and suggestive plants. Unchanging
over centuries, the original recipe is apparently locked in a bank vault
in Switzerland. It was fashionable in the 1920s – it is cited by both
Evelyn Waugh and F. Scott Fitzgerald – and despite its price (£30+)
worth investing in as nothing is quite like it. Art of Choke (page 106),
Bijou (page 107), Spring Green (page 135), Tipperary (page 137),
Widow's Kiss (page 140), Champagne Cocktail (page 222), Brandy Fix
(page 152), Champs-Elysées (page 155), Last Word (page 170),
Nuclear Daiquiri (page 174), Chartreuse Swizzle (page 195),
Green Wing (page 198).

Chartreuse (yellow)

It may be less celebrated than its enigmatic green sibling, but yellow Chartreuse is still a delicious elixir. It comes in at a lower ABV (40%) and has a more arboreal taste, redolent of pine trees and flowering meadows. It goes well with gin, grapefruit and lemon. Alaska (page 103), Pacific Coast Highway (page 129), Skid Row (page 135), Widow's Kiss (page 140), Last Word (variation, page 170), Naked and Famous (page 173).

Cherry brandy

One of the more useful liqueurs, luscious and ripe at its best and excellent in non-cocktail contexts too. Comes dry and sweet. The most praised brand is Cherry Heering from Denmark; I also like Luxardo's. Its most classic uses come in the Blood & Sand (page 150) and the Singapore Sling (page 211), while a Cherry Bomb (page 156) is a good way of bringing it to the fore. Also Pablo Alvarez de Canas Special (page 129), Remember the Maine (page 132), Rose (page 132).

Cider brandy

The English style of **apple brandy.**

Chocolate liqueur

See **crème de cacao.**

Coffee liqueur

Coffee liqueurs can be made from a neutral base (Tia Maria), rum (Kahlua), tequila (Patron Café) and even cognac (Grand Brulot). In coffee cocktails such as the Espresso Martini (page 163) or White Russian (page 214), I'd always opt for fresh coffee rather than liqueurs (which can taste a bit 'instant'). Still, **Kahlua** does chime interestingly with lime in the Daiquiri Mulata (page 161) and a number of Tiki-style drinks too.

Cognac

Superior **brandy**, made in the Cognac region of France, rated VS (expensive), VSOP (really expensive) and XO (taking the piss). The market is dominated by a few large houses – Courvoisier, Hennessey, Martell and Remy Martin, principally – but you'll find more value with smaller producers.

Cointreau

By far the most useful **orange liqueur**, thrice distilled, colourless, absolutely razor sharp in flavour. It's not cheap (c£25) but you rarely need more than 15ml at a time so one bottle will last a while. The sweetness should not blind you to its strength (40% ABV), meaning it is a more than willing accessory to mischief in Margaritas and White Ladies. See **orange liqueur** for the full recipe list.

Crème (general)

Crèmes are liqueurs made in south-east France. The term has nothing to do with cream but is used in the 'crème de la crème' sense to mean the best part of whatever fruit, nut, flower or leaf they lob into their vats. Superior producers include Edmund de Briottet, Marie Brizard, Giffard and Gabriel Boudier. Nowadays, their ranges run into exoticisms such as papaya and hibiscus flower but look out too for local specialities such as coqueillage (poppy) and sapin (fir tree).

Crème de cacao (white)

The lighter style of chocolate liqueur – at its best fairly dry. Chocolate Martini (page 110), Florida (page 165), Grasshopper (page 166).

Crème de cacao (dark)

The richer style of chocolate liqueur, usually sweeter and more viscose and as such mainly used in liquid desserts such as the Brandy Alexander (page 151) and my Ginger Alexander (page 165). It's also good in a Daiquiri Mulata (page 161) while a dash works well as a sub for **Bénédictine** in rich drinks such as the Vieux Carré (page 139).

Crème de cassis

Blackcurrant is one of the most popular liqueurs, partly due to its

inclusion in the Kir and Kir Royale (page 223). It's also good as a
sweetener for brandy (see BCC, page 107). Gabriel Boudier's is
excellent, and available widely for not very much money. Also: Charco
di Sangre (page 110), Sangre di Agave (page 180), Teresa (page 182).

Crème de fraise
Strawberry liqueur is fairly common but has limited use in classic
cocktails (fresh strawberries usually work better). Still, adding 10ml to
a Negroni (page 62) is good.

Crème de framboise
Raspberry liqueur. Goes well with brandy – a touch of vermouth will
bridge the gap.

Crème de menthe
Among the most popular liqueurs at 1970s dinner parties, partly due to
the palate-cleansing qualities of mint. It comes either clear ('blanche')
or green ('verte'), the colour being the only difference (instead of
investing in a bottle of each, purchase some a clear menthe and a small
bottle of green food colouring). You can make your own easily by
leaving around 30 mint leaves to macerate overnight in 250ml vodka
(any longer and the mixture will turn bitter), sweetening with white
sugar syrup to taste. Pre-eminent in the Grasshopper (page 166) and the
Stinger (page 136) as well as the Eye-Opener (page 116).

Crème de mure
Blackberry liqueur. Combines with gin to form a taste of an English
hedgerow very effectively in the Bramble (page 151).

Crème de noisette
Hazelnut liqueur. Good in Flips and Alexanders and White Russians.

Crème de noyaux
Made from the kernels of apricot or peach stones, which have an
almond-like taste (they're also used in **amaretto**). It's pale pink in colour

and hard to source outside of France – sub anything almondy if you can't find it. Old Etonian (page 128).

Crème de peche
Peach liqueur. The superior stuff is called Crème de Peche de Vigne. A drop in a Mint Julep (page 71) is heavenly. It goes superbly with sparkling wine too and works in most apricot brandy contexts too. See also Consolation (page 111), Moonraker (page 126), One Way (page 175) and Baby (page 192).

Crème de roses
If you overdo rose it can taste like soap but a little can be poetic. You can make a serviceable homemade version by leaving a ten lumps of (good) Turkish delight to melt over a week in 250ml vodka and straining the results. See Pink Rabbit (page 130) and Campari Smash (page 154).

Crème de violette
Indigo in colour, with a taste like My Little Ponies and grandmothers, violette is one of those vintage ingredients that was impossible to find until a few years ago and is now a little overused. (At the time of writing, one of Jamie Oliver's restaurants is offering a 'Parma Violet Spritz'. No.) Use it sparingly, however, and it's wistful and compelling in gin contexts – Arsenic & Old Lace (page 105), Trilby (page 138), Aviation (page 146) – and it's worth trying a drop in place of the orange flower water in a Ramos Gin Fizz too (page 87) which gives you a Violet Fizz. Also weirdly good with dark rum.

Cuaranta y Tres
AKA Licor 43. A delicious toffee/vanilla scented Spanish liqueur.

Curacao
A Dutch style of orange liqueur from the Caribbean island of the same name. Most styles (whether clear, orange or blue) are sweet but you can buy Dry Curacao. See **orange liqueur.**

Cynar

An Italian **amaro,** much prized among discerning barkeeps and notable for the inclusion of artichoke in its list of ingredients (not that you can really taste it). Use in place of Campari or Aperol – or appreciate its particular dark-hued affinity with rum in the Art of Choke (page 106) with chocolate in the Edward I (page 115) and with sherry in the Dunaway (page 113).

Dark rum

I've used dark rum here to mean aged rum of the sort used in traditional punches and Tiki drinks. Styles vary according to the colonial sphere of influence (English rums tend to be heavier than Spanish rums, for example), the specific island (English rums from St Croix and Antigua might be lighter than those from Jamaica and Barbados) and then the distillery, age and expression. One year of ageing in the wild Caribbean climate is said to be worth three in a chilly Scottish barrel so it makes a huge difference whether a rum is five or 12 years old. A medium-bodied dark rum such as El Dorado 8-year (Guyana), Havana Club 8-year (Cuba) or Appleton V/X (Jamaica) will cover most cocktail bases – but look out too for the premium styles from Ron Zacapa (Guatemala), Angostura (Trinidad) and Diplomatico (Venezuela). See Corn'n'Oil (page 112), Suburban (page 136), Dickens's Flaming Punch (page 225), Fish House Punch (page 226), Planter's Punch (page 227), Airmail (page 220), Daiquiri-Mulata (page 161), Daiquiri de Maracuja (page 161), Kingston Cocktail (page 169), Pina Colada #2 (page 206), Sangre de Agava (page 180), Jungle Bird (page 200), Navy Grog (page 204), Rum Punch (page 208), Mai Tai (page 202), Zombie (page 214). Rum loves to mix so will work well in place of any other brown spirit in Rum Old Fashioneds, Rum Manhattans, Rum Juleps, etc.

Drambuie

A Scotch whisky liqueur sweetened with honey, heather and herbs. In the golden age of the cocktail, Drambuie was among the most prized of liqueurs, a sort of Scotch take on Bénédictine. (Charles H Baker cited it as his favourite). Somewhere down the years, the recipe changed and it became oversweet so should be used sparingly. Hopefully its new owners will reformulate the recipe to its former glory. Until then, you can approximate old Drambuie by stirring 90ml blended Scotch (Chivas if you want to be accurate) with 10ml Islay malt and 20ml of the best honey you can find and leaving a fresh rosemary sprig to macerate in it for a day or two before straining. See Bobby Burns (page 108), Rusty Nail (page 133), Cotonian (page 157).

Dubonnet
The most widespread variety of **quinquina** much loved by the Queen of England who has two baths in it per day. (Her signature Gin & Dubonnet is equal parts of each with a slice of lemon). It's delicious stuff and versatile too but the Royal connection and a slightly naff label means it doesn't quite get the credit it deserves. Due a reboot? Recipes under **quinquina**.

Eau-de-vie
The generic name for fruit- or grain-based distillate, literally 'Water of Life'. You'll find varieties all over Europe. Plum from the Balkans is **slivovitz**. Cherry from Germany is **kirsch**. Pear eaux-de-vie are particularly worth tracking down – the best I have tasted is made by Slovenian monks and known as Pleterje. It comes complete with a whole Williams Pear in the bottle and consorts happily with Zubrowka, apple brandy and orchard flavours.

Elderflower liqueur
I'm not sure who has been marketing elderflower these past few years, but fair play. What was once a niche country pursuit has now supplanted orange squash as the cordial of choice in fashionable English households. It also makes a lovely liqueur – the brandy-based St Germain is preeminent and comes in an elegant art deco-style bottle. It chimes very effectively with gin, Zubrowka, pear eau-de-vie and orchard liqueurs. Elderflower Martini (page 115), Referendum (page 131), Spring Green (page 135), Jalisco Flower (page 223), Wah-Wah (page 186), Twinkle (page 224).

Falernum

A low-alcohol (10–15%) rum-based liqueur/cordial from Jamaica and Barbados flavoured with lime, almond, cloves and ginger. Taylor's Velvet Falernum is the most common variety (available online for £10 or so) and is among the essential weapons in the Tiki bar. Its simplest application is in the Corn'n'Oil (page 112) in which it sweetens dark rum. See also Nuclear Daiquiri (page 174), Chartreuse Swizzle (page 195) and Zombie (page 214).

Farigoule

Dry thyme liqueur from Provence, well worth the investment if you happen to be in that part of the world. Good in place of Chartreuse in Last Word variations (page 170) while a dash or two lends a dry herbal mystery to a G&T (page 90). See also Consolation (page 111).

Fernet-Branca

Love-it-or-hate-it Italian **amaro**, distinctive for its medicinal taste of menthol and tree bark and its relative lack of sweetness. In Argentina it is the national drink (they tend to mix it with Coke). In cocktails it tends to be used exceedingly sparingly – see the Fernando (page 116), Hanky Panky (page 118) and Stomach Reviver (page 136) – but it takes centre stage in the alien soda Fernet Sling (page 196). A dash in an Old Fashioned (page 63) gives you a Toronto and it is an optional note in the Ping-Pong (page 130) and the Stinger (page 136).

Fino

The driest style of **sherry** is capable of standing up to headier cocktail ingredients and works almost equally well as a low-alcohol base and as a superdry alternative to French vermouth (with a tiny dash of sugar, perhaps). Sherry Cobbler (page 210), Baby (page 192), Adonis (page 103), Bamboo (page 106), Dunaway (page 113), Pablo Alvarez de Canas Special (page 129), Spring Green (page 135), Tuxedo (page 139), Figaro (page 164), Bloody Mary (page 193).

Frangelico
An indulgent Italian hazelnut digestif (ie **crème de noisette**) that comes in a silly bottle shaped like a monk. Use in Flips and Alexanders.

French vermouth
The drier style of vermouth. See Preliminaries (page 38). It is the difference between gin and a Martini (page 57), but tends to be used to bridge the gap between base spirits and other modifiers – though it is the star player in the Chrysanthemum (page 111). See Bronx (page 77), Clover Club (page 69), Affinity (page 103), Algonquin (page 104), Arsenic & Old Lace (page 105), Bamboo (page 106), Old Pal (Boulevardier variation, page 108), Brooklyn (page 109), Earl Grey Martini (page 114), Elderflower Martini (page 115), El Presidente (page 115), Journalist (page 120), Kangaroo (page 121), Lucien Gaudin (page 124), Obituary (page 128), Ping-Pong (page 130), Poet's Dream (page 131), Rose (page 132), Tuxedo (page 139), Chanticleer (page 155), Cotonian (page 157), Holland House (page 168), Scofflaw (page 180).

Galliano L'Autentico
An Italian herbal liqueur with notes of butterscotch and vanilla in the same loose family as **Yellow Chartreuse** and **Strega** (though sweeter). The formula has recently been revised back to its old proof meaning it's a lot more subtle than it was. Fernando (page 116).

Genepi
A French herbal concoction. You can pick it up in French supermarkets either in the form of liqueurs or sometimes as a cordial. Close to **Yellow Chartreuse** in taste.

Genever
The Dutch style of gin is markedly different from the English styles that it spawned. Although juniper berries are the predominant botanical influence in both, genever has a much more pronounced grain flavour that's malty and rustic, closer to whisky or pre-industrial styles of vodka. Bols Genever dates back to 1575 and tastes suitably historical.

If you make a Genever Old Fashioned you're making the original 'cocktail' (page 63). Genever also makes an interesting variant on the Martinez (page 125) and the Tom Collins (which makes it a John Collins, page 74). See also Skid Row (page 135), and Holland House (page 168).

Gin

Mother's ruin. See Preliminaries (page 35). Martini (page 57), Negroni (page 62), Sour (page 65), Green Park (page 67), Clover Club (page 69), French 75 (page 72), Tom Collins/Gin Fizz (page 74), Bronx (page 77), Ginger Rogers Punch (page 81), Gimlet (page 84), Army & Navy (page 86), Ramos Gin Fizz (page 87), Gin & It (page 89), Gin & Tonic (page 90), 'Pin' (page 92), English Breakfast Martini (page 94), Alaska (page 103), Ampersand (page 105), Arsenic & Old Lace (page 105), Bijou (page 107), Celery Cocktail (page 109), Cucumber Cocktail (page 113), Earl Grey Martini (page 114), Gin Cocktail (page 117), Gin & Pine (page 117), Hanky Panky (page 118), Harry's Cocktail (page 118), Journalist (page 120), London Cocktail (page 123), Lucien Gaudin (page 124), Obituary (page 128), Old Etonian (page 128), Pink Gin (page 130), Poet's Dream (page 131), Rose (page 132), Sylvanian Martini (page 137), Trilby (page 138), Tuxedo (page 139), Purl (page 228), Aperol Sour (page 146), Aviation (page 146), Bacardi Special (page 147), Barbara West (page 148), Barnum Was Right (page 148), Bee's Knees (page 149), Bramble (page 151), Chanticleer (page 155), Charlie Chaplin (page 155), Corpse Reviver #2 (page 156), Golden Dawn (page 166), Ideal (page 168), Last Word (page 170), Monkey Gland (page 173), One Way (page 175), Opal (page 175), Pegu Club (page 177), Red Lion (page 179), Silver Bullet (page 182), Vesper (page 185), White Lady (page 187), Pink Lady (page 178), Apricot Rickey (page 192), Black G&T (page 193), Fog Cutter (page 197), Green Isaacs Special (page 198), Long Island Iced Tea (page 201), Shaky Pete's Ginger Brew (page 210), Singapore Sling (page 211), Southside Fizz (page 212), Twentieth Century (page 241).

Ginger liqueur

The King's Ginger is a fabulous example. Substitute ginger syrup (page 117) if you don't have. See Ginger Alexander (page 165) and Penicillin (page 177).

Ginger wine

A favourite of wartime granddads, not bad with hot water when you're under the weather in a country pub. See Whisky Mac (page 140).

Gold rum

The term for **dark rum** that is dark but not that dark… usually aged three to five years. Sometimes called amber rum. I've tended to use the term dark rum as a catch-all but gold rum work well in light contexts such as El Presidentes too (page 115).

Grand Marnier

A venerable **orange liqueur** made from a base of aged **brandy** which gives it a rather more august taste than **Cointreau** or **curacao**. While these orange liqueurs tend to be used to sweeten cocktails, almost like sugar syrup, Grand Marnier works better as a warming herbal note, used sparingly (a bit like **Bénédictine**) to add depth and grandeur. It's worth trying a teaspoon in cocktails such as the Gin & It (page 89), the El Presidente (page 115), the classic Champagne Cocktail (page 222), or even a Sidecar (page 181). See also Ampersand (page 105), Bamboo (page 106), East India (page 114), Dulchin (page 162), Red Lion (page 179), Cosmopolitan (page 157).

Grappa

A clear, dry Italian spirit made from the leftover bits from winemaking (pips, seeds, stalks). It's a fine digestivo and makes a good Sour too (page 65… a grappa sour is known as a Fellini). The Nardini brand is recommended and makes some wonderful infused grappas such as **Mandorla**.

Holland(s) gin
See **genever.**

Irish whiskey
I feel sorry for Irish whiskey, which sort of falls between two stools when it comes to cocktail making. It's less distinctive than **Scotch** but lacks the homely sweetness of **bourbon,** and as such has tended to end up in St Patrick's day specials and Irish Coffee. Still, you can use it in place of either with success (a Manhattan made with Irish whiskey is called an Emerald) and the Tipperary makes it a star (page 137).

Islay Scotch
The finest single malt Scotches are wasted as base ingredients in cocktails (go for a decent blend instead) but the smoky-peaty profile of Islay malts (eg Laphraoig, Bowmore, Kilchoman) makes them useful for seasoning. A tiny dash is transformative in a Grosvenor (page 118) and a Penicillin (page 177) and it's worth trying the same technique with any other cocktail you would like to taste 'smoked' (see Jack Rose, page 168). As a base, Islay makes a weird and wonderful Last Word variant, too (page 170).

Italian vermouth
See Preliminaries, page 38. Recipes: Manhattan (page 59), Americano (page 61), Negroni (page 62), Bronx (page 77), Gin & It (page 89), Adonis (page 103), Affinity (page 103), Ampersand (page 105), Bijou (page 107), Bobby Burns (page 108), Boulevardier (page 108), Corpse Reviver #1 (page 112), Hanky Panky (page 118), Harry's Cocktail (page 118), Journalist (page 120), Louisiana (page 124), Martinez (page 125), Metropolitan (page 126), Ping-Pong (page 130), Remember the Maine (page 132), Rob Roy (page 132), Rosita (page 133), Saratoga (page 134), Tipperary (page 137), Trilby (page 138), Vieux Carré (page 139), Sbagliato (page 223), Blood & Sand (page 150), La Florida (page 165), Ideal (page 168), Vowel (page 186), Bloody Mary (page 193), Fernet Sling (page 196), Papa Ghiradelli (page 205).

Jagermeister

A bitter German liqueur. While it is widely seen as a punishment drink, you can use it a little like **Fernet-Branca.**

Jamaican rum

Any rum made on the island of Jamaica. The big distilleries are Appleton Estate, Myers and J. Wray and Nephew. In old recipes, it will always denote **dark rum** of the richest and spiciest kind.

Japanese whisky

Japan's whisky industry is now considered to be a serious rival to Scotland's at the upper end. Save the expensive stuff for home sipping or drink in a Japanese-style Highball (with fizzy water) or Mizuwari (page 202).

Kahlua

There's a lovely scene in the latter series of *Mad Men* where Don arrives at Megan's new place in Los Angeles and finds a bottle of Kahlua. He looks at it a little disgusted... what is this? It's rum-based **coffee liqueur,** popular in Tiki drinks (coffee + lime + rum = surprisingly good). See **coffee liqueur** for full list of recipes.

Kamm & Sons

Devised by London bartender and man-about-town Alex Kammerling, Kamm & Sons is a unique liqueur-spirit hybrid with an inscrutable list of ingredients including ginseng and manuka honey. It's very well balanced on its own but works well as a light **amaro.** See Brit Spritz (page 222) and the Grosvenor (page 118).

Kina Lillet

The old name for **Lillet,** specified in numerous vintage cocktails including Ian Fleming's Vesper (page 185) – for which reason old bottles are highly sought after. Lillet reformulated the recipe in the 1980s and many claim that Cocchi Americano is closer to what it once was.

Kirsch or Kirschswasser

German cherry eau de vie, required in *Schwarzwaldekirshtorten* and in fondue. Tends to fade in all but the lightest cocktails.

Kummel

A historic style of caraway liqueur from Northern Europe, popular among Russian nobility and a mainstay of 19th century liqueur cabinets. (It used to come in a variety of bear-shaped bottles.) It also has a cult following among golfers. The leading brand now is Wolfschmidt which has one of my favourite bottles. In cocktails it's easily overbearing so the best bet is to cast it as the lead player, as in the Silver Bullet (page 182) or the Vowel (page 186) but it slips well into a tropical context in the Kingston Cocktail (page 169) and the Martiki (page 125). The Stomach Reviver (page 136).

Light rum

Light rum has a much livelier and fruitier flavour than dark rum. It's usually aged but only for a short while and then charcoal filtered to remove the colour. It's the most playful spirit and tends to be made best in the Spanish Caribbean (Cuba, Puerto Rico, Guatemala, etc) though light rums from Guyana are sensational. Sadly, it is not well represented by the leading brand (Bacardi), which betrays a noble heritage with an inferior product. Opt instead for Havana Club 3-year, Flor de Cana Extra Dry or El Dorado 3-year and you will see why people once got so crazy for the stuff. The quintessential expression is the Daiquiri (see page 158) while the aromatic El Presidente (see page 115) makes a delectable summertime alternative to a Martini. See also: Art of Choke (page 106), Martiki (page 125), King's Jubilee (Aviation variation, page 147), Bacardi Special (page 147), Between the Sheets (page 149), Daiquiri Frozen (page 160), Daiquiri Passion (page 161), Daiquiri Strawberry (page 160), Florida (page 165), Hemmingway Daiquiri (page 167), Hurricane (page 200), Mary Pickford (page 172), Nuclear Daiquiri (page 174), Oh Gosh! (page 175), Santiago (page 180), Long Island Iced Tea (page 201), Mojito (page 203), Navy Grog (page 204), Pina Colada #1 (page 206).

Lillet Blanc

A bright, lemony aromatised wine with a pronounced sauvignon blanc flavour, formerly known as **Kina Lillet**. It's similar to **sweet white vermouth** in style so feel free to sub. Celery Cocktail (page 109), Nymph (page 127), Corpse Reviver #2 (page 156), Vesper (page 185).

Limoncello

Italian dessert liqueur made by leaving Amalfi lemon peels to macerate in grain spirit and then adding sugar. Best drunk straight from the freezer. Look out too for orange and grapefruit versions of the same (arancello and pompelcello).

London Dry gin

The dominant style of mixing gin. See Preliminaries, page 36, for a fuller explanation.

Mandorla

A variety of 50 per cent ABV almond-infused grappa made by the Nardini family that comes into its own in the Mandorla Sour (page 171).

Maraschino

A sweet, clear liqueur made from marasca cherries (flesh and stones) from Croatia. The Luxardo brand is the most common but hasn't made it to the supermarkets (yet). It has a strong and distinctive taste – funky, floral, a little almondy – and was used all the time by old-time bartenders as a general purpose sweetener. These days, you can generally tell someone who's serious about cocktails by whether they own a bottle of maraschino. It is most distinctive in the Aviation (page 146) and the Last Word (page 170) and adds a dash of sweetness to the Martinez (page 125). See also Brooklyn (page 109), Dunaway (page 113), East India (page 114), Improved Brandy Cocktail (page 119), Tuxedo (page 139), Daiquiri Frozen (page 160), Hemingway Daiquiri (page 167), Holland House (page 168), Ideal (page 168), Lima Sour (page 167), Mary Pickford (page 172).

Mezcal

Like tequila but rougher, mezcal is an (over-rated) agave-based spirit from Mexico with a large hipster cult. It is usually unaged and has a potent flavour of smoke, petrol and rubber but the better varieties (there are numerous artisanal producers) will give way to a spiky agave hit. Like single malt Scotches, it works better as a smoky side note than as a base in cocktails. See Oaxaca Old Fashioned (page 127) and the Pacific Coast Highway (page 129). The Naked and Famous brings it into head-on collision with other strong flavours (page 173). A drop in a Bloody Mary and a Margarita works well too.

Midori

Green melon liqueur, popular in pretentious Asian restaurants. Approach with caution.

Mozart Dry

Mozart is an excellent Austrian producer of chocolate liqueurs and spirits. The brown crème de cacao is the gold standard but look out too for their unique chocolate distillate which is made a little like gin – it's full of chocolate flavour but completely dry. See Chocolate Martini (page 110), Edward I (page 115).

Navy rum

The term used to denote the potent style of **dark rum** found in British Navy rations. Pusser's from the British Virgin Islands is a good example.

Old Tom gin

The most popular style of gin in Victorian London, symbolised by a black cat and made to a sweeter recipe than the classic London Dry style that prevails today. The sweeter style means this was mainly sipped neat or with water – but it's used in plenty of old cocktails, notably the Tom Collins (page 74). Hayman's is recommended. Use in gin contexts, especially in the Green Park (page 67), Ampersand (page 105), Gin Cocktail (page 117), and Trilby (page 138).

Orange bitters

A very common style of bitters that disappeared from view in the cocktail dark ages but has been revived by canny producers such as Fee Brothers, Gaz Regan and Bitter Truth. While Angostura-style bitters are usually used to deepen flavours, orange bitters bring brightness and lift most notably to the traditional Martini (page 57). They can be a little shy, so use a liberal hand. If you have none, you can approximate the effect with a spritz of orange peel. Adonis (page 103), Alaska (page 103), Ampersand (page 105), Chopin (page 111), Consolation (page 111), London Cocktail (page 123), Metropolitan (page 126), Old Etonian (page 128), Ping-Pong (page 130), Suburban (page 136), Trilby (page 138), Tuxedo (page 139), Opal (page 175), Pegu Club (page 177) and Scofflaw (page 180).

Orange liqueur

The single most versatile liqueur there is, pre-eminent in the Sidecar (page 181), the Margarita (page 171) and the White Lady (page 187). Like maraschino, orange liqueur is used almost analogously to sugar syrup to sweeten both sour and aromatic style cocktails while imparting a citrusy warmth. The Dutch style is known as **curacao**, the French as **triple sec** and you can find more specifically formulated varieties such as the rhum agricole-based Clement Creole Orange Shrub and the brandy based **Grand Marnier**. I favour **Cointreau** as a general purpose orange liqueur. See Journalist (page 120), Lucien Gaudin (page 124), Between the Sheets (page 149), Corpse Reviver #2 (page 156), Florida (page 165), Knickerbocker (page 169), Oh Gosh! (page 175), Opal (page 175), Pegu Club (page 177), Cosmopolitan (page 157), Long Island Iced Tea (page 201), and Mai Tai (page 202).

Ouzo

Rank Greek anis liqueur. See **anisette**.

Overproof rum

Ordinary rum is distilled to very high proofs and then watered down so as not to kill anyone. With overproof rum, they don't water it down, meaning it comes in as high as 70% ABV, packing in a ton of flavour as well as body. The classic light overproof is Wray & Nephew's, ubiquitous in Jamaica, but there's dark overproof rum too which is used to add richness to Tiki drinks and punches – look out for Lemon-Hart 151 (Guyana) and Gosling's Overproof (Bermuda). It's great in a Swizzle (page 213). The high alcohol also means its highly flammable, so it's often carefully layered on top of cocktails and set on fire. It will keep a Christmas pudding burning until Epiphany too. See Hurricane (page 200), Nuclear Daiquiri (page 174), Rum'n'Ting (page 209).

Parfait Amour

Perfect love. A style of violet liqueur with hint of orange.

Pastis

Pastis was what the French turned to after **absinthe** was banned. It has no hallucinogens and much lower alcohol content but it has the same predominant aniseed flavour and is typically watered down in the 'louche' style like absinthe (which makes it look 'like a cloud trapped in a glass,' as Edward St Aubyn describes it in *Never Mind*). It's also much cheaper so is a good substitute for absinthe if you can't stretch.

Peach liqueur

See **crème de peche**.

Peach schnapps

The most common kind of **schnapps** used in a variety of abominable cocktails.

Pernod

The leading brand of **pastis** is sometimes called for by name in cocktail recipes. Since pastis is a sub for absinthe in itself, it's fine to use absinthe in these contexts.

Peychaud's bitters
One of the oldest varieties of bitters, compounded by a New Orleans apothecary and as such widely used in local favourites such as the Sazerac (page 134), Louisiana (page 124) and the Vieux Carré (page 139). It is bright red in colour and a has a distinct anise note that marries well with Scotch. Bitter Truth make a version called Creole Bitters. Affinity (page 103), Algonquin (page 104), Bobby Burns (page 108), Referendum (page 131), Rob Roy (page 132).

Pimento dram
A Jamaican allspice liqueur made by macerating allspice berries and cloves in rum. It has a very strong taste so must be used sparingly but a dash in a Rum Old Fashioned works a treat. Don the Beachcomber used to batch this up with vanilla-infused sugar syrup as one of his 'secret' spice blends. See Daiquiri de Maracuja (page 161), Kingston Cocktail (page 169) and Swizzle (page 213).

Pisco
An unaged grape brandy made in Peru and in Chile, once popular in the Wild West too. At its best – I adore the Pisco brand from Chile – it comes with great bouquets of flora and consorts well with all manner of fruity contexts. The Pisco Sour (page 179) is one of the classic sours, while the Pisco Punch (page 207) had Rudyard Kipling in raptures. Try stirred in a Consolation (page 111), Pink Rabbit (page 130) or in place of brandy in an Ampersand (page 105) but mostly in fruity contexts: the Dulchin (page 162), the Wah-Wah (page 186) and the Papa Ghiradelli (page 205).

Plymouth Gin
A delectable citrus-forward gin distilled in the English port, distinct enough to warrant its own category. It's what I tend to ask for in a Martini (page 57).

Port
Any of a number of styles of Anglo-Portuguese fortified wine –
underrated as a cocktail ingredient. Port of distinguished vintage should
be drunk on its own (though watch out for the hangover). However, the
drier tawny style makes a fuller-bodied alternative to Italian vermouth
in aromatic-style cocktails such as the Suburban (page 136), while the
jammier ruby ports work well in fruity contexts. It's also worth subbing
French vermouth for white port, simply lengthening with sugar, bitters
and water for an old school Port Sangaree, or lobbing into a Bloody
Mary (page 193).

Punt e Mes
A particularly bitter **Italian vermouth**, bordering on an amaro. It's good
in Manhattans etc (page 59) but its unique menthol/caramel profile is
called for in the Grosvenor (page 118) and my Bloody Mary (page 193).

Quinquina
A French style of aperitif wine made from red grapes (which gives it a
luscious ripeness) and flavoured with quinine. **Dubonnet** and **Byrrh** are
the leading brands. If in doubt, use like **Italian vermouth**, but try it in
the Chopin (page 111) and the Moonraker (page 126).

Raki
Turkish style of **anisette**.

Reposado tequila
See **tequila**.

Rhum agricole
Rum from the French Caribbean (Martinique, Guadeloupe, Haiti, etc)
distilled from sugar cane juice. Aged rhum agricole is the secret to a
true Mai Tai (page 202). Unaged rhum agricole finds its truest
expression in the Ti' Punch (page 183).

Rum

Distilled sunshine. Rum counts as any aged or unaged spirit made from fermented sugar molasses and sometimes fresh sugar cane juice. A by-product of the sugar trade, it originated in the plantations of the Caribbean and comes with all the bad associations (piracy, slavery) as well as the good (palm trees, fiestas). There are three main schools of Caribbean rum, varying according to local colonial influences: French (see **rhum agricole**), Spanish and English (which has further subcategories of **Jamaican rum**, Demerara rum from Guyana and **Navy rum**). There are also rums made all over the world, notably in Brazil (see **cachaça**), India and the Phillippines. In simple cocktail terms, however, it divides into **light rum** and **dark rum.**

Rye

Bourbon's hardier big brother – American whiskey made predominantly of rye. See Preliminaries, page 36.

Saké

Japanese rice wine. A drier and floral style will make an interesting **French vermouth** alternative in the Japanese Martini (page 120).

Sambuca

A vile Italian **anisette,** usually employed as a punishment shot in Britain, but presumably sales of the Luxardo brand help subsidise the **maraschino** operation so I'll forgive it.

Schnapps

Sweet northern European style of clear liqueur. Peach flavour is often used in rubbish throwback cocktails.

Scotch

The complexities of Scotch whisky are, naturally, worth more than a paragraph. In a cocktail context, however, there are two principal uses for Scotch. When using Scotch as a base spirit (which is rarely) I would stick to a good blend such as those by Compass Box. When classics such as the Affinity (page 103), the Blood & Sand (page 150) and the Rob Roy (page 132) were devised, it was mellow blended Scotch that prevailed – only many years later did the Single Malts come to be the most prized expressions. However, a subsidiary use is to use a little to add smokiness – in the same way that absinthe adds dryness. See **Islay Scotch** for recipes.

Sherry

Spanish fortified wine from Xeres, wonderful in cocktails and often excellent value (how many other 25-year-old bottles can you purchase for £15?). There are numerous styles, from the bone dry **fino** and the delicate manzanilla to the nuttier oloroso and **amontillado** styles all the way through to the Christmas pudding-like flavours of Pedro Ximinez (use more like **Bénédictine**). When a classic cocktail recipe calls simply for sherry (see Sherry Cobbler, page 210), it is a good bet that the author had in mind 'cream' sherry, the sweet blend your grandmother might enjoy.

Shochu

Japanese rice spirit – an interesting base spirit to play with in gin and vodka contexts.

Slivovitz

Plum **eau-de-vie** from the Balkans.

Sloe gin

A gin liqueur made by macerating the plum-like fruits of the sloe tree in gin and adding sugar. It's great simply with champagne (or better, English sparkling wine). In cocktails you can use it in place of regular gin too, you will need to dial down the sweetness elsewhere (for example, in a Sloe Gin Negroni, use dry French vermouth in place of Italian). There are some good classics such as the Charlie Chaplin (page 155), Ping-Pong (page 130) and Sloe Gin Fizz (page 211).

Soju
A clear rice spirit. It's only really drunk in Korea but they knock it back in sufficient quantities they claim it the world's best-selling spirit.

Sparkling wine
Champagne (or prosecco, cava, cremant, etc) adds a subtle acid to sparkling cocktails. See French 75 (page 72) and the full section of Sparklers, pages 220–224.

Spiced rum
Spiced rums normally contain prominent vanilla, cinnamon and coconut and tend to be blended for mixing with Coca-Cola. Don Papa from the Philippines and Chairman's Reserve from St Lucia are subtler examples. Use like **dark rum.**

Strega
A herbal Italian liqueur along the lines of **Galliano L'Autentico** and not a million miles away from yellow **Chartreuse.**

Swedish Punsch
A phase-3 cocktail geek ingredient. Swedish people drink it alongside their traditional split pea soup but it's also a key reference in the *Savoy Cocktail Book*. It is made from a base of **arrack**, sweetened and spiced and diluted with chamomile tea, which gives a yellow colour. As a sweetening element it adds intrigue to old-school sours such as the Diki-Diki (page 162) and One Way (page 175) but like a lot of austere northern ingredients (**aquavit, kummel, Chartreuse**) it also goes well in rum contexts. It's worth using as an alternative sweetener in a Daiquiri (page 158), for example.

Sweet white vermouth
The sweeter style of light vermouth is known as blanc in France and bianco in Italy. Most of the vermouth houses (Dolin, Martini & Rosso, Noilly Prat, Belsazar) produce a version. There are additional styles of aperitif wine that are, to all intents and purposes, sweet vermouths

including **Lillet Blanc** (which is fresh and lemony) and Cocchi Americano (which has more vanilla and spice). You can also use rosé vermouths in this context. See Algonquin (page 104), Fernando (page 116), Nymph (page 127), Old Etonian (page 128), Corpse Reviver #2 (page 156), Vesper (page 185), Twentieth Century (page 241).

Tequila
Mexico's national spirit is made from the blue agave cactus and has a spiny, vegetal flavour that is not really found anywhere else. It comes in three main styles: silver is transparent and unaged and has a fresh flavour that works best in simple sours such as the classic Margarita; reposado is rested in barrels and lends an austere elegance to mixed drinks such as the Rosita; anejo is aged for three years and more and is usually sipped neat. I'm sure bartending elite would disagree but I don't mind using reposado and silver interchangeably.

Many people think they hate tequila. I blame Jose Cuervo, the leading brand, which is horrific. Still, the overpriced Patrón pulls things too far in the other direction. There are many delightful tequilas in between, my preference being Aqua Riva. Whichever you choose, make it 100% agave which means it will be made from cactus and not mouldy tortillas.

Tequila only really entered the cocktail canon in the 1930s but has been making up for lost time. See Charco di Sange (page 110), Oaxaca Old Fashioned (page 127), Pacific Coast Highway (page 129), Rosita (page 133), Jalisco Flower (page 223), Margarita (page 171), Mexican Jumping Bean (page 172), Sangre de Agave (page 180), Tommy's Margarita (page 183), Toreador (page 184), Two-One-Two (page 185), Long Island Iced Tea (page 201), Paloma (page 205), Tequila Sunrise (page 240).

Triple sec
The French style of **orange liqueur**. The name means 'triple dry' which is mysterious as it's mostly pretty sweet.

Velvet Falernum
See falernum.

Vermouth
See **Italian vermouth, French vermouth, sweet white vermouth.**

Violet liqueur, Violette
See **crème de violette.** The acquisition of this particular ingredient usually means a line has been crossed.

Vodka
'Neutral spirits, so distilled... as to be without distinctive character, aroma, taste or color,' according to the US licensing authorities. 'The most impressive marketing campaign America has ever seen' according to David Embury. See Kangaroo (page 121) for a fuller history. Although it is reviled by certain bartenders, there are some vodkas with character (Konik's Tail, Vestal) and otherwise, you can use the designer blandness to allow other strong ingredients to come into play. It's also useful for homemade infusions. See Campari Smash (page 154), Chocolate Martini (page 110), Edward I (page 115), Japanese Martini (page 120), Cucumber Gimlet (page 158), Espresso Martini (page 163), French Martini (page 165), Nursery Plush (page 174), Teresa (page 182), Vesper (page 185), Cosmopolitan (page 157), Sgroppino (page 224), White Russian (page 214), Bloody Mary (page 193), Long Island Iced Tea (page 201), Abominable Cocktails (passim, page 238).

Whiskey/Whisky
See **Irish whiskey, bourbon, rye, Japanese whisky, Scotch.**

Wine
Fermented grape juice. Dry white wine is called for in the Spritz (page 75) and the Kir (page 223), red wine in the Sangaree (page 209). As with beer, there are few wine cocktails that I'd take over wine on its own.

Zubrowka
Both the leading brand and a style of vodka made in Poland and scented with the delicate bison grass that grows in the Bialoweszka

forest region (Grasowka is also good). It goes wonderfully with fresh orchard flavours such as pear and elderflower and worth trying as a Sour too (page 65). Chopin (page 111), Cucumber Cocktail (page 113), Elderflower Martini (page 115), Tatanka (page 213).

NON-ALCOHOLIC INGREDIENTS

Agave Syrup
A sweetener made from the blue agave cactus. It relatively low G.I. (and scorching sweetness) make it a favourite sugar substitute among orthorexics and a good way of making tequila and mezcal more obliging. Oaxaca Old Fashioned (page 127), Tommy's Margarita (page 183), Mexican Jumping Bean (page 172), Cucumber Soda (page 232).

Apple
Moving swiftly past the Appletini (page 239), there are surprisingly few apple juice cocktails. The Tatanka pairs it with Zubrowka (page 213), while if you lengthen a Rum Old Fashioned (page 63) with apple juice you have yourself a Treacle. Wassail Punch (page 229) makes use of the real fruit.

Banana
Banana is by no means a classic cocktail ingredient but it's worth trying a Banana Daiquiri (once). Simply follow the recipe for Daiquiri de Fresa (page 160) with sweet ripe banana in place of the strawberry. You can lob half a banana into a Pina Colada #1 too (page 206) and upgrade a plain old banana milkshake with a splash of rum too. For a subtler flavour, infuse dark rum with a few banana chips for a couple of days.

Basil
Basil brings a heady Mediterranean intrigue to a drink – it's wonderful in a Green Park (page 67). It's worth adding a few leaves to the shaker when you're making light rum and tequila drinks too.

Blackberries
Go well with gin in the Bramble (page 151) and the Black G&T (page 193). Otherwise good for garnishing smashes and cobblers.

Butter
A delicious ingredient if you can get the chemistry of oil and water right... see Hot Buttered Rum (page 198).

Cardamom
The seeds in green cardamom pods emit a mellow fragrance that goes sumptuously both with cream (Nursery Plush, page 174) and with tropical flavours (Kerala Fizz, page 233). Make a cardamom tincture by toasting a few pods in a dry pan and leaving them to infuse in some rum for a few days before straining – a drop or two will do wonders to a Gimlet (page 84) or Daiquiri (page 158).

Celery
A core component of the Bloody Mary (page 193), celery has a savoury bite that comes into its own in the Celery Cocktail (page 109).

Cherry
Cherry flavours usually enter cocktails via cherry brandy, maraschino liqueur, kirsch or the cherry garnish (see page 46 for how to make your own.) A little syrup from the cherry jar is always a tempting addition to bourbon cocktails in particular, while fresh cherries are good in cobblers, smashes and juleps.

Cinnamon
A dusting of cinnamon (or even better, a grating of a cinnamon bark) makes a good garnish for Flip (page 164) and Plush (page 208). If you dissolve a little cinnamon into sugar syrup, it adds an interesting depth. See Purl (page 228), Wassail Punch (page 229), Zombie (page 214).

Cloves
Clove can be domineering but when used subtly, it brings a peppery bite to the BCC (page 107) and the classic Pisco Punch (page 207) as well as Victorian drinks such as Purl (page 228). Make your own clove tincture by leaving a few cloves to infuse in some strong vodka/gin/rum for a few days before straining. Store in a dropper bottle and apply the merest drop.

Coca-Cola
If you take away all the sugar and chemicals from Coke, you're left with a mix of herbs, spices, rinds and roots that isn't a million miles away from an interesting amaro. Still, you'd need some complicated equipment to do that. See the table on page 190 for the various Coke drinks and Long Island Iced Tea (page 201) for full silliness.

Coconut cream
Coco Lopez cream is one of the classic Tiki ingredients and something of a guilty pleasure. You can order it from specialists or approximate your own by mixing the much-easier-to-find coconut milk with sugar syrup. See Pina Colada #1 (page 206).

Coconut water
It may be ludicrously overpriced, but coconut water is (frustratingly) delicious. You can take it in a sweet, limey direction (Green Isaacs Special, page 198), pull out the drier, chocolate notes (Martiki, page 125) or dress it up for the evening (Pina Colada #2, page 206).

Coffee
Proper fresh coffee will help deliver on the Espresso Martini's promise to 'wake you up then f*** you up' (page 163). It's also at the core of the Mexican Jumping Bean (page 172) and the White Russian (page 214). Coffee beans also make good quick infusions: see the Bamboo (page 106).

Cranberry
Dry and tart, cranberry was the quintessential 1990s juice and is a star player in the quintessential 1990s cocktail, the Cosmopolitan (page 157). I always like it best when it's mixed half and half with orange juice (which is also the basis of the Sex on the Beach... which you may have to google).

Cream

I find single cream works best in cocktail contexts, double is a little too gloopsome. See Ramos Gin Fizz (page 87) if you want to know how to mix it with lemon without it curdling. Most cream drinks are desserts: Nursery Plush (page 174), Brandy Alexander (page 151), Ginger Alexander (page 165), Grasshopper (page 166).

Cucumber

A slither of cuke makes a fine garnish for a Gin & Tonic (page 90), a Brit Spritz (page 222) and a Sherry Cobbler too (the drinking person's alternative to the Pimm's Cup, see page 210). Its flavour shimmers through the Cucumber Cocktail (page 113), Cucumber Gimlet (page 158), and the non-alcoholic Cucumber Soda (page 232).

Date syrup

Coming into vogue as a sweetener – it's rich and dark and good in place of sugar syrup in Old Fashioned contexts (page 63).

Egg (white)

See Green Park (page 67) for general discussion on how to use egg whites. (I often leave them out as they're sort of messy.) Still: Clover Club (page 69), Silver Fizz (under Gin Fizz, page 75), Ramos Gin Fizz (page 87), English Breakfast Martini (page 94), Angostura Sour (page 96), Absinthe Suissesse (page 145), Amaretto Sour (page 145), Aperol Sour (page 146), Eagle's Dream (under Aviation, page 146), Chanticleer (page 155), Cherry Bomb (page 156), Mandorla Sour (page 171), Pisco Sour (page 179), Silver Bullet (page 182), White Lady (page 187), Delicious (page 196), Pink Lady (page 178).

Egg (yolk)

It's hard to persuade a 21st-century drinker to suck egg yolks, but the Victorians couldn't get enough of them. See the Flip (page 164) and the Purl (page 228) or add them to Gin Fizz for a Golden Fizz (page 74).

Elderflower cordial

A much cheaper elderflower iteration than the liqueur (page 283) and almost as effective (you can cheat a liqueur by mixing in a little vodka or brandy in any case). See Brit Spritz (page 222) and Twinkle (page 224).

Fig

The fig has some lovely affinities with dark spirits – especially bourbon – but it can be a faff to muddle and strain (see Figaro, page 164). Leave some dried figs in a dark spirit for a few days and strain well (ie through a coffee filter) for an interesting infusion.

Fizzy water

The simplest way of adding effervescence. Americano (page 61), Tom Collins/Gin Fizz (page 74), Spritz (page 75), 'Pin' (page 92), Aperol Spritz (page 221), Apricot Rickey (page 192), Baby (page 192), Brandy Daisy (page 195), Brit Spritz (page 222), Delicious (page 196), Fernet Sling (page 196), Mojito (page 203), Papa Ghirardelli (page 205), Pisco Punch (page 207), Sangaree (page 209), Sloe Gin Fizz (page 211), Southside Fizz (page 212), Sprezzamatura (page 212), Navy Grog (page 204), Cucumber Soda (page 232), Green Lemonade (page 233), Kerala Fizz (page 233).

Ginger beer

For my money, the most useful and versatile mixer. (I'd always go for spicy ginger beer over pale ginger ale too). It goes with almost any spirit in Buck form but you can make it a bit fancier in a Ginger Rogers Punch (page 81) or the classic mocktail, Shirley Temple (page 234).

Ginger syrup

I usually have a bunch of syrups on the go in the fridge and ginger is the one I end up remaking most often (see page 117 for the recipe). It's included here in the Gin Cocktail (page 117), Penicillin (page 177), Shaky Pete's Ginger Brew (page 210) – but it's rarely a bad sub for sugar syrup in Daiquiris and suchlike (page 158) and in non-alcoholic drinks such as Cobra's Breath (page 232), it lends such a fiery kick, you miss the alcohol much less than you'd think.

Golden syrup
The contents of the green Tate & Lyle tin at the back of your cupboard makes a dandy sweetener – as with honey, it will need loosening in hot water to mix. See Ti' Punch (page 183).

Grapefruit
Tart and bitter, grapefruit has become the discerning cocktailer's choice of citrus juice. It adds complexity and aroma while a fat wedge makes a great garnish for a G&T too. See: Charco di Sangre (page 110), Pacific Coast Highway (page 129), Brown Derby (page 153), Diki-Diki (page 162), Hemingway Daiquiri (page 167), Ideal (page 168), Two-One-Two (page 185), Wah-Wah (page 186), Sprezzamatura (page 212), Jalisco Flower (page 223), Navy Grog (page 204), Sangaree (page 209), Zombie (page 214).

Grapefruit soda
Either make use of a can of San Pellegrino Pompelmo or Ting – else fashion your own with fresh grapefruit, sugar and fizzy water. For use in the Paloma (page 205) and Rum'n'Ting (page 209).

Grenadine
A lush pink syrup made from pomegranates. I've never found a good commercial variety so the only sane option is to manufacture your own (page 83). It can then be used just like a pink version of sugar syrup: Avenue B (page 82), East India (page 114), El Presidente (page 115), Bacardi Special (page 147), Dulchin (page 162), Florida (page 165), Golden Dawn (page 166), Jack Rose (page 168), Mary Pickford (page 172), Monkey Gland (page 173), Pan-American Clipper (page 176), Red Lion (page 179), Santiago (page 180), Scofflaw (page 180), Ward Eight (page 186), Zombie (page 214), Shirley Temple (page 234), Cobra's Breath (page 232), Pink Lady (page 178), Tequila Sunrise (page 240).

Honey

There are a huge range of honey flavours available, from fragrant orange blossom to medicinal thyme honey and rich dark manuka honey. I'd recommend the honey-forward Bee's Knees if you want to experiment with them (page 149). For most other purposes (Don the Beachcomber used honey a lot) simply use a workaday runny honey, remembering to loosen it with a little hot water for mixing ease. See Brown Derby (page 153), Penicillin (page 177), Hot Buttered Rum (page 198), Hot Toddy (page 199), Airmail (page 220), Navy Grog (page 204).

Ice cream

A scoop of vanilla ice cream shaken into a Silver Fizz (page 75) will give you a Silver Stallion. Also worth blending with rum if that's the kind of person you are.

Lavender

A sprig makes a superior garnish to a Gin & Tonic (page 90); leave a few in pisco, light rum or gin for a day and you will have an interesting infusion.

Lemon

According to the online Cocktail Database, lemon juice is the most commonly used cocktail ingredient of them all, comfortably ahead of gin and Angostura bitters. A lemon twist is also the most common garnish. For this reason, I treat running out of lemons with the same urgency as running out of loo roll. Sour (page 65), Green Park (page 67), Clover Club (page 69), French 75 (page 72), Tom Collins / Gin Fizz (page 74), Jerry Thomas Gin Punch (page 79), Army & Navy (page 86), Ramos Gin Fizz (page 87), 'Pin' (page 92), English Breakfast Martini (page 94), Amaretto Sour (page 145), Aperol Sour (page 146), Aviation (page 146), Barbara West (page 148), Barnum Was Right (page 148), Bee's Knees (page 149), Between the Sheets (page 149), Bramble (page 151), Campari Smash (page 154), Champs-Elysées (page 155), Cherry Bomb (page 156), Corpse Reviver #2 (page 156), Figaro (page 164),

Holland House (page 168), Jack Rose (page 168), Knickerbocker (page 169), Mandorla Sour (page 171), One Way (page 175), Paper Plane (page 176), Penicillin (page 177), Santiago (page 180), Scofflaw (page 180), Silver Bullet (page 182), Trinidad Sour (page 184), Ward Eight (page 186), White Lady (page 187), Delicious (page 196), Fernet Sling (page 196), Fog Cutter (page 197), Brandy Fix (page 152), Hot Toddy (page 199), Long Island Iced Tea (page 201), Papa Ghirardelli (page 205), Pisco Punch (page 207), Shaky Pete's Ginger Brew (page 210), Sloe Gin Fizz (page 211), Southside Fizz (page 212), Dickens's Flaming Punch (page 225), Fish House Punch (page 226), Wassail Punch (page 229), Green Lemonade (page 233), Pink Lady (page 178), Twentieth Century (page 241).

Lime

Lime is happiest as a consort for warm climate liquors – rum, tequila, pisco, cachaca – as well as gin (which travels well). It's worth trying lemon recipes such as the Clover Club (page 69) or the Jack Rose (page 168) with lime too. Ginger Rogers Punch (page 81), Gimlet (page 84), Ramos Gin Fizz (page 87), Gin & Tonic (page 90), Angostura Sour (page 96), Art of Choke (page 106), Corn n' Oil (page 112), Bacardi Special (page 147), Batida (page 148), Brandy Fix (page 152), Caipirinha (page 153), Charlie Chaplin (page 155), Cosmopolitan (page 157), Cucumber Gimlet (page 158), Daiquiri Classic (page 158), Daiquiri Frozen (page 160), Daiquiri de Fresa (page 160), Daiquiri de Maracuja (page 161), Daiquiri Mulata (page 161), Dulchin (page 162), Florida (page 165), Hemingway Daiquiri (page 167), Last Word (page 170), Margarita (page 171), Naked & Famous (page 173), Nuclear Daiquiri (page 174), Oh Gosh! (page 175), Pan-American Clipper (page 176), Pegu Club (page 177), Pisco Sour (page 179), Red Lion (page 179), Sangre de Agave (page 180), Teresa (page 182), Ti' Punch (page 183), Tommy's Margarita (page 183), Toreador (page 184), Rickey (page 190), Mule (page 190), Buck (page 190), Cuba Libre (page 190), Batanga (page 190), Apricot Rickey (page 192), Black G&T (page 193), Green Isaacs Special (page 198), Jungle Bird (page 200), Long Island Iced Tea (page 201), Mojito (page 203), Paloma (page 205), Rum Punch (page 208), Rum 'n' Ting (page 209), Sangaree (page 209) Singapore Sling (page 211), Swizzle (page 213), Airmail (page 220), Planter's Punch (page 227), Wassail Punch (page 229), Chartreuse Swizzle (page 195), Hurricane (page 200), Mai Tai (page 202), Navy Grog (page 204), Zombie (page 214), Cobra's Breath (page 232), Kerala Fizz (page 233), Porn Star Martini (page 240).

Mango
It's best to muddle soft fruits like mangeos (and peaches, kiwis, papayas, guavas etc). For full impact, add a drop of lemon or lime. See Batida (page 148) and also Daiquiri de Fresa (page 160).

Maple syrup
A delicious alternative to sugar syrup. See Bacon Old Fashioned (page 95), Brown Derby (page 153) and Plush (page 208).

Milk
Whole milk please. See Nursery Plush (page 174), Plush (page 208) and White Russian (page 214). Warm milk is a comforting veil for sweet liqueurs such as Drambuie, Crème de cacao and Cuaranta y Tres.

Mint
The Mint Julep (page 71) is the classic fresh mint cocktail, the Mojito (page 203), the modern equivalent. A sprig is an excellent garnish for long drinks (smack it gently to release the aromas) while a well chosen leaf is good on short drink and alters the aroma sufficiently to be considered a vital ingredient. Jerry Thomas Gin Punch (page 79), Ginger Rogers Punch (page 81), Art of Choke (page 106), Cucumber Cocktail (page 113), Fernando (page 116), Harry's Cocktail (page 118), Widow's Kiss (page 140), Absinthe Suissesse (page 145), Bramble (page 151), Campari Smash (page 154), Cucumber Gimlet (page 158), Miami (see Daiquiri, page 159), Stinger (page 136), Green Wing (page 198), Singapore Sling (page 211), Southside Fizz (page 212), Fish House Punch (page 226), Grasshopper (page 166), Chartreuse Swizzle (page 195), Mai Tai (page 202), Zombie (page 214), Cucumber Soda (page 232).

Nuts

You can use just about any nut in place of almonds to make orgeat (page 86) if your bent is that way inclined; cashews and macadamias are particularly good in tropical contexts even if less pronounced. Nuts also work in infusions: toast a handful of pecans in a dry pan, leave to cool, and then infuse in a small bottle of bourbon for a couple of days before straining and decanting.

Nutmeg

A grating of nutmeg is a traditional garnish for punches and for creamy drinks. See Jerry Thomas Gin Punch (page 79), Flip (page 164), Hot Buttered Rum (page 198), Pina Colada #2 (page 206), Rum Punch (page 208), Swizzle (page 213), Dickens's Flaming Punch (page 225), Planter's Punch (page 227), Purl (page 228), Wassail Punch (page 229), Brandy Alexander (page 151), Chartreuse Swizzle (page 195).

Orange blossom water

A fragrant hydrosol made from the flowers of the orange tree. It adds a gentle perfume to the Avenue B (page 82), Ramos Gin Fizz (page 87) and Opal (page 175). It's also an optional note in orgeat (page 86) and grenadine (page 83).

Orange

As mentioned before, my preference is for blood oranges when in season. Do not countenance using orange juice from a carton for cocktails unless it is of supreme quality. Bronx (page 77), Casino (see Aviation, page 146), Blood & Sand (page 150), Golden Dawn (page 166), Kingston Cocktail (page 169), Monkey Gland (page 173), Opal (page 175), Vowel (page 186), Ward Eight (page 186), Fog Cutter (197), Tequila Sunrise (page 240).

Orgeat

A rich, buttery, nutty syrup made from almonds, used in a wide variety of cocktails. Trader Vic pioneered its use in rum drinks. It's always worth subbing in as a sweetener in Margaritas, Daiquiris, etc. See page

86 for the recipe. Also: Army & Navy (page 86), Japanese Cocktail (page 120), Absinthe Suissesse (page 145), Daiquiri de Marcuja (page 161), Trinidad Sour (page 184), Swizzle (page 213), Mai Tai (page 202).

Passion fruit

The subtle acid and fragrant blush of passion fruit make it among my favourite fruits for cocktails. Usually, I spoon out all the pulp into the shaker and strain away the crunchy black seeds, but if you're blending, it's worth straining these away first. A typical passion fruit will yield about 20ml of pulp complete with crunchy edible pips but when it's passion fruit season in the tropics (usually April–June or so) you sometimes find one that's three times the size and weight. If you come across a recipe calling for passion fruit syrup, I'd just use half passion pulp and half sugar syrup. Avenue B (page 82), Batida (page 148), Cotonian (page 157), Daiquiri de Maracuja (page 161), Hurricane (page 200), Cobra's Breath (page 232), Porn Star Martini (page 240).

Peach

Used in puréed form in the Bellini (page 221). Otherwise, treat like strawberry.

Pineapple

Pineapple juice adds a mellow tropical acid to cocktails and has an additional property of frothing into a foamy head which lends a pleasing texture to pineapple fizzes. (Usually, I'll give the carton itself a thorough shake to save the rigmarole of pouring everything into the cocktail shaker.) Chunks of pineapple are good in punches too and a wedge is a nicely OTT garnish – ideally with an umbrella sticking out? 'Pin' (page 92), Algonquin (page 104), French Martini (page 165), Holland House (page 168), Mary Pickford (page 172), Jungle Bird (page 200), Pina Colada #1 (page 206), Pina Colada #2 (page 206), Pisco Punch (page 207), Sherry Cobbler (page 210), Chartreuse Swizzle (page 195), Kerala Fizz (page 233).

Pineapple syrup

Once much used as a sweetener by Jerry Thomas et al... Though the availability of fresh juice seems to have put paid to that. See Brandy Fix (page 152) for the recipe plus Algonquin (page 104).

Raspberries

Raspberries most often turn up in cocktails in the form of raspberry syrup – an old-time ingredient that's called for in a number of punches and sours. These days, it's much easier to find fresh raspberries so feel free to use two or three actual fruits and make up the quantity with regular sugar syrup (same applies to other soft fruits such as blueberries, passion fruits, etc). Clover Club (page 69), Jerry Thomas Gin Punch (page 79), Knickerbocker (page 169), Sherry Cobbler (page 210), Parisian Pousse-Café No.1 (page 237).

Rose water

Rose water is a cheap way of adding sophistication (a bottle is usually £2 in decent grocers) though should be used sparingly, otherwise your cocktail will taste of your grandmother's bathroom cabinet. It's good in a gin context such as the Rose (obviously... page 132) as well as in place of the orange blossom water in the Ramos Gin Fizz (page 87). It's an optional note in both grenadine (page 83) and orgeat (page 86).

Salt

The salt rim is the distinctive feature of the Margarita (page 171) and helps bind the sweet/sour flavours together. It's worth trying in a Gin Rickey too (see table, page 190). The saltiness of olive brine adds a more savoury quality to the Dirty Martini (page 57).

Sorbet

Considering lemon sorbet contains lemon, sugar and egg white, all you really need to add is spirit to give you a Sour. The White Gin Fizz works on this principle (see Gin Fizz, page 74).

Strawberries

A good muddling fruit – works well with mint. See Daiquiri de Fresa (page 160) and Campari Smash (page 154).

Tea

Tea leaves makes a great quick infusion: leave them in spirit for a few minutes much as if you were making tea with boiling water. It's worth experimenting with different types: chamomile, assam, gunpowder tea etc. See English Breakfast Martini (page 94) and Earl Grey Martini (page 114) for the principle. Freshly brewed tea is a slightly more interesting way of lengthening a punch too: Jerry Thomas Gin Punch (page 79), Green Wing (page 198), Fish House Punch (page 226), Planter's Punch (page 227).

Tomato

The Bloody Mary and its variants (page 193).

Vanilla

A drop of vanilla extract adds comfort to the Ramos Gin Fizz (page 87) and also works in the Plush (page 208), Flip (page 164) and, erm, the Porn Star Martini (page 240). A vanilla-scented sugar syrup will be good in all manner of aromatic dark drinks and rum punches: simply scrape the seeds from a fresh vanilla pod into the pan while you're making a regular golden sugar syrup (page 44). One of Don the Beachcomber's secret blends involved one part vanilla sugar syrup to one part pimento dram... a useful mixture.

INDEX

Here is an index of all the drinks in this book, including the variants.

ACKNOWLEDGEMENTS

I'd like to thank my agent, Georgina Capel, for being such a shining light and to Rowan Yapp, Rosemary Davidson, Marion Moisy and all at Vintage for seeing the book through. Thank you to Andy Forshaw for his delectable illustrations – and a special thanks to Will Webb too, both for dreaming up such a stylish design and being so patient when I said 'Can we just try this...?' We always could...

I have, all things considered, drunk well in the last few years. Thank you to my old colleagues at the *London Evening Standard* for indulging my sideline, sparking ideas and putting up with all the related hangovers: in particular Sarah Sands, Charlotte Ross, Andrew Neather, Jackie Annesley, Andrew Barker, Emilie McMeekan, Kara Dolman, Nick Curtis, Zach Leonard, Victoria Stewart, Jasmine Gardner and Karen Dacre.

Thank you too to all the generous people in and around London's Martini industries, whose wisdom (and booze) has found its way into this book. I've learned much from Cleo Rocos, Stuart Freeman, Pleurat Shabani, Damian Barr, Alex Kammerling, Edgar Harden, Hilary Whitney, Tony Conigliaro, Sam Galsworthy, Erik Lorincz, Tom Walker, Paddy Renouf, Ryan Chetiyawardana, Henrietta Lovell and Emma Currin.

I owe debts to any number of cocktail writers dead and alive. Aside from the obvious candidates, I'd single out three resources that have changed my approach: the revolutionary *Beta Cocktails* e-book by Maksym Pazuniak and Kirk Estopinal; Jeff 'Beachbum' Berry's *Total Tiki* iPad app; and the British Library, where I spent many happy hours scanning out-of-print editions by David Embury, Trader Vic and friends. Bravo to my parents, Rachel and Paul, and a large Gin & It for my mother-in-law Annie for all her support too. And thanks too to everyone who has cocktailed with me. There would be no joy in drinking if it weren't for good company – which is why most special thanks go to Johanna and Edward, who are the best company of all. An El Presidente and a bottle of milk coming up!